LOST AT SEA

A. A. Hoehling

Rutledge Hill Press®
Nashville, Tennessee

Published in Nashville, Tennessee, by Rutledge Hill Press®, 211 Seventh Avenue North, Nashville, Tennessee 37219.

Distributed in Canada by H. B. Fenn & Company, Ltd., 34 Nixon Road, Bolton, Ontario L7E 1W2.

Distributed in Australia by The Five Mile Press Pty., Ltd., 22 Summit Road, Noble Park, Victoria 3174.

Distributed in New Zealand by Tandem Press, 2 Rugby Road, Birkenhead, Auckland 10.

Distributed in the United Kingdom by Verulam Publishing, Ltd., 152a Park Street Lane, Park Street, St. Albans, Hertfordshire AL2 2AU.

Typography by Roger A. DeLiso, Rutledge Hill Press®

The original version of this book was published in 1984 by Stackpole Books of Harrisburg, Pennsylvania.

Jacket photograph. Artist's concept of the sinking of the *Lusitania*, published in the *London Graphic*. The liner assumed the acute angle, confirmed by survivors' testimony, when her bow buried itself in the sand and mud of the sea bottom only three hundred feet below, not even half the great ship's length. This reproduction is from U.S. Navy Archives.

Library of Congress Cataloging-in-Publication Data
Hoehling, A. A. (Adolph)
    Lost at sea / A. A. Hoehling.
        p.   cm.
    Originally published: Harrisburg, PA : Stackpole Books, c1984.
    Includes bibliographical references (p.   ).
    ISBN 1-55853-744-9 (pbk.)
    1. Shipwrecks. I. Title.
G525.H77   1999
910.4'52–dc21   99-11922
                                      CIP

Printed in the United States of America

1 2 3 4 5 6 7 8 9—03 02 01 00 99

CONTENTS

*"O God, thy sea is so great,
and my boat is so small."**

—from a Breton fishermen's prayer

Introduction

"Hello, Donna—this is Bob!"

It was midnight, October 24, 1980. Donna Gove had answered the phone to hear a familiar but unexpected voice—that of her husband of three months. Robert Gove, twenty-six, was third mate on the American freighter, *Poet*. His call came as a surprise since he was some two hundred miles out in the Atlantic east of Delaware Bay, en route to Port Said. This was their first separation since their honeymoon.

Bob said he missed her. He hoped to be home in another three or four weeks. He did not allude to the vessel, his shipmates, or the weather.

Loaded with yellow grain corn, a Department of State AID shipment to the troubled Middle East, *Poet* displaced, altogether, some twenty-one thousand tons. Thus deeply laden, the World War II C-4 transport had put Cape Henlopen astern this gray, lowering Friday in the face of gale warnings. A large "disturbance" was howling up the coast.

Bob's good-bye to Donna in this radiotelephone conversation would be his final one. It was also the last known message ever transmitted from the *Poet*. In spite of sea and air sweeps that would cover nearly three hundred thousand square miles of the Atlantic Ocean, not a trace, not so much as one identifiable life jacket was ever found.

Independent investigations conducted by the U.S. House of Representatives, by the Coast Guard, and by the National Transportation Safety Board all came to the same unsatisfactory conclusion, through different and diverse phraseology: *Poet*'s disappearance was a complete mystery. The Safety Board, for example, observed that it was "unable to determine the probable cause of this accident...." In fact, this governmental entity, along with the Coast Guard, found it could develop a fairly convincing thesis to show why the *Poet* should still be afloat.

But, where *was* she?

Though the most recent disappearance of a major merchant vessel, the loss did not write maritime history. The disappearance of the *Poet* was but another tragic chapter in the annals of the sea. As long as man has dared deep waters and the elements, families have waited on shores across the world for ships that never would come home. They had foundered, broken up, burned—vanished without a clue.

Immigrants booking passage for America, on sailing vessels and steamers alike, could praise the Lord simply for their safe crossing of the Atlantic. All too many were never heard of again: for one, the ornate steamship *President*, distinguished by a figurehead of George Washington at her bowsprit plus an American eagle and British lion at the stern. The British and American Navigation Company's entry in the transatlantic carriage trade, as it were, sailed on March 4, 1841, from New York, carrying thirty passengers and a crew of about ninety. Lord Lynnox and the well-known Irish actor Tyrone Power were among the former. She vanished as though swallowed *in toto* by a voracious and merciless ocean.

Thirteen years later, in 1854, the *City of Glasgow* was considered as modern a steamer as had ever slid down the ways. Passengers and crew on her fateful voyage totaled nearly five hundred, an unusually large number for one vessel. Like the *President*, the *City of Glasgow* paddled into nowhere, to become a bafflement to her underwriters and a vexing question mark in the lore of the sea.

Then, in the twentieth century, in 1909, the *Waratah*, a brand-new, good-sized liner plying the London-Australia trade, disappeared as totally as the *President*, the *City of Glasgow*, or the *Poet*. To this day there are a few who believe she drifted helplessly to Antarctica to become a silent, barely recognizable ice sculpture of an early twentieth-century steamship. Below decks, presumably, in her ghostly saloons, cabins, and fo'c'sles would be found passengers and crew frozen by natural cryogenics on a notably interrupted voyage to London, awaiting only the "resurrection" to thaw.

The resting places of some "lost" ships, such as the *Lusitania*, are known, but certainly not the full circumstances, the scenarios surrounding their tragedies. Another example—the *Morro Castle*, which drifted ashore at Asbury Park, New Jersey, in 1934, burning incandescently. But *what* or *who* had set the luxury Ward liner afire?

Then there is the yet more baffling situation of the abandoned ship. Consider the *Mary Celeste*, sailing on, in 1872, without crew, past the Azores...

1

Mary Celeste

The missing log

When captain benjamin spooner Briggs, his wife Sarah, and two-year-old daughter Sophia left Rose Cottage in Marion, Massachusetts, that crisp autumn of 1872 for their little ship, outfitting and loading in New York, they had an appointment with a bizarre destiny.

At Pier 50, East River, the 282-ton, two-masted half-brig *Mary Celeste* ("Heavenly Mary") went lower and lower into the water as sweating dock hands trundled seventeen hundred barrels of alcohol into her holds. Certified at 93.35 proof, the intoxicating liquid was contained in partly porous red oak casks. Although the vessel's overall length was but one hundred feet, her capacity was listed as twice as many barrels as this shipment. For thirsty Europeans, American alcohol or rum was not an unusual cargo, although a portion would predictably be consigned for industrial use. Carrying these heady spirits via Jamaica, Cuba, and Bermuda had been big business for blockade runners during the Civil War.

Mary Celeste as a half-brig, or brigantine, was a curious craft. Her foremast was bluntly square-rigged, her aft sporting graceful schooner sails, blending, on whatever tack, more with the lines of the ship herself.

Briggs, already a veteran master of sail at thirty-seven, was preparing for a routine voyage to Genoa—his first on the *Mary Celeste*—against a backdrop of peace and prosperity in a land committing the

There are no known photographs of *Mary Celeste*. This, however, is an artist's rendition of a half-brig approximately the size of *Mary Celeste*, sporting the unusual mix of schooner and square-rigged sails. (Author's collection)

war to memory. Appomattox was now seven and a half years into history—in some respects not far enough into the shadows to suit Benjamin Briggs.

He had become sick and tired of being asked during the long, bloody conflict why he wasn't "down there fightin'?" At first, he would retort that someone had to keep commerce going. Then he stopped trying to explain altogether.

The town of Marion, along with the ample three-storied Rose Cottage, where the old sea captain Nathan Briggs raised five sons and a daughter, bespoke the good life as the nineteenth century approached its final quarter. Sometimes called Sippican Village, from the Sippican Indians who first dwelt on these calm shores of Buzzard's Bay, Marion with its shaded streets had been home to some one thousand residents—merchants, farmers, shipbuilders, and sailors like the Briggses. Until recently, most had been whalers. The great whaling port, New Bedford, was but ten miles to the west.

Like others in New England, those of Sippican Village could readily satisfy their wants, whether necessities or extravagances. The Boston papers, for example, were thick with advertisements: human hair, corsets, clothing of every description, "matched fast horses," and "choice" church pews, Colt revolvers, or books—Horatio Alger's *Luck and Pluck* had just gone on sale. This and others in the Alger series promised "true pictures of life with a manly purpose woven into them." For those contemplating foreign travel, Madame Leonide Lafitte was resuming French lessons at her Berwick Park residence, Beacon Hill.

The needs of Sarah Briggs, thirty, who happened to be her husband's cousin, were more simple. She had brought along a small sewing machine, now in vogue nationally, as well as a melodeon (a rather diminutive reed organ). The daughter of a clergyman, the Reverend Leander Cobb, Sarah planned to accompany much hymn singing to bring cheer and comfort to the long, lonely voyage. This was agreeable to Benjamin, a serious teetotaler and indeed ascetic who, like Cotton Mather, found his release in somber and weighty religious tracts.

The captain's cabin was further improved by the addition of lockers for Sarah's and the baby's clothing. However, this was not a new experience to Sarah, who was seawise from having accompanied Benjamin across the Atlantic on their honeymoon ten years earlier. In the days of sail his was not an unusual opening scene for marriage. He then commanded the three-master *Forest King*. Later, Sarah was by his side on several voyages of the brig *Sea Foam*.

One member of the family would be left at home with Grandmother. Seven-year-old Arthur must tend to his schooling.

The master could do pretty much as he pleased with *Mary Celeste*, since he was part owner along with Captain James H. Winchester, of New York, a former master turned ship broker, and two others. What they had paid for the vessel in 1872 was not a matter of public record, although she was rumored to have been a bargain.

Insurance on *Mary Celeste*'s hull was said to be as high as $15,000, as low as $7,000, measured against a traditional desire on the part of owners to overvalue their hulls. Either figure contrasted with the insurance drawn against the cargo: $37,000, also listed as $1,000 above that figure. But by any yardstick the *Mary Celeste* had already proven a hard-luck craft. Underwriters had to know that she wasn't worth a great deal.

Originally named the *Amazon*, the half-brig was built in Nova Scotia. She was launched in 1861—about the time of the firing on Fort Sumter—under a manifestly evil star. Her first captain, Robert McClellan, fell ill and died within hours. While no specific cause was given, nothing suspicious was recorded.

In 1867 the ship was wrecked in Glace Bay, Cape Breton Island, Nova Scotia. Since her insurance excluded coverage in these treacherous waters, her owners were unable to pay salvage costs. She was abandoned.

Others did refloat the *Amazon* and subsequently sold her to American owners. An upper deck was added among various other alterations and a new name given: *Mary Celeste*, under United States registry. No reason was offered, although religious motivations had to be assumed.

Name changing in itself was sufficient to deter many a tar from signing on, to say nothing of stranding and sudden, mysterious death. But jinxes and superstitions did not matter a whit to Winchester. Her principal owner, in fact, was well pleased with ship and crew.

The first mate, Albert G. Richardson, happened to be related to him by marriage. The twenty-eight-year-old Stockton Springs, Maine, native had served in his state's coast artillery during the war. Winchester praised the crew, seven altogether including the cook, as "all German, the nicest set of men I ever saw on board a ship."

He was partly correct since four seamen did list Germany as their place of birth. Their average age was about twenty-seven.

November arrived. *Mary Celeste* was readied for her voyage. On Sunday, the third, Briggs wrote to his mother. His father, Captain Nathan Briggs, had been killed just two years previously, in 1870. He had walked out of the front door of his house during a summer storm and had been struck by a bolt of lightning.

"It seems," Benjamin penned in bold, legible strokes, "like home since Sarah and Sophia have got here and we enjoy our little quarters…we seem to have a very good mate and steward…and I hope shall have a pleasant voyage…we enjoy our melodeon and have some good sings." (The steward was Edward Head, a twenty-three-year-old New Yorker who, like the other crewmen, had just wandered aboard and signed on.)

He was, Briggs asserted, caught up in "the busy whirl of business life," impeded, however, by the lack of horse cars in the city. An influenza-like disease known as the "epizootic" had stricken many horses. Nonetheless, he managed to locate one carriage long enough to go riding with Sarah in Central Park.

"We finished loading last night and shall leave on Tuesday morning if we don't get off tomorrow night, the Lord willing. Our vessel is in beautiful trim and I hope we shall have a fine passage, but as I have never been in her before can't say how she'll sail. Shall want you to write us in about twenty days to Genoa care of Am. Consul.

"Hoping to be with you again early in the spring, with much love…"

Monday evening he and Sarah dined at the popular Astor House, on Broadway at Barclay in the shipping and wharf district, with an old friend, Captain David Reed Morehouse. The latter, thirty-four, distinguished by a full, flowing beard as contrasted with Briggs's neat, sparse one, captained the Nova Scotian brigantine *Dei Gratia* ("Thanks to God"), of about the same tonnage as the *Mary Celeste*. She was bound for Gibraltar with a cargo of petroleum. The thick, oily stuff was already gushing in great volumes from the fields of Pennsylvania and into West Virginia, Ohio, and Illinois.

That same Monday, Richardson, the mate of the *Mary Celeste*, returned to his Brooklyn home to say good-bye to Fanny, his bride of one year. Kissing her repeatedly, as she herself would recall, "he wished his things weren't on board as he did not like to go."

It seemed a singular change of desire for a man who earned his living through the sea. However, just three weeks previously their first baby had been stillborn. Too, Richardson had already commanded his own ship. There was thus a certain reason for his reluctance.

Even so, Fanny's mother, who shared the residence, appreciated Albert's instincts. She was certain he was no coward. Something, she did not know what, must be wrong. She said if he "felt that way he should not go." Nonetheless, with heavy heart, the mate took leave of his family.

A loaf of salt pork and some freshly baked bread slung over his shoulder, he walked out into a dark, windy night. The gas lamps flickered and cast their fading, wavering shadows as he vanished down the rough, rutted streets of Brooklyn.

Mary Celeste eased away from Pier 50 at 4:30 A.M., Tuesday, November 5, as cold rain squalls swept over New York Harbor from the northwest. This was election day, which would be marked by President Grant's decisive victory, for his second term, over Horace Greeley, the editor of the *New York Tribune* and famed abolitionist. Only eight states gave Greeley the edge, as the rival *Herald* crowed: "The battle won. Another Appomattox!"

That night one of Grant's most trusted lieutenants, Major General George Gordon Meade, died in Philadelphia, still on active duty. He had blunted the Confederate tide at Gettysburg, although he had neglected to pursue Lee's broken, bleeding army.

The half-brig sailed no farther than Staten Island where she hove to until the seventh. A letter from Sarah, dated that Thursday, addressed to Mother Briggs and handed to the pilot, elaborated:

"We anchored about a mile or so from the city, as it was strong head wind...it looked so thick and nasty...accordingly, we took a fresh departure this morning...we had some baked apple (sour) the other night about the size of a newborn infant's head. They tasted extremely well. Please give our love to Mother and the girls, Aunt Hannah, Arthur and other friends, reserving a share for yourself...."

Eight days after his friend's brig put American shores astern, Captain Morehouse cast off *Dei Gratia*'s heavy hawsers. The passage would be rough.

Steamers arriving in New York or in European ports reported severe storms all the way across, from the Maine coast to the North Sea.

The White Star Liner *Baltic* and the Cunarder *Batavia* both took aboard survivors from foundering schooners in mid-Atlantic. There was "great loss of life in Denmark," the *New York Times* and also the *Herald* reported. The British Isles were lashed by winds of near-hurricane intensity.

The Norwegian bark *Dagmar* sank off Ireland, although her crew was rescued by the steamer *Idaho*. Lashed by gales, the steamship *Helvetia* from New York drifted helplessly off the Isle of Wight with flooded engines. Life station boats, at their supreme peril, put out from shore to rescue the passengers. One passenger was drowned; others were injured.

Perhaps the continuing newspaper attention accorded these winter storms and ship accidents was responsible for a nightmare of Fanny Richardson's on November 24.

"I dreamed," she would recall, "that I was going on a wrecked, dilapidated-looking ship that had no masts and that I had to walk aboard on a square joist of timber. In the distance I could see a large ship with white sails bearing down upon us. When I reached the deck a hideous-looking man came up to me and put something like a snake around my waist, and said, 'That is part of your husband and is all you will ever see of him.' "

Little wonder that Fanny "awoke screaming" and called out for Albert's mother.

Coincidentally enough, that very night, off the Azores, Albert had started a letter to Fanny. He was going on watch at 8:00 P.M. during "a terrible storm," a storm so furious that "rubber boots and coats" were "of no consequence."

The next morning, November 25, either Richardson or Andrew Gilling, the second mate, presumably made entries on a "log slate," a daily supplement to the log book: "comes in fresh...got in Royals and top G [gallant] sail...rainy, at 5 made the island of St. Mary's bearing E.S.E....at 8 [A.M.] Eastern Point bore S.S. W. 6 miles distant." (St. Mary's or Santa Maria was the easternmost of the Azores, and Eastern Point probably Pontado Castelo, fronting a rough 700-foot range. This island, volcanic as the rest of the archipelago, was some 870 miles west of Lisbon.)

There would be no more entries.

Ten days later the *Dei Gratia* was herself nearing European shores, about 590 miles west of Gibraltar. Her position, specifically, had just been dead reckoned as 38° 20' N. and 17° 15' W. The watch noted this Thursday, December 5, "fresh breeze and clear, sea still running heavy but wind moderating." The log continued:

"Saw a sail to the E 2 P.M. Saw she was under very short canvas steering very wild and evidently in distress. Hauled up to speak to her and render assistance if necessary, at 3 P.M. hailed her and getting no answer and seeing no one on deck [got] out boat and sent the mate and 2 men aboard."

The stranger was sailing west on the starboard tack under but two sails, the jib and fore-topmast staysail. One sail hung loose; the remainder were furled or had been blown away. She was hardly "in neat trim."

Through rough seas, *Dei Gratia*'s mate, Oliver Deveau, a handsome, bearded man of thirty-five, rowed over to the derelict. He soon established her identity as the *Mary Celeste*. His reactions and, subsequently, those of Captain Morehouse in confirming the half-brig's abandonment, were at the least laconic:

"I found three feet and a half of water in the pumps...I found the forehatch and the lazaret hatch both off," Deveau would shortly testify before Vice Admiralty Court in Gibraltar. "The binnacle stove in, a great deal of water between decks—the forward house full of water to the coaming [framing around the hatchway].

"I found everything wet in the cabin in which there had been a great deal of water—the clock was spoilt by the water—the skylight of the cabin was open and raised—the compass in the binnacle was destroyed. I found all the Captain's effects had been left—I mean his clothing, furniture, etc.—the bed was just as they had left it, the bed and the other clothes were wet."

Subsequent inspections, however, would elicit that everything was "perfectly dry," not "affected by water."

Deveau "judged" that a woman had been on the derelict, also located the Captain's charts and books, " a number of them, in the Cabin, some were in two bags under the bed. I found no charts on the table."

But he did find the logbook in the mate's cabin "on his desk—the log slate I found on the cabin table." He noted "an entry in the log book up to 24th November, and an entry on the log slate dated 25th November showing that they had made the Island of St. Mary...."

Based on the last entry of November 25, the *Mary Celeste* would have sailed herself some four hundred miles, on course, before being hailed by the *Dei Gratia.*

Deveau did not locate the ship's register or other papers, "but only some letters and account books." He discovered the mate's notebook containing cargo receipts, "etc."

Deveau also noticed two charts in the mate's cabin, at least one of which showed the track of the *Mary Celeste* up to the twenty-fourth of the month. He thought one was hanging above the bed, the other under it.

"There seemed to be everything left behind in the cabin as if left in a hurry, but everything in its place, I noticed the impression in the Captain's bed as of a child having lain there."

One could speculate, on the other hand, if the inconsequential weight of a two-year-old on an old sailing ship's normally hard bunk could, in fact, leave an "impression."

Deveau observed children's clothing and toys as well, also "female clothing—an old dress hanging near the bed...the dress was dirty, as if worn; it was not wet. The bedding was wet." He found a box packed with men's and women's clothing.

Food—and sailors' pipes—also caught Deveau's fancy. While he recorded no edibles spread out on the cabin table or other "preparations," there were "preserved meats in the pantry." In the galley, "all the things: pots, kettles, etc. were washed up...there was a barrel of flour, one-third gone...she had, I should say, six months' provisions...there was plenty to eat."

The mate was especially puzzled by the fact that "the men's clothing was all left behind: their oilskins, boots, and even their pipes, as if they had left in a great hurry or haste...a sailor would generally take such things, especially his pipe if not in great haste."

If the crew abandoned, how? Deveau found a spar strongly lashed to the davits[1] where a boat normally would have been. While such a craft could have been secured to the main hatch, "that was not the right place for her...there were no lashings visible." Thus, "I cannot swear that the *Mary Celeste* had any boat at all," also, "there was nothing to show how the boat was launched...no signs of any tackles to launch her."

He attached significance to the fact that "the peak halyard[2] was broken and gone." Could it, for example, have been used as a painter, or line, for the missing small boat?

Summing, the mate from *Dei Gratia*, pronounced the cargo "in good condition and well stowed, and had not shifted"; he located an extra compass in the mate's cabin to replace the smashed one in the binnacle[3]. He also found two quadrants[4], but the chronometer[5], sextant[6], navigation book, ship's register, and other papers all remained missing.

That same Thursday, December 5, Deveau pumped out the

---

[1] A *davit* is an upright from which a small boat is hung.
[2] A *halyard* is a rope used nautically.
[3] A *binnacle* is a case for a compass.
[4] A *quadrant* is an instrument used for measuring angle of elevation and altitude in navigation.
[5] A *chronometer* is the ship's clock.
[6] A *sextant* is a device used for celestial navigation.

derelict. In fact, it was his hunch that the water provided a clue to the mystery: "There was a panic from the belief that the vessel had more water in her than she had." Eight days later, on the thirteenth, the mate brought *Mary Celeste* into Gibraltar, where a British Vice Admiralty Court took custody. Captain Morehouse surprised no one by filing for salvage rights.

On that date, Horatio J. Sprague, U.S. Consul at Gibraltar, cabled the Board of Underwriters, in New York: "Brig *Mary Celeste* here derelict important send power attorney to claim from Admiralty Court." He dispatched much the same message to the consul in Genoa. The families of those aboard the ill-starred ship, however, would have to wait. Word did not filter, for example, to Fanny Richardson until Christmas Eve. It seemed almost a deliberate act of cruelty.

Consul Sprague, a tall, reserved, distinguished-appearing gentleman, had the distinction in American diplomacy of representing the smallest consular post of the United States. The State Department's eyes and ears at "the Rock" since 1850, he had kept Washington advised during the Civil War of the movements of Confederate raiders and blockade runners into and out of the Mediterranean. He had been active in trying to persuade the British to deny coal and supplies to such vessels.

Moving to center stage now, however, was a remarkable figure with an equally remarkable name, Solly Flood. It sounded almost a *nom de plume*, certainly out of Dickens. The seventy-some-year-old Irishman was advocate and proctor for Queen Victoria, in Vice Admiralty Court, Gibraltar. The rotund, bouncy little man with muttonchop whiskers, by the measure of Consul Sprague, "has always been considered an individual of very vivid imagination, and to have survived, to some extent at least, the judicious application of his mental faculties."

When the court convened on December 18, primarily to hear testimony from Mate Deveau, Flood reacted as though he had been waiting his entire tour at "the Gib" for such a break in colonial monotony. Even while the naval jurists were examining the *Dei Gratia*'s mate, Proctor Solly gathered and unleashed an investigative troupe that included surveyors, naval officers, other lawyers (or proctors), a registrar, a diver, a surgeon, as well as those of no especial identification or qualifications who appeared to be mere camp followers of Flood.

He would explain that his formation, at considerable official expense, of this platoon was inspired by the allegation that Deveau's account "of the soundness and good condition of the derelict was so extraordinary that I found it necessary to apply for a survey."

Solly's minions swarmed through the brig, probing, exploring, gawking, making notes, even idly kicking such extrusions as cleats, capstans[7], or deadeyes[8]. The diver, Ricardo Portunato, dared several plunges into the murky chill waters and thereby enriched his indifferent fortunes.

After negative findings of any damage to hull, keel, or rudder, the "experienced" diver submitted an affidavit assuring his employer that he had "remained under water...for a time amply sufficient."

According to the Queen's proctor, his coterie had sniffed out some overlooked items: nine of the alcohol casks were empty, one "tampered with"; some peculiar, if minor, damage to the bows; and—of all things!—a real sword half hidden beneath Captain Briggs's bed. With manifest satisfaction, Solly Flood scratched off a report to London:

"From the survey it appears that both bows of the derelict had been recently cut by a sharp instrument but that she was thoroughly sound, staunch, strong, and every way seaworthy...well provisioned and that she had encountered no seriously heavy weather and that no appearance of fire or of explosion or of alarm of fire or of explosion or any other assignable cause for abandonment was discoverable.

"A sword however was found which appeared to me to exhibit traces of blood...my own theory or guess is that the Crew got at the alcohol and in the fury of drunkenness murdered the Master...and wife and Child and the Chief Mate—that they then damaged the bows of the Vessel with the view of giving it the appearance of having struck on rocks or suffered a collision."

The survivors, Flood concluded, managed to "escape on board some vessel bound for some North or South American port or the West Indies."

What about that sword? Why had not Deveau reported it in his original testimony, even though he noted "two bags" under the captain's bed, where the sword was located? Survivors of Captain Briggs recalled that the weapon, emblazoned with the Cross of Navarre, had been picked up by Benjamin and Sarah while touring the battlefield at Fiume, Austria. Fanny Richardson contradicted this, attesting that it was her husband's, a "trick sword" given to the mate, Albert Richardson, "by a juggler."

Whatever its pedigree or origin, Solly Flood considered the sword the ultimate discovery. He commissioned a surgeon, Dr. J. Patron, to

---

[7] *Capstans* are drums used for hauling cables.
[8] A *deadeye* is a wooden (at that time) contrivance through which cables were passed.

analyze the bloodstains, as well as other blotches found on the deck "about a millimeter thick." His conclusion: "rust (carbonate of iron) and some fragments of vegetable substance (fibers of wood)."

However, if indeed the sword had "been wiped," the doctor's efforts had been doomed. Too, the tools at his disposal as a chemical detective—1872–1873—were, at the very least, limited, certainly ancestral.

The stains could indeed have been blood.

Then, Proctor Flood compounded the sword mystery by sealing Dr. Patron's findings—for twelve years.

Since an American man o' war, the USS *Plymouth*, happened to be in the harbor, Consul Sprague invited her commanding officer, Captain R. W. Shufeldt (scourge of blockade runners in the Civil War), to examine the *Mary Celeste*. After "a cursory examination," the rather senior naval officer speculated that the brig "may have strained in the gale," which induced her to leak "so much" that Captain Briggs hailed a passing ship and transferred to it family, crew, and self. Since this hypothetical rescue vessel may have been "bound to a distant port," Shufeldt evinced no surprise that nothing had been heard from the master.

Expressing the belief that the "damage about the bows" was nothing more than the wear of the sea itself, the officer concluded, "I reject the idea of a mutiny from the fact that there is no evidence of violence about the decks or cabins."

And the USS *Plymouth* steamed for home, its captain quite confident he might in the months ahead be encountering Captain Briggs in some American port.

On January 13, 1873, James Winchester, as principal owner of the derelict, arrived in Gibraltar to retake possession. The complex litigation was still pursuing its tedious pace. With claims for salvage unresolved, the court would not release the *Mary Celeste*.

Frustrated and fuming about British admiralty law, Winchester soon booked passage for a return voyage in early February. He had reason to hurry home. His wife was bedded with a bad "coff" which Winchester feared to be "consumption."

As, bags in hand, he quit "the Rock," the old sea captain grumped to an immigration officer that should perchance he ever discover any "English blood" in his veins he would "open them" and "drain it out."

He might have been patient a bit longer.

The *Mary Celeste* was released from custody on February 25 (although the records remain ambiguous as to whether or not Winchester had to post a bond). She sailed March 10 on her interrupted voyage to Genoa, under a captain—George W. Blatchford—and crew dispatched by steamer from New York. It had not been a simple matter to convince the average, superstitious seaman that the craft was not jinxed. Few had applied for berths on the half-brig.

The next month, Vice Admiralty Court awarded Morehouse his salvage fee: the equivalent of about $8,300. One-fifth the total value of ship and cargo, it seemed modest enough.

It was now time for amens and postscripts, if not solutions. John Austin, Surveyor of Shipping for the Crown, concluded:

"The Vessel was thoroughly sound, staunch and strong and not taking water to any appreciable extent...having carefully weighed and considered the contents thereof and all and singular the matters aforesaid I am wholly unable to discover any reason whatever why the said Vessel should have been abandoned."

Deveau had said much the same: "It is difficult to account for her abandonment in face of the apparent seaworthy condition of this vessel."

Consul Sprague's efforts in the *Mary Celeste* affair had not been on a par with his services during the Civil War. Compared with the fevered output of Solly Flood, Sprague's approach became one of inaction and apathy. Nonetheless, he went on record:

"This case of the *Mary Celeste*...is startling since it appears to be one of those mysteries which no human ingenuity can penetrate sufficiently to account for the abandonment of this vessel, and the disappearance of her Master, family, and crew about whom nothing has ever transpired."

Eloquent, perhaps, by its omission was the failure to involve Captain Morehouse in the testimony. More singular yet—none mentioned friendship between Morehouse and Briggs, and the former did not volunteer this pertinent intelligence. Surely Morehouse did not have to send a boarding party to ascertain the identity of the "strange sail" he had sighted that December 5. He well knew the *Mary Celeste.*

Thus, dark rumors of collusion between the two captains would never be fully laid to rest—and this in spite of the ridiculously low salvage award.

Dr. Oliver W. Cobb, of Easthampton, Massachusetts, a young cousin of Captain Briggs, would voice his own doubts (in a booklet he wrote, *Rose Cottage*):

"We are quite dependent upon the evidence of the salvors as we try to construct the story. We must be mindful of the fact that Mr. Deveau and the two sailors who with him brought the *Mary Celeste* to Gibraltar, where they went into the Admiralty Court suing for salvage compensation, were coached by an attorney, and it was or seemed to be to their advantage to make the situation or condition as bad for the vessel as possible. There must have been some reason why Captain Morehouse of the *Dei Gratia* stipulated that he was not to be called into court."

Too, there was only Deveau's word that *Mary Celeste* was completely abandoned. Could not a few—even one or two—have remained on board, to be secreted on the *Dei Gratia* pending award of salvage money?

Weeks turned into months without survivors being landed, as Captain Shufeldt had forecast, at "a distant port." Some corpses found afloat on a raft in the Bay of Biscay by Portuguese fishermen caused momentary speculation in the local press. But identification proved impossible. Indeed, the imaginations of writers and editors had already been inflamed. They sharpened their pencils or filled their pens and went to it.

As early as February 24, 1873, the *Boston Post* leapt ahead of the pack to report confidently, "the general opinion is that there has been foul play on board." A piratical attack by a drunken crew, which had broken into the cargo, was the gist of the article.

Two days later the *New York Times* reprinted the *Post*'s story verbatim.

On March 12, the *New York Sun* headlined, "The Abandoned Ship—No Mutiny but a Scheme to Defraud the Insurance Company." One of the newspaper's reporters had been informed that the *Mary Celeste*, "improperly cleared," had sailed "under false colors." Overinsured, by the daily's claim to the amount of $13,400, the vessel, the journalistic ferret concluded, was worth only $2,600.

This in turn inspired the Treasury Department to question if there had been "fraud" somehow in the listing and/or taxing of the cargo. It was a low-key growl, since the department did not attempt to follow up.

Meanwhile, during the remainder of 1873, Sprague was itemizing the contents of the footlockers of the officers and crew of the *Mary Celeste* and arranging to have them shipped back to the United States. There were shirts, coats, trousers, underwear, socks, shoes, all types of clothing (including infant's wear), books, pipes, other private possessions, even the melodeon and the sewing machine. Perhaps the most provocative legacy was the unfinished letter commenced by Albert Richardson the night of the twenty-fourth of November. But his widow, Fanny, did not come upon it until a year later when she found it tucked "in an old log in the false bottom of his footlocker."

"I always believed and always will believe," she told a reporter for the *Brooklyn Eagle* (in 1902), "that my husband, Captain Briggs, Mrs. Briggs, her baby, and the cook were murdered by the crew."

At the same time, she claimed that her husband had asserted to her that the crew were "as bad a looking lot as ever swabbed a deck...Italians,

Turks, and Portuguese." Since, however, the four seamen were certified as German, Fanny's memory must have been playing tricks.

These were disastrous months both for the Briggs family and for sea transportation generally. Oliver Briggs, Benjamin's brother, was lost when his brigantine, the *Julia Hallock*, foundered in the Bay of Biscay about the same time those aboard the *Mary Celeste* disappeared.

In March 1873 the big White Star Liner *Atlantic* smashed aground off the entrance to Halifax Harbor, Nova Scotia, claiming more than five hundred lives. In November, the "luxury" French steam packet *Ville-du-Havre* collided at sea with a large schooner and sank quickly. A total of 226 perished.

The years passed—with fresh disasters and question marks at sea. The last day of January 1880, the British trading frigate *Atalanta*, some three hundred cadets, officers, and crew aboard, put out of Hamilton, Bermuda, and was never heard from again. In this decade, however, the dormant name *Mary Celeste* rang out once more. The half-brig herself was wrecked on a reef off Haiti in January 1885, as her new owners pleaded guilty to barratry—deliberate stranding.

Solly Flood, who by now was well into his mid-eighties, commenced dunning the State Department for compensation for his efforts on behalf of the *Mary Celeste*. Although his importunings were eminently without fruit, his reemergence underscored the notable fact of his tenure, as well as Consul Sprague's. Both Emissaries remained at their old posts, watching the ships pass "the Gib."

However, it was none other than Conan Doyle himself who focused worldwide attention on the half-brig. In *Cornhill's Magazine*, London, the creator of Sherlock Holmes published anonymously, in 1884, "J. Habakuk Jephson's Statement."

"I am Joseph Habakuk Jephson, Doctor of Medicine of the University of Harvard and ex-Consulting Physician of the Samaritan Hospital of Brooklyn," is the pretentious beginning of Conan Doyle's meticulous spoof. The author rewrites history, placing, for example, the climactic battle of Gettysburg prior to Antietam. He creates a new captain, one J. W. Tibbs, adds some Negroes to the crew, and loads the *Marie* [sic] *Celeste* with a cargo of clocks and tallow.

Nonetheless, the author leans on the Civil War to set the stage for a magical "old black stone," given to Jephson by an ancient black woman while recuperating from his wounds. Also put aboard the hapless vessel is "a very tall, gaunt" passenger, Septimius Goring, a spooky mulatto who, it turns out, is a homicidal maniac bent on nothing short of the extermination of the white race. Indeed, murder—in volume—

and voodoo spice Conan Doyle's lurid tale, coming to its grisly conclusion at a black "Mahometans'" colony in Africa. Jephson's mystical stone accounts for his own salvation and escape to make possible the "Statement" in *Cornhill's*.

At least as compelling as the yarn was its acceptance as fact by so many. Newspapers and periodicals accorded it serious reviews, as next of kin predictably denounced Sir Arthur's mischief. Even the aging Solly Flood paid implicit tribute to the escapade by complaining that it was "nothing less than a fabrication."

With the fine honing of his imagination, Conan Doyle nonetheless did not create a sea monster. But one inevitably broke water from out of the literary depths—in 1904.

"Back in the sixties," wrote a Briton, J. L. Hornibrook, in the London publication *Chambers' Journal*, "Spanish authorities near the Straits of Gibraltar boarded a ship which appeared to be sailing aimlessly." It turned out to be the *Marie* [sic] *Celeste*, with, among other authorial contributions, "not a single boat missing," a "half-consumed dinner" sitting on the table, "the captain's watch...ticking on a nail above his berth," and the port of departure logged as Boston.

(At that the writer missed a few of the popular myths, including a "half-burnt" chicken on the stove, cackling fowl in their crates, a rocker moving to and fro, and an occasional ghostly strain emanating from the small organ.)

Since Hornibrook was of the mind that every mystery must have its solution, he found that unnamed "American scientists" had finally concluded that the "disappearance of the crew" could be attributed to "the agency of a huge octopus or devilfish...one by one they [those on board] are caught by the waving, wriggling arms and swept overboard."

Or perhaps it was a giant squid?

Bizarre in its own fashion was the story of one Abel Fosdyk, published by the *Strand Magazine*, London, in 1913. It was reprinted, with illustrations, in the *New York Times* magazine section in November of the same year. Obviously, this was a parcel of "all the news that's fit to print."

A measure of dignity, perhaps, if not veracity, was lent by the fact that a professor of Magdalen College, Oxford (and also headmaster of the Peterborough preparatory school), one A. Howard Linford, had supposedly contributed the manuscript. He said it was the diary of a deceased servant, Abel Fosdyk.

Fosdyk, who places himself aboard the *Mary Celeste* as a passenger, weaves a fanciful tale of captain and mate, fully clothed, participating in a swimming race around a becalmed *Mary Celeste*, only to be attacked by sharks. Entering the plot here is a morsel of imaginative brilliance—"baby's quarter-deck."

This contribution to marine architecture Fosdyk claims to have been constructed near the bow to keep the Briggses' daughter from falling overboard. However, the others, crowding onto this little deck to watch the race, themselves plunged into the sea. Fosdyk is saved by nothing less than the wonderful quarter-deck, on which he floats to Africa—and salvation. How else could he have survived to weave his yarn?

All that can be confirmed of this tale is the existence of Professor Linford himself. Oxford records show that indeed, such a scholar was a Magdalen professor and the headmaster of a boys' school.

One "posthumous" account was foreordained to spawn another—but it was a decade coming. A sailor named Triggs bequeathed, via a Royal Navy captain, a story published once more in the magazine section of the *New York Times*, which by now should have known better. It purports to describe the findings by the *Celeste*'s crew of a safe containing at least $17,000 aboard a derelict steamer. The amount was then split, with Captain Briggs's implied assent. The ship's company scuttled the sailing vessel and sloshed by open boats their various, guilt-ridden routes to European ports.

In 1929, an Englishman, who signed himself variously by the dual names of Laurence J. Keating/Lee Kaye, published *The Great Mary Celeste Hoax*. It was accorded mingled awe, denunciation, and even some respectful approbation. He had not labeled his efforts fiction.

Keating peopled his brig with hulking, sinister characters such as Toby Hullock, the mate; Carl Venholdt, "shanghaied lubber"; and the cook, John Pemberton. The last named had supposedly at the age of ninety-two, broken silence in his Liverpool snug harbor to tell Keating/Kaye "the truth."

Sudden death, possible murder, and collusion skulk through this book. There was no baby aboard, only a "baby piano," and this, in a storm, broke loose, killing Mrs. Briggs—"she was as dead as mutton." The crew rejoiced since her hymn banging and singing had driven them, apparently, even madder than their Creator had made them. As for Captain Briggs, according to Pemberton, he "had suicided and fed a shark."

The *Buffalo Evening News*, commenting on the "preposterous statements" in the book, thumped, "there is scarcely a correctly stated fact in it," while the *Evening Standard*, of London, dubbed "Pemberton's tale...a product of a lively imagination and utter disregard for the facts." Families of those who had sailed aboard the ill-starred half-brig joined in the protest, avowing that Captain Briggs especially had been libeled.

Yet Keating's detractors were not the only ones lacking a sense of humor—there were those others, for example, who took the author more or less seriously. The *Saturday Review*, of September 21, 1929, featured an appreciation by one Captain David W. Bone under the heading: "A Forecastle Classic." According to the reviewer, "his tale is ingenious and quite credible and he has apparently been at considerable pains to search for and examine all the evidence...."

He might as logically have been discussing *Twelfth Night*.

In this decade, a respected writer of the sea, John Gilbert Lockhart, while denying Keating's reconstruction, seized upon the melodeon and various books of religious flavor found in the cabin of the *Mary Celeste* as tattletales in his "solution" of the mystery.

"In a terrible fit of homicidal religious mania," Lockhart theorized, Captain Briggs "became obsessed with the idea that it was his duty to release from the miseries of life his wife, his child, and the seven men."

Presumably, the sailing master from Marion, Massachusetts, used the sword to dispatch his family and shipmates, one by one. Why he did not encounter resistance, certainly from the strong, young seamen, the author did not attempt to resolve.

Neither clergy nor devout laity was much amused by Lockhart's casual "slander." But then, one so-called writer or another besmirched the reputations of almost all on board through a virtual potpourri of charges. The least libelous was, in effect, the quality of being bird-brained. Only Sarah Briggs—and the baby Sophia—had escaped the fusillades of calumny over the decades.

One author, Harold T. Wilkins, could not rid himself of the conviction that Captain Morehouse was the guilty party. "It must seem strange," he wrote for the *Quarterly Review* in 1931, "that the authorities at Gibraltar in 1872–73 did not set in motion legal machinery in London which would have led to the arrest of the Captain, mate and crew of the British brig, *Dei Gratia*. It is evident that in the hands of a skillful cross-examiner at the Old Bailey, acting for the Public Prosecutor of his Crown contemporary in the 1870s, Deveau, mate of the *Dei Gratia*, might have been forced to tell the truth, and thereby have put the police on the track of the criminals who made away with the captain, his wife and family, and the officers and crew of the *Mary Celeste*."

Since Morehouse, in the euphemism of the sea, had slipped his cable in 1905, the old captain wasn't around to refute charges of his criminal proclivities.

By 1933, Mr. Hornibrook, who had thumped for sea monsters at the turn of the century, now had many years and an intervening World War to chew over his case. These creatures just may have been a bit improbable. After all, no British or German submarines, to say nothing of surface warships, had logged sighting such a denizen during those four terrible years—on any of the world's seas.

Now, it was the Riff pirates, out of Algiers, who boarded the *Marie* [sic] *Celeste*, cutlasses and all. When they discovered the cargo of alcohol, "anathema to the Moslem Moor," that sealed it for passengers and crew, who were removed as prisoners. Indeed, "one shudders to think of the fate in store for the captives." Hornibrook then delivered his amen: "That is the true story of the *Marie Celeste.*"

But—what *had* happened or might (within the bounds of elemental reason) have occurred?

Mary Celeste was not unique in maritime history by the mere fact of her abandonment. In the last decades of the nineteenth century, several ships sailed impressive distances without benefit of crew. For example:

The schooner *Twenty-one Friends,* abandoned in March 1885 off Chesapeake Bay, was last seen nine months later off Cape Finisterre, the westernmost point of Spain. It was estimated that she had drifted more than thirty-five hundred miles.

The *William L. White,* another schooner, abandoned off Delaware Bay during the great blizzard of March 1888, sailed five thousand miles in a ten-month period. Based on sightings, it was believed she averaged as much as thirty-two nautical miles on some days.

The schooners *Ethel M. Davis* and *David W. Hunt,* both abandoned off the east coast of the United States in November of the same year, 1888, each cruised without benefit of human guidance about the same distance as the *William L. White.*

A record surely was set by the *Fannie J. Wolsten,* abandoned in 1891. The schooner drifted an estimated nine thousand miles in four years before breaking up off the New Jersey coast. It was remarkable that none of these lumbering vessels or others like them, thrashing mindlessly across the world's seas, had collided with ships that were under control.

But there was a signal difference in every one of these abandonments, as compared to the *Mary Celeste.* The crew, or a portion of it, reached safety—or their fate was clearly established. These derelicts were remarkable, not for inherent mysteries, but because they remained afloat so long and covered such prodigious mileage.

The number of "missing" ships was considerable. London's Board of Trade figures for the year 1879–80, for example, list seventy-five vessels, sail and steam, British registry, aggregating more than forty-one thousand tons "missing." For the year ended 1890, the comparable figures were fifty-two ships and twenty-four thousand aggregate tons respectively.

Over the years, James Winchester evolved his own theory, inspired in part by talking with other captains who professed to similar experiences. In February 1913, shortly after the shipowner's death, the *New York World* paraphrased his reconstruction:

"Under pressure caused by high temperature, the alcoholic fumes [of the cargo] had escaped through the porous red-oak casks. Mixing with the foul air in the hold they had generated a gas which blew off the fore hatch. Volumes of vapor resembling smoke belched forth, leading Captain Briggs to believe that his vessel was on fire and about to blow up.

"Knowing the explosive nature of the cargo, he lost no time but with his wife, child, crew, chronometer and papers dropped into the jolly boat astern."

The Briggses' cousin, Dr. Cobb, who dedicated disproportionate hours of his long life in an effort to unravel the riddle, was much in agreement with Winchester. He wrote during the first half of this century a number of articles, the principal ones for the *Outlook* and *Yachting*, and a summary in his small book, *Rose Cottage*. The thoughts were identical, many of the paragraphs interchangeable. The following is a much condensed composite:

"A cargo of alcohol sometimes explodes, and it usually rumbles before exploding...we do not know why, but I think that...the cargo of alcohol having been loaded in cold weather at New York early in November and the vessel having crossed the Gulf Stream and being now in comparatively warm weather, there may have been some leakage and gas may have accumulated in the hold.

"It may well be that after the breakfast had been cleared away in the cabin...the cargo began to rumble...and indeed an explosion may have already occurred, blowing off a hatch and throwing it upside down on deck where it was found...having care for his wife and daughter [Briggs] was unjustifiably alarmed...determined to take his people in the boat...being on the davits across the stern...from the vessel until the immediate danger should pass....

"The boat was launched on the port side. The captain got his wife and daughter into the boat and left them in charge of Mr. Richardson with one sailor in the boat while the captain went for his chronometer, sextant, *Nautical Almanac,* and the ship's papers.

"Mr. Gilling with one sailor would be getting the peak halyard ready to use as a tow rope...the cook gathered up what cooked food he had on hand, some canned goods."

Cobb then went into some detail as to the trim—or lack of trim—of the *Mary Celeste.* "He would have laid the squaresails aback to deaden the headway…the royal and topgallant sail, the flying jib, main topmast staysail, middle staysail, gaff topsail and mainsail were furled…[all this indicating] good seamanship and preparation to leave the vessel.

"The embarkation must have been in great haste as the captain left his watch and his money and three sailors left money in their chests. The main staysail was not furled. The wheel was left loose. The binnacle was displaced and the compass broken, probably in a clumsy attempt to get the compass quickly.

"It is evident that the boat with ten people in her left the vessel and that the peak halyard was taken as a tow line." When this line parted, by Cobb's theorizing, "the vessel sailed away from them, leaving ten persons in a small boat a hundred miles from land without compass, food or water. They perished; how we shall never know."

Certainly not fanciful, within the realms of plausibility, what Cobb and Winchester concluded was just a theory. Nonetheless, it was echoed by a number of seafarers and historians alike. Among them was John Lockhart, who had already gone on record with his religious maniac theory. Now he had quite diametrically reversed himself.

Yet to subscribe to this reconstruction one must accept the premise that Captain Briggs was prone to panic, surely to hysteria to some degree. Against the captain's proven background as a competent, apparently phlegmatic sailing master, the proposition becomes, at the least, shaky, suggesting the need for further substantiation.

Besides, alcohol does not "explode." It can expand and blow lids off. Its flash point for spontaneous ignition is far too high—several hundred degrees Fahrenheit—to meet the cool conditions of the Atlantic Ocean in winter.

But Winchester and Cobb were sailors, not chemists.

Apparently, the most palpably simple possibility was not considered of merit by Cobb, Winchester—anyone: that one or more had fallen overboard in the storm and that the remainder had perished in vain efforts at rescue. Such tragedies or variations on them are in the news regularly to this day. This hypothesis, nonetheless, leaves unanswered other questions. Why was the ship's boat missing? Where were certain of the ship's papers, including *Mary Celeste*'s register? Why was the compass in the binnacle destroyed? Why were the sailors not wearing those boots and oilskins that were left behind?

Thus, every explanation, or even suggestion, offered over the last

125 years is vulnerable to being challenged, if not demolished. And by the same token, like mutiny, murder, voodoo, avarice, baby's quarterdeck, collusion, sea serpents, subsurface upheavals, or merely the urge to abandon in favor of a remote island, such as Tristan da Cunha—one is quite unable to present hard countering evidence in rebuttal.

So, the answer was always a vexing question mark. But, it did not necessarily have to be, or perhaps should not have been, once.

Meticulous, like some fussy, aging headmistress of a girl's school when it came to trivialities, Admiralty Court neglected to heed what might have been the most revealing tattletale.

On May 2, 1873, Sprague wrote O. M. Spencer, consul at Genoa, that he was forwarding the *Mary Celeste* logbook by steamer, and "shall feel obliged by your allowing the parties concerned to peruse and afterwards please retain it yourself and hold it subject to the orders of the Department of State...please acknowledge the receipt of said log book."

Consul Spencer, if indeed he ever received the log, never acknowledged.

During the proceedings, only that part of the log that had been continued by Deveau appeared to be of any investigative interest. The main portion, chronicling the voyage from New York, was ignored *in toto*. No pages or excerpts were quoted in the testimony, much less a copy produced for the record.

Solly Flood, who in retrospect could have been considered a character out of Gilbert and Sullivan—with scant makeup or costumery necessary—had become peevish and nearly hysterical in seeking the log of the *Dei Gratia*.

"I have asked for the log twenty times a day and not been able to receive it!" he complained to the court. With that, he was finally handed a copy.

But of what use was the *Dei Gratia*'s log? *She* had not been abandoned.

No one seemed to have studied the log of the *Mary Celeste* any more than casually—if that—much less had it copied. Then, to compound the Admiralty's mingled indifference and ineptitude as well as Consul Sprague's carelessness, the log was lost.

Or was it stolen?

Or was it destroyed?

In either of these possibilities, by whom? And, why?

The *Dei Gratia* had sailed from Genoa by the time the log should have arrived. *Mary Celeste*, with relief captain and crew, was still there, unloading.

But, had the log *ever* reached Consul Spencer over that moderate distance, a few days' steamer passage?

Indeed, was the log really sent to Genoa from Gibraltar?

Considering that Sprague had successfully returned across the Atlantic Ocean crates and chests of personal possessions such as pipes, socks, thread, boots, even the melodeon—why could not one little log-book have safely traversed less than half of the Mediterranean?

For that matter, who *was* Consul Spencer in Genoa? Department of State records in the National Archives indicate only that he was an Iowan. And there his so-called biographical information ends. Had this man ever known Captain Morehouse or Captain Briggs?

What about Sprague (who would die at his old post in 1901)? Had *he* any past acquaintanceship with either of the two captains?

What was in those pages of the voyage from New York, commencing November 7, 1872?

Did the handwriting change at any time between the sailing date and that of the last entry, November 25? This could have been easily determined. Only the captain, Richardson, and Andrew Gilling, the second mate, kept the log. Samples of their handwriting were in Winchester's offices, among other places.

No effort manifestly was made to ascertain this salient bit of evidence. Was this an omission of carelessness, abject stupidity, or willfulness?

Had someone noticed something *in* the log or *about* the log that caused it to disappear irretrievably?

Aside from its loss, how could so important a piece of evidence have been ignored at the inquiry?

A positive answer to even a very few of these questions might resolve much as to the fate of those aboard the *Celeste.*

Yet another riddle endures within the greater overall mystery. Fanny Richardson, who found the start of a letter in the footlocker, or sea chest, thought her husband also had begun something else, these four words:

"Fanny, my dear wife..."

That was all. She understood that the words had been scribbled on the cabin wall. Another version, in fact suggested by Oliver Cobb, held that the same words were written on a sheet of paper found lying across the log book, which Deveau had said he retrieved from the desk in the mate's cabin. To Cobb, the tantalizing words seemed merely the start of a letter Richardson wanted "ready to mail on arrival at Gibraltar."

But Deveau never mentioned "Fanny, my dear wife." How did

Richardson's widow, much less Cobb, know about it, if indeed this incomplete message *did* exist?

Obvious and eloquent was Richardson's unhappiness or concern, which caused him to visit his "dear wife" just before sailing and profess his desire not to make this voyage. Did he have an actual premonition? If so, what had inspired it? What was wrong?

Somehow, Albert Richardson, his worries, and his attributed fragmentary messages all seem telling components in the vexing jigsaw puzzle that is the mystery of the *Mary Celeste.*

But the principals are all gone now and so are their children, perhaps their children's children—and other descendants.

Fanny Richardson died in New York at the age of ninety-one, in 1937. Arthur Briggs, whom the captain left behind to tend to his schooling, expired in 1933. A prominent New England banker, the sixty-eight-year-old Arthur had spent much of his own income attempting, without success, to solve the mystery of the disappearance of his father, mother, and baby sister. Oliver Cobb survived until 1949. The squire of Easthampton was ninety. James Franklin Briggs, nephew of Captain Briggs, passed on in New Bedford in 1952.

No longer is there even "hand-me-down," word-of-mouth memory. The descendants of the Briggses, the Cobbs, the Richardsons, the Winchesters are removed from the fact by more than a century. For that matter, where are they?

"[I] am sorry I don't know of any one around here that would [be of assistance,]" wrote Madge Trundy to this author, from Stockton Springs, Maine. There are a number of Trundys in that coastal town, who in various, brittle ways trace their lineage back to Albert Richardson.

Her inability to help is typical of the thinning threads that link today's generation with the *Mary Celeste.* There are grandchildren now and great-grandchildren who can speak, like Madge Trundy, of yesterday's nieces and half-brothers, aunts, and cousins, all of whom once, seventy-five or even one hundred years ago, knew that ghostly band that set out from Pier 50, East River, one blustery November day, 1872.

They are all gone now....

Remaining only can be mute, inanimate testimony. But such might turn up some day in an attic, in the dusty back shelves of a library or historical society—then at long last the mystery of the *Mary Celeste* will be, if not entirely solved, better understood.

2

SS *Waratah*

"As safe as a church!"

THAT JULY OF 1909, almost a decade into the twentieth century, the Boer War had been over for seven years, and King Edward VII was entering the last ten months of his short, late-in-life, often sybaritic reign.

In the splendor of the Royal Hotel, Durban, Claude G. Sawyer awoke in a cold sweat from another nightmare. The elderly company director of London and Australia "saw a ship in heavy seas, and one big roller came over the bows and pressed upon her. She rolled over on her starboard side and vanished."

It was very early Tuesday morning, July 27. These dreams, or perhaps visions—he was not entirely sure—had caused him to debark in South Africa before journey's end from the new liner, *Waratah,* and register in this overstuffed Victorian hostelry on Market Square. Sawyer stretched his short legs down from the ample mattressing of his brass bed and walked over to the window.

Through heavy drapes he saw that it was still nighttime. Gas lights of the great port city glowed. The rattle of morning trams had not yet begun. Somewhere out there, waiting to cross the bar and enter Durban Harbor past the Point, a tramp ship was wailing plaintively for a pilot, like a cow needing to be milked.

Sawyer knew the *Waratah* herself was also out in the blackness of the Indian Ocean. He had seen the big ship off from St. Paul's Wharf, shed C, at eight o'clock the past night and, "as usual," he noticed, "a slight list to starboard." She was never upright, he had concluded on the long, strange passage from Adelaide. But even that had not precipitated his premature departure.

It was those dreams while on board—three times.

"I saw a man clad in a very peculiar dress which I had never seen before, with a long sword in his right hand which he seemed to be holding between us. In his other hand he had a knife, covered with blood. I saw this three times in succession the same morning."

The third time the whole apparition was so clearly etched "I could even now draw the design of the sword, the dress of the man—in fact every detail of his appearance."

Perhaps twice the figure also clutched a rag or cloth saturated with blood.

Trouble was, Claude Sawyer was not sure whether these *were* dreams or nightmares. In thinking back, he became increasingly certain they were actual visions in daylight. However, this early Tuesday morning, Sawyer knew he had much to do to continue his long voyage home to Phoenix Lodge Mansions, Brook Green, London. He must rebook to Cape Town, then on to Britain. He also wanted to talk to a doctor about those pains, which he vaguely attributed to neuritis.

Or was it neurosis, or even psychosis?

* * *

Less than a year earlier, on September 12, 1908, the band had played "God Save the King" as the beautiful *Waratah* slid down the ways of Barclay, Curle & Co., Whiteinch, Scotland, on the Clyde. The veteran ship constructors had built nearly five hundred vessels, including those carrying such distinguished flags as the Peninsular and Oriental, Canadian Pacific, and Union Castle Lines. The last named happened to be Lund's Blue Anchor Line's most earnest competitor.

At some 9,339 tons net, 465 feet overall, with a beam of 60 feet, and costing about $760,000, *Waratah* at once became the queen of Lund's. According to its sailing announcements, it would now be operating eight cargo liners from England to South Africa and Australia. Over the years they had borne quaint Australian names, such as the *Bungaree, Geelong, Narrung, Wakool, Warrambool, Murrumbidgee, Wilcannia, Warrigal, Yarrawonga,* or the virtually unpronounceable *Woolloomoolloo.* As if for leaven, there was the disarmingly obvious *Commonwealth.*

Waratah, among the simplest of the christenings, happened to be

Australia's patron wildflower. Appropriately, a large painting of a waratah in brilliant oils hung in the first-class dining salon.

She offered the finest in top-fare accommodations, spread over three decks, including two promenades, with roomy cabins, none fitted with more than two berths, and an open-air lounge. Plush saloons with fluted, gilded columns, teak paneling, and heavy carpets were designed to make the traveler believe that he was in some posh international hotel rather than at sea. Alice in Wonderland joined Hansel and Gretel in colorful sketches splashed across the nursery walls, rather a novelty in itself.

A tall funnel stamped with the line's blue anchor distinguished the *Waratah*, as others of the fleet. She should be the fastest. Her twin propellers could drive her at 13.5 knots or better.

By Lund's pronouncement at the launching of their latest pride, all vessels added since 1896 had been "fitted with Bilge Keels, which make them exceptionally steady at sea; and they are also lighted throughout with electricity, and have special refrigerated chambers for the carriage of all kinds of fresh provisions, fish, game, etc.; ice is also supplied during the voyage when required."

There were cavernous dry-food bins aboard the *Waratah* and a technically advanced distilling system geared to fifty-five hundred gallons of fresh water daily. First- and cabin-class passengers were spoiled with the tastiest Edwardian menus—kippers, tender New Zealand mutton, roast beef, topped off with porridge at any hour of the day or night. And a bargain: First-class passengers could book from London to South Africa for as low as $125.

Yet the *Waratah*'s owners still did not go as far in extolling her virtues and services as one newspaper reporter. He penned: "Seven watertight bulkheads, with complete double bottom, ensure practical immunity from any danger of sinking." But should worse come to worst she carried sixteen lifeboats, with a capacity of eight hundred persons.

Notably lacking, however, was that miraculous new invention of the Italian, Marconi—the wireless. A few of the latest superliners, however, were so equipped, including the huge new *Lusitania* and *Mauretania* and Germany's corpulent, waddling challengers, *Kaiser Wilhelm II* and *Kronprinz Wilhelm.*

Waratah's captain was an obvious choice—J. E. Ilbery, the line's commodore, a salty type with a generous white beard and a voice that commanded respect. Marking some thirty years under the Blue Anchor, Ilbery was slated to retire after a few more voyages, if he so desired.

Waratah, with the code identification "HNGM," was almost

Waratah was described by those who knew her as a more handsome vessel than this photograph—perhaps the only one in existence—suggests. With plush saloons and comfortable cabins, she was relatively fast for the time. (Author's collection)

perfunctorily classed "100 A1" by a Lloyd's survey and certified by the Board of Trade as fit to carry passengers. It meant as well that her hull and machinery had passed their tests. There was some discussion among the owners, builders, and the captain on the new liner's ability to be shifted from berth to berth without permanent coal and water ballast on account of her several decks and potential for top-heaviness. Under cargo, however, she drew from twenty-nine to thirty-five feet, which seemed to ensure stability in the worst storms.

Besides, early sea trials had inspired Captain Ilbery to observe that "she had a very fine righting power or stability." He was seconded in this thought by F. W. Lund Jr., a partner in W. Lund and Sons and general manager—also, as might have been expected, by the builders.

On the other hand, the master thereupon qualified his remarks by noting, almost as an oblique aside, that the *Geelong*, a slightly smaller, plainer "sister," demonstrated a "somewhat improved stability" and was "more responsive to steering."

Whatever the characteristics or "personality" of the latest addition to Lund's Blue Anchor Line, *Waratah* set out on her maiden voyage to Australia on November 6, less than two months after her launching. Attractive, no doubt because of her newness and speed in the "Down Under" service, she hosted a record booking. There were more than

760 passengers, but mostly emigrants jammed into dormitory-like accommodations.

But what matter? She was fast, cheap, and immune "from any danger of sinking."

There would be postscripts to her first passage. It was especially trying for a bedroom steward, H. C. Herbert: "She seemed to roll excessively....I did not like the large amount of crockery that was broken." One early morning after a particularly heavy roll a "terrific crash of crockery" led Herbert to believe that all the dishware aboard had splintered to bits. He felt he was sweeping up pieces of china much of the time.

Herbert was seconded by B. J. Shore, a steerage steward, who asserted he had "a job to keep the tables laid sometimes." She could "change her list three or four times in an hour."

Worse yet, Herbert observed that portions of the promenade deck had moved so much that he could squeeze his fingers between the planks. He figured that some of the bolts had broken. His theory was bolstered by the fact that one bolt fell down and hit "the baker's head." The latter being manifestly hard, the passengers continued to enjoy their fare of baked goods. The big vessel certainly creaked a great deal, but then the steward philosophized that "all new ships creaked."

Others of the crew snickered that "old 'Arry" (Herbert) was "prone to exaggeration."

This probably could not be said, however, about a first-voyage passenger, Sir William Bragg, physics professor at the University of Leeds, Fellow of the Royal Society, and winner of the Nobel Prize. Sir William was informed (assuming that he did not possess the knowledge at first hand) that the ladies could not take baths for several days at a time since the *Waratah* rolled so badly that all the water slopped out of the tubs. In their attributed dripping nudity, the females were both frustrated and angry.

Yet, what intrigued the distinguished physicist more than the women's unwashed nakedness was the fact that the passage had been marked by no serious storms. The sea had remained for the most part relatively calm. Why should the liner cavort so, like a stricken creature? As he would recall, he "continued to query the captain at breakfast whether he could not do something about the list."

Ilbery obliged, following the professor's suggestion that he balance the water ballast tanks. The ship thereupon came upright and, with much groaning and creaking, settled down to a more or less permanent list on the *other* side.

The determined physicist then asked Ilbery if he had any "stability curves." The master replied that these "curves" were not on board when he left Cape Town.

The continuing list sparked a pleasantry among the travelers, one calling to another, "How are you up there?"

To which would come the obvious answer, "How are you *down* there?"

Obtaining no satisfaction, obviously, from the captain, Professor Bragg asked Chief Engineer C. W. Hodder about this peculiarly behaving liner. With a tug at his walrus mustache and a deep draw on his large, evil-smelling pipe, Hodder replied cheerily, "Why, she's as safe as a church—sir!"

But a seaman, one E. H. Pask, privately contradicted the chief engineer, swearing that the liner was top-heavy and that he "never remembered her to be completely upright."

Two passengers, Gerald Steel and W. Church, were in agreement that the ship *was* top-heavy. The former, who had traveled to the United States several times, asserted that the *Waratah* "did not roll comfortably but would get down on either side and hang there." Church thought she "stood very high out of the water…usually listed on one side even in good weather. She shivered or shook at the end of a roll…most of the ladies were much affected by the rolling."

Of less concern or annoyance was a fire in the starboard lower coal bunker that smoldered for three days before being brought under control. The smoke, fortuitously, blew astern.

However, the *Waratah*'s impressive, moderately high silhouette with the black hull and white superstructure, was welcomed to Melbourne in early January. The "Down Under" land was glad to count another link to the world beyond this big, remote continent.

There were even those aboard the maiden voyage with a positive word. "Indeed she seemed to be everything that a first-class sea-going liner should be. In a storm off Freemantle, although it was one to try a big steamer like the *Waratah,* I did not even have my elbows brought in contact with the sides of the bunk. She was not a bad roller."

So averred C. S. Sanders, a New Zealand businessman.

And Alexander Reader, an able seaman, "noticed nothing out of the normal" in her "behavior." She "behaved wonderfully," and he heard "no complaints."

H. M. Bennett, third mate (or officer), asserted the *Waratah*'s "behavior was nothing extraordinary. She frequently had a list with a strong wind, and on account of her bunkers…four or five degrees at most." He characterized her normal roll as a "slow" one.

Conspicuous by their absence were any comments from the six hundred and some passengers who emerged pale and manifestly shaken from steerage.

The harbor master at Melbourne cast his acid eye over the *Waratah* and subsequently delivered himself of an oblique appraisal. Captain Inglis did not like "the large awning on the shelter deck, which gave too much space to the wind…but still I wouldn't say she had an excessive top-hamper."

Captain Ilbery himself replied that every vessel possesses her own "peculiarities," and the *Waratah* was entitled to her own. He agreed that her ballast was "rather much," but that, too, did not seem to disturb him unduly.

More routine was her homeward voyage, which inspired no adverse comments of record. Mr. Lund came down from London for a welcome banquet at Durban. When she berthed in the Thames, again the Blue Anchor liner was inspected and recertified as fully seaworthy—this in spite of some affidavits presented to the Board of Trade declaring that the ship "behaved in a most extraordinary manner in apparently calm weather."

Able seaman Edward Dischler found, for one, that it was "the general opinion among sailors…that she was unsafe for a long voyage." He was told that "none of the sailors on the first voyage would go on the second." This in turn was sparked by the wholly unfounded rumor that neither the master nor mate would risk a return passage.

However, Fraser Chapman, an engineer, maintained the *Waratah* was "a very steady ship" and that he had signed off only because his wife was in poor health.

Since the Jeremiahs, or crepe hangers, were apparently balanced by others claiming *Waratah* "behaved well," the whole batch of negative comments or statements was filed away in Lund's offices in a lower drawer labeled "No Action Required."

The Lund's liner sailed on her second voyage to Australia on April 27, 1909. She carried a full cargo and complement of passengers, suggesting that the company had every reason to consider its fleet queen a highly successful moneymaker. Her "bugs"—such as ballasting—apparently were licked, and she could settle down to an anticipated humdrum of dependable ocean commerce.

She arrived without incident in Australia, although then the familiar disparagements and concerns surfaced once more. For example, F. E. Thomas, a Melbourne businessman who journeyed from there to Sydney, commented on "a list to starboard," adding:

"She was discharging rusty-looking water and I inquired of the Chief Engineer. His explanation that they were pumping out the tank to rectify the list was good enough in words but did not seem to put the matter right completely." He also had overheard sailors grumbling that the ship was "a crank."

Another traveler within Australian waters, E. Crossley, a marine inventor from Melbourne, quoted the same engineer, Hodder, as confessing that he was "very dissatisfied"; that the *Waratah* had "a peculiar way of getting on one side without righting herself immediately."

Too, a rumor worried along the Australian waterfront about a seaman named Nicholson. When he was about to sign on in London, Chief Officer C. Owen had allegedly warned him, "If you can get anything else, take it, because this ship will be a coffin for somebody."

H. Duncan Mason, who happened to hold an engineer's certificate, was a passenger on this second voyage. While he admired the *Waratah*'s machinery, he believed the liner "did not recover herself properly, and was not quick enough." At one time he observed to the chief officer, "Owen, if I were you I would get out of this ship. She will be making a big hole in the water some of these days."

To which he said Owen replied, "I'm afraid she will."

All in all, it was more than surprising that Chief Officer Owen continued to hang his ticket on the *Waratah*.

When she sailed from Sydney on June 26, *Waratah* was laden to her Plimsoll line—drawing 35 feet of water—with 6,500 tons of cargo taken on there, at Melbourne, and at Adelaide. It included 7,800 bars of lead, 400 bales of wool, considerable quantities of skin, 1,000 boxes of butter, frozen carcasses, leather strips, tallow, and timber. It was insured altogether for nearly $700,000, which, curiously enough, was about the value of the ship herself.

Topsides around her bridge were stowed 300 tons of bagged coal—a common practice to provide a safety margin of fuel for any large steamer's voracious furnaces.

Her bookings for Durban, Cape Town, and London were somewhat less than one hundred passengers. Included was Claude Sawyer, who would wish he had remained in Australia or else berthed on another steamer.

Sawyer, who had airily remarked to the purser that he traveled by sea "a great deal," observed the first day into the Pacific that the *Waratah* "wobbled about a great deal, going through some disturbed water." When she listed to starboard "she remained there for a very long time."

After he ascended to the vantage position of the boat deck the liner heeled over "till the water was underneath…and remained so long." Altogether she "rolled in a very disagreeable way. She rolled and then remained for a long time on her side before recovering; while she was recovering when the deck had become horizontal she often gave a decided jerk."

Because of these abrupt motions, according to Sawyer, "several of the passengers had bad falls on the deck."

One morning the cabin steward informed him that the ship had "rolled very much during the night." Sawyer believed him since, by his estimate, the water in his bathtub had slid off to an angle of forty-five degrees. Inquiring of an officer of the exact angle of list he "got no satisfactory answer." He asked if there were an instrument on the bridge, such as an inclinometer, to measure the *Waratah*'s rolls. He understood that there was not.

"The builders would have seen to the roll. It is all right," was the reply.

Another passenger, named Ebsworth, a former seaman and subsequently a solicitor, swore that he had "never seen such pitching." He went forward one morning to watch the *Waratah* butting through heavy seas. She would take a "big roller," then put her bow into the trough, only to remain there and "seemed to keep her nose into the next wave and simply plow through it."

Even as the two men gaped at this disturbing spectacle—of a ship that could not seem to recover her equilibrium—two passengers were knocked onto the deck and badly bruised. A third, Mrs. Caywood, fell and apparently broke her hip.

It was then, about ten days out of Durban, that Sawyer decided that he "better be off that ship."

When he began his dreams—or visions—his resolve was strengthened. At breakfast he mentioned the man with the sword and knife to another passenger, Mrs. Alexandra Hay, of Coventry. She expressed immediate shock, if not disbelief.

He also confided the experience to his friend Ebsworth, who agreed that it must be some sort of portent and perhaps should be taken seriously. On the other hand, Father Fadle, a South African priest, burst into laughter as he assured Sawyer he was "quite droll."

The London businessman persisted. He sought out Ilbery and repeated what was already an oft-told tale. The veteran master saw no humor in the matter whatsoever. Sawyer was worse than absurd. The old salt would listen to none of it. In forty years at sea he had been cornered by far too many oddballs. He had heard them all. His patience had long since worn thin. Besides, reposing on his desk was a report he was preparing for the Collector of Customs, Port Natal (Durban):

> I do hereby declare to the best of my knowledge and belief, that my steamship *Waratah* has sustained no damage from any cause whatever since leaving her last port, Adelaide, and I have nothing special to report.

Undeterred, Sawyer tried to persuade Mrs. Hay, as well as her daughter, "Miss H. G.," to abandon the ship with him. They thanked him for his solicitude, but said they would continue on home. Sawyer's resolve was firm. When *Waratah* docked on July 24, he debarked with all of his baggage and went directly to a cable office where he advised his wife in London:

Think *Waratah* top-heavy. Coming Cape Town. Landed at Durban. Claude.

The clerk at J. Rennie & Sons, Durban agents for Lund's Line, was dumbfounded when Sawyer said he was canceling his passage, willing to forfeit the balance of his fare. However, Rennie offered to pass the matter along to the Blue Anchor London home office.

Sawyer then went across the street to the Union Castle Line to book on the *Kildonan Castle*, sailing for Cape Town and London in a couple of days. Heartened by the availability of a first-class cabin, if not as well a bit giddy, the recent *Waratah* passenger endeavored to explain his dreams to the incredulous gentleman behind the counter. While he volunteered little, the latter's reaction was much the same as Captain Ilbery's.

At least two others left the *Waratah* at Durban. Mrs. Caywood, who had injured her hip, was removed in a wheelchair to continue on to Johannesburg. Frederick Little, a "general servant" in the crew, signed off. He explained this was merely to seek other, more remunerative employment. He could remember "no accidents to passengers." He suggested that when the liner rolled it was only in response to "a heavy beam sea."

He thought the *Waratah* "a fine ship."

As if in endorsement of the seaworthiness of the big Lund's liner, a number of passengers—three or four from her first voyage— embarked at Durban, including Mr. and Mrs. David Turner and five of their children, plus a nursemaid. Turner was a local landing and forwarding agent, formerly with the Scottish railways. There was also

Mrs. Nora Connolly, of Dublin, widow of a coal miner, en route home with her daughter. Worried about carrying money with her, she cabled $5,000 to the National Bank of South Africa in London.

"Just precautionary, you know," she confided to the cable clerk.

The most illustrious of those boarding at Durban was Dr. Carrick, a well-known geologist, who had discovered gold in the Orange Free State. He believed this intelligence would be of far more than passing interest to British investors.

Altogether, the *Waratah* now manifested 92 passengers and a crew of 119.

She readied to sail at eight o'clock Monday evening, July 26. But among those who saw her off, or preparing to cast off, there would be another in addition to Claude Sawyer who became obsessed with the notion of impending doom.

Robert Dives, a member of the Institute of Mechanical Engineers, Newcastle-on-Tyne, had lived in Durban the past twelve years. Ships interested him. He spent idle hours wandering on the dock area and the bluff, seeing the steamers putting out past the Point into the Indian Ocean. This late July afternoon his "attention was drawn to [the *Waratah*] by her exceedingly high navigating bridge." He had "a sort of premonition or presentiment that if he did not go and see the vessel then he would never have the chance again."

He stood there at St. Paul's Wharf in the late-afternoon air pungent with tar, soft coal smoke, and the potpourri of smells at any dock-side from hides to fertilizers. The *Waratah* was being "buttoned up," tarpaulin battened back on those hatches where there had been minor offloadings of cargo. A few more bags of coal were added to her topside stowage. Porters were trundling aboard the last steamer trunks and lighter baggage of the Durban passengers.

Dives thought the liner, with her towering funnel, "very high out of the water." Indeed, he had "never seen a vessel with such a high bridge." However, it was not his affair. He shook his head and walked back into the city.

(Dives, whatever the strength of his intuition, needed his vision checked. With more than 2,300 tons of coal now on board, plus 40 tons of scrap metal added at Durban, *Waratah* carried a total of nearly 10,000 tons of fuel and cargo. Added to her own gross, *Waratah* was in effect a 20,000-ton vessel. She *had* to be riding *low*, not high as Dives thought. She was deep in the water, more than 35 feet, equivalent to at least a two-story house.)

The last gangplanks were hauled back onto the pier promptly at

Durban Harbor at the turn of the century (circa 1900). *Waratah* sailed from here on her final voyage. (Naval Archives, Pietermaritzburg, South Africa)

8:00 P.M. Her hawsers were unloosened from the dock's bollards. Thick, black smoke poured from her funnel to flatten out under a mounting southerly wind. Then from her deep bass horn, *Waratah* blew three throaty blasts. Her twin propellers bit into the murky harbor waters and she started to back out from her slip, aided by the tug *Richard King*.

In contradiction to Claude Sawyer's impression this same evening, John Rainnie, the port captain as well as the master of the tug, thought the liner was in fine trim, showing "no list" whatsoever.

Shouts of "Good-bye," "Bon voyage!" echoed from the pier as friends and relatives of the passengers waved handkerchiefs, hats, whatever they held in their hands. The women's long dresses; wide, lacy hats; and parasols together with the men's bowlers lent a festive coloring to the occasion. Little children were held high over their parents' heads. As a matter of fact, there were upwards of twenty youngsters onboard the liner, including infants in arms.

When the *Waratah* was well into the stream, there was another blast from her horn. Then the tug kept her in tow toward the Point and ultimately the bar, where it would release her.

After she was safely across, Mr. Lindsey, the pilot, handed command back to Captain Ilbery and climbed down a rope ladder to his own waiting launch, ready to guide the next ship into the harbor. Chief Officer Owen, as customary, took the first watch. He set the liner on a southward course toward Cape Hermes, off Port St. John's. It was about 160 miles down the coast of Pondoland, or the Transkei, a self-governing territory within the South African Republic.

With increasingly strong headwinds, *Waratah* might not realize her customary 13.5 knots. Nonetheless, the night was clear. Lighthouses and buoys winked reassuringly.

About four o'clock the next morning, a wet, blustery Tuesday, *Waratah* was sighted by the small cargo vessel, *Clan McIntyre*. She had also steamed out of Durban on Monday. Under no obligation to challenge the larger ship, the master—Andrew Weir—nonetheless blinked by light: "What ship?"

"*Waratah* for London," came the clear reply through a murky predawn.

"*Clan McIntyre* for London," the introductions finished. Then the watch on the 4,800-ton steamer continued, "What weather had you from Australia?"

"Strong southwesterly and southerly winds across."

"Thanks, good-bye. Pleasant voyage," *Clan McIntyre* signed off.

"Thanks. Same to you. Good-bye."

This ended the conversation across the dark green, roiling seas flecked with whitecaps. However, *Clan McIntyre* kept the tall, hulking shape of the Lund's liner in sight for several hours. At 7:00 A.M. the two were roughly abeam of Cape Hermes, about thirteen and a half miles distant, steering southwest. The visibility must have improved or the familiar landfall would not have been distinguishable. Also, the *Waratah* could not have made the 160-mile run without being aided by the four- to six-knot Agulhas Current sweeping down the southeast African shores.

And still the ships steamed in view of one another, the *Waratah* about ten miles ahead. Since the *Clan McIntyre* could not approach the thirteen and a half knots of the big liner—eight or nine knots was closer—the latter must have slowed down. This fact, however, did not seem to be of especial note to Captain Weir of the *Clan McIntyre*, who would merely observe later that the *Waratah* "appeared to be perfectly upright and to be in no difficulty, steaming rapidly."

Her uprightness, nonetheless, was contradicted by an apprentice on board the freighter, *S. P. Lamont*, who noted "a list to starboard and sailing along like a yacht—heeled over. She was showing her propellers above the surface now and again and pitching."

About 9:20 A.M., *Waratah* altered course, crossing from the *Clan McIntyre*'s starboard to port bow. Some estimated she came as close as two miles. *Waratah* then seemed to pick up speed and was lost in the mists. At this time, *Clan McIntyre* calculated she was about twelve miles off the mouth of the Bashee River.

However, the freighter now had her own concerns. The strong winds and heavy seas from the southwest were building up. Solid water cascaded across her bow and geysered in frothy spindrift over king posts. She had to make sure hatches were securely battened, the booms double-lashed. Her speed was cut back to one-half.

About 7:30 P.M., this Tuesday, the small British freighter *Harlow*—a shade over four thousand tons—was also thrashing through these stormy seas close inshore to Cape Hermes, not more than a mile or two abeam. Captain John Bruce observed through the darkness and clouds two masthead lights gaining astern "and the red light of a vessel eight or ten miles away." Presumably, these lights belonged to the same ship.

In spite of the storm, the master thought he saw bush fires burning on shore, a common occurrence during the "dry season." Then he watched two red flares shoot up as high as one thousand feet.

His second officer, Alfred E. Harris, saw the same spectacle as "a glow among the smoke...then a large flare up in the heavens lasting a minute or two." Robert P. Owens, the chief officer, thought the "flames" were "narrow at the bottom, mushrooming out on top."

It was all over so quickly that the three—captain and two mates—agreed that their visual memories could play tricks on them. However, they decided that the lights and/or flares probably were coming from a signal station on Cape Hermes, while the glow was from bush fires.

The *Harlow* steamed on through the night and the wild sea.

However, *if* the sighting of flares, masthead lights, fires, or whatever had any connection with the *Waratah*—as Captain Bruce would speculate—the Lund's Blue Anchor liner would have been hove to for some eleven hours since the *Clan McIntyre* had sighted her off the same Cape Hermes at 7:00 A.M. Barring engine trouble, the ship that the *Harlow* reported could not reasonably have been the *Waratah*.

About two and a half hours later, logged at precisely 9:51 P.M., the 5,000-ton Union Castle liner *Guelph*, inbound for Durban, sighted "a large passenger ship" abeam of Hood Point, adjacent to East London. This was some 140 miles below Cape Hermes. Captain James N. Culverwell ordered Chief Officer Thomas R. Blanchard to "raise" the other vessel, now about five miles distant.

Blanchard blinked his signal lamp repeatedly, but the only letters he could make out from the stranger were these: "T A H." In any case, Culverwell decided the big steamer was "on course for Cape Town," and there was no reason to keep on attempting to identify her, even though Master Culverwell suspected she was the *Waratah*.

Guelph plodded on for Port Natal.

But, *how* could the second ship have been the *Waratah*? Not conceivably if the masthead lights sighted by the *Harlow* were actually those of the Lund's liner. But two and a half hours separated these loggings by the two small vessels—and a distance of 140 miles!

If the *Guelph* had actually "spoken" *Waratah*, then the *Harlow* had seen some other ship, or none at all. It was reasonable and conceivable, however, that both the *Clan McIntyre* and the *Guelph* could have hailed the *Waratah*.

By Wednesday morning, *Clan McIntyre* was butting into a storm of "hurricane intensity...with tremendous seas." The southerly gales had now shifted to the northeast, tossing the small freighter onto her beam ends. Other ships were wallowing in this same Indian Ocean fury. The *Bannockburn*, for example, en route from New York to New Zealand, listed the storm as one of "unprecedented violence." Most of her deck cargo, including supplemental coal bags, was washed overboard.

Curiously, perhaps, it was the loss of her super cargo, which tended to make her top-heavy, that helped to save the ship.

The *Magdala*, bound for Sydney from Durban, was having a hard time of it, as was the German steamer *Furth*. The small French coaster *Menaranda*, plying between Madagascar and East London, was so delayed that for several days she was reported overdue. The British *Illovo* logged "mountainous seas and cyclonic weather."

On the tail of the great storm was the *Solveig*, inbound for Durban from Norfolk. She logged "extremely rough weather." The *Kildonan Castle* missed much of it. But the angry seas must have been peculiarly familiar to one passenger: Claude Sawyer.

Waratah should have rounded Table Bay some time on Thursday, the twenty-ninth, and tied up in Cape Town. But not until Saturday, the last day of July, did agents for Lund's Blue Anchor Line begin to worry.

Where was the queen of the fleet?

The salvage steamer *Sir Thomas Fuller* was chartered to sniff the coastal waters from Cape Town to Durban, upwards of nine hundred miles to the east, while the tug *Harry Escombe* thumped out of Durban on the same quest. Perhaps *Waratah* was stuck on a sandbar, awaiting only a good push or a towline.

"Have you spoken the *Waratah*?" the masters of the two vessels called through megaphones to passing ships. Without exception the answers proved negative. Continuing rough weather forced the small craft to return to port.

The Royal Navy was alerted. Three cruisers of varying speed and obsolescence put out from South African ports. They were HMS *Pandora*, *Hermes*, and *Forte*.

Although as July ended and August commenced there had been no formal announcement that *Waratah* was overdue, the fact was already common knowledge along the Cape Town and Durban waterfronts. One man, whose wife and children were aboard, had haunted the end of the Cape Town breakwater since Friday morning, July 30, waiting for the long black hull and superstructure to loom into view.

Then, on August 4, the London *Times* noted, "It may safely be assumed that the vessel's machinery was in some way broken down...the case is admitted to be serious." A spokesman for Lund's, however, was quoted as saying the owners "do not consider there is cause for anxiety."

Two days later, Lund's Blue Anchor Line admitted, "Concern is felt for the safety of the *Waratah*." On Sunday, August 8, in Melbourne, there was so much "concern" that prayers and hymns for the safety of those onboard the missing liner were offered in all the churches. "Intense anxiety prevails," noted a Reuter's dispatch.

The churches along South Africa's coasts and some in Great Britain also prayed that *Waratah* would again make port. But when the last bars of "O God our help in ages past" and "O hear us when we cry to Thee for those in peril on the sea!" grew silent and the worshippers filed out, the liner's fate still remained a question mark.

On Monday, the British press carried a report that a ship resembling the *Waratah* was "slowly making for Durban." When nothing materialized, the shamefaced editors did not bother even to bang out a correction.

Nonetheless, Lund's would not publicly abandon hope.

"There has been very bad weather off the coast," read an official announcement. "We are of the opinion that some part of the machinery has been disabled, such as the main steam-pipe, which would take several days to repair. The vessel is probably drifting."

And a London editorial counseled, "the need for wireless stations at Cape Town, Port Elizabeth, and Durban…[and] on board liners…is especially great."

Now en route from Cape Town to London, Claude Sawyer was rather enjoying his passage aboard the *Kildonan Castle*. The weather in the South Atlantic was favorable. Besides, he wouldn't know about the missing *Waratah* until he docked in the Thames.

Meanwhile, London reporters had gathered at Phoenix Lodge Mansions in Brook Green, Sawyer's London home. In their hands were *Waratah* passenger lists, wheedled and bullied out of a very reluctant Lund's. They read with all the inherent doom of tombstone inscriptions. Like a very Charon, the local vicar, heavily in black, accompanied the somber little group, according to one writer.

But none was prepared for his reception. Reporters and minister were greeted rather cheerily by Maude Prudence Sawyer herself, who also clutched a piece of paper to wave at *them*: the cablegram from Durban announcing that Claude was en route home by another ship.

"I expect," she was quoted, "my husband will be along soon, don't you think?"

Far less confident, the National Bank of South Africa, in London, in receipt of Nora Connolly's cabled $5,000, was not at all sure what to do with it except hold on. And that's what they did.

All ships departing from South African ports were ordered to keep "a sharp lookout" for the big Lund's liner. One was the 4,500-ton freighter *Tottenham*, Antwerp-bound. Charles Edward Cox, the master, dutifully passed the word to his mates.

Early on the morning of August 11, about twenty-five miles south-east of East London, the captain and John Noble Day, the second mate, were called to the bridge by an apprentice, Curtis, at the wheel. He reported he had seen in the water "a little girl—ten or twelve—dressed in a red gown." In fact, she was so close as to be caught in the vessel's wash.

Master Cox and Mate Day then studied the seas through their binoculars. The master would report "all round the ship pieces of flesh floating on the water, one piece larger than the others with an alba-tross" sitting on it. He thought that was indeed "the trunk of a body."

Officers and crewmen, now aroused, lined the decks. E. F. Humphrey, the third officer, was certain he was looking at "two human bodies face downward," with seagulls perched on their heads. As the ship plowed on, since the master thought the seas were too rough to attempt retrieval or positive identification, more chunks seemingly of flesh were passed, with sharks coursing around them.

Chinese stokers, momentarily abandoning their steamy domain, would exclaim, "Plenty dead bodies seaside!" And this was about the extent of their English or their comprehension.

There was, on the other hand, some difference of opinion. Chief Officer David Evam saw nothing of the sort. Maybe "a big skate" or "blubber" in the water, or a school of large fish such as the big, oval sun-fish being torn to pieces by the ravenous sharks. Chief Engineer John Hammond was certain the "little girl" was nothing else than a roll of red paper. When the third mate, Humphrey, thought more about it, he decided he had seen only what "looked like bodies." He could not be fully certain.

By the next morning, all on board the *Tottenham*, except perhaps the Chinese, were wholly in doubt as to what, if anything, had passed by their ship. Accosted by the cruiser *Forte* as to sighting of the *Waratah*, Captain Cox replied he had "seen nothing" that could be linked to the missing liner.

At the same time, the mate of the 3,000-ton freighter, *Insizwa*, out of Aberdeen, reported to Captain W. O. Moore the sighting of four fully clothed bodies. The ship's position then was off the Bashee River, some 125 miles east of the *Tottenham*'s sightings. The master, however, tended to the opinion that he was looking at blubber or "the refuse from whales."

On August 18, three full weeks after the *Waratah* should have tied up at Cape Town, Lund's persisted publicly that "something of a favor-able nature would yet be heard." She was probably "disabled" and "drifting." One thing seemed certain: The passengers and crew would not go hungry. If the cargo of frozen hides were taken into consideration, passengers and crew could count on provisions sufficient for at least a year.

Lund's pinned their corporate hopes for survival of the liner on the strange case of the *Waikato*, 1899. Between June 6 and September 15 of that year, the disabled steamer drifted two thousand miles across the South Indian Ocean, borne along by the westerly "Roaring Forties." She was finally picked up off Freemantle, generally in good shape. Those aboard were hungry but well.

On the chance that the *Waratah*, with engines cold, was following the same track, the line chartered the 3,800-ton Union Castle ship *Sabine* and piled 4,000 tons of coal onto her. On her bow was mounted a large searchlight. On September 11, with naval officers and Lund's representatives aboard, she cast off from Cape Town to sniff out sea-lanes swelling past such outposts as St. Paul, the Crozets, and Kerguelen Island, all the way to the Australian coast.

And even as the *Sabine* steamed off in search, so did the *Waratah* drift out of the news columns.

Weeks turned into months—September, October, November passed. The chartered Union Castle ship searched three thousand square miles of open ocean. In early December, she returned in frustration. The official postscript to her long cruise read like an obituary. The *Sabine* had found "no trace...no wreckage, or anything of that sort." She spoke only four other vessels, none of which had sighted anything resembling the *Waratah*. With her distinctive black hull and high white superstructure, how could there be any mistake?

The *Sabine*'s searchlights had picked up penguins on the icy shores of Kerguelen Island, the desolate French possession on the outer ramparts of Antarctica. The bare bones of sailing vessels lost long ago had been seen on other uninhabited islands, but nothing that conceivably could have once been part of the *Waratah*.

Geelong, the liner's smaller "sister," returned from a much less extensive search with similar lack of success.

Thus, in mid-December, rather belatedly, the historic Lutine Bell was rung in Lloyd's of London. *Waratah* was formally "posted missing," a preliminary to treating insurance claims, commencing with those involving liner and cargo.

One by one the survivors—widows, children, parents, a few husbands—came forward. In Dublin, the probate court awarded Nora Connolly's $5,000 and other sums and property to those sharing in the estate. In London, the widow of Arthur Edward Bellringer, a coal trimmer, was granted $55 a week for twelve months for herself and the care of two children. The balance of some $750 was to be invested and held in trust. Harriet M. Skailes, the widow—who happened to be in delicate health—of the purser, S. G. Skailes, was granted an outright $1,500 for her family.

And so on and so on. But even as the next of kin of the 211 souls who had sailed on the *Waratah* entered courts or insurance or legal offices, one last, forlorn effort was put forth to find the vanished liner. Since her loss had brought sorrow to so many homes "Down Under," it was not surprising that a "committee of citizens" would be formed at Melbourne. By popular subscription, $25,000 was raised—enough, seemingly, to charter the brand-new cargo vessel *Wakefeld* for an "exhaustive search."

The 4,000-ton freighter sailed from Cape Town on February 22, 1910. When she returned in June, after mostly retracing the *Sabine*'s course, the *Wakefeld* had nothing to report save the sighting of "a large herd of cattle" on New Amsterdam Island. She also did some soundings of hitherto uncharted bays and channels of the remote islands in the southern reaches of the Indian Ocean.

And while the *Wakefeld* plowed through the loneliness of distant seas, the world itself changed. The man who lent his name to an era died on May 6. Edward VII, almost seventy, succumbed to heart failure, bronchitis, and a lifetime of excesses. The British press "turned the rules" as London waited two weeks for international and Empire leaders to assemble for the awesome, as well as interminable, spectacle of his funeral and final burial at Windsor Castle.

During these days, Halley's Comet, which had not been seen for seventy-six years, made its fiery-tailed visitation. The astrologically minded, or perhaps the simply superstitious, pondered its meaning, if any. Appearing at this solemn time of transition, was it a portent of good, evil, or conceivably some blander state in between?

Although the *Wakefeld* and the *Sabine* had encountered nothing, hints of the *Waratah* continued for some months to drift ashore. In March, for example, a cushion marked "W" was picked up at Mossel Bay, to the east of Cape Town, along with a hatchway bearing no identification. A deck chair plainly marked *Waratah* floated into Coffee Cove, thirty-five miles south of Port St. John's. A life belt, also stamped with the name of the missing liner, washed onto the beach at Manukau Harbor, New Zealand.

But there wasn't much. And any of these items could easily have fallen overboard without implying danger to the ship. Some five messages in bottles picked up along the Australian coast, purporting to have been tossed from the liner, were dismissed as hoaxes.

Certainly, these were disastrous, at best chancy, times for those who journeyed by sea or earned their livelihood through it: 23,274 human beings had been lost at sea—in steam and sailing vessels—in the *two decades* through 1909, Lloyd's announced grimly. This involved 2,420 steam and 5,911 sailing ships of United Kingdom and colonial registry. Causes included foundering, stranding, collisions, fire, or simply "missing" like the *Waratah*. The net tonnage of steamships lost was nearly two million.

Marine insurance rates continued to soar. And underwriters sniffed it was scant wonder.

Finally, almost seventeen months after the liner's disappearance, a formal inquiry was convened by the Board of Trade in Caxton Hall, Borough of Westminster. Under Magistrate John Dickinson, the proceedings continued from mid-December until early January 1911. Depositions, mostly, were presented—from former passengers and crew, from Lund's officials, the builders, inspectors, insurers, harbor pilots, stowage representatives, marine engineers and architects—indeed, almost anyone who had ever seen or merely contemplated the *Waratah* and had some comment to proffer.

Not until February 23 were the findings announced. They surprised no one. *Waratah* was "lost in the gale of July 28, 1909, which was of exceptional violence for those waters and was the first great storm she had encountered...the precise manner of her loss could not be determined upon the evidence available." But those who sifted the evidence were "on the whole inclined to the opinion that she capsized," while the "particular chain of circumstances" leading to the disaster eluded the investigators. Certainly, the sinking "must have been sudden" since no wreckage was found.

She "should" be lying somewhere off the Bashee River in perhaps six thousand feet of water—more than a mile deep, many times below diving range.

Purported sightings after the *Clan McIntyre* hailed her were discounted. After that, "so far as the court had been able to ascertain...[she] was not seen or spoken by any other vessel."

The search missions had served a negative purpose since, had the *Waratah* merely been "disabled," she "would have been found." The court decided the liner was in paradoxically fine shape, from trim to the functioning of her engines:

"She had sufficient stability as laden. She was in proper trim for the voyage she was about to undertake. She was in good condition as regards structure, and so far as the evidence went in a seaworthy condition; but there was not sufficient evidence before the Court to show that all proper precautions such as battening hatches, securing ports, coaling doors, etc. had been taken...the cargo was properly stowed."

Not only did it sound as though the Board of Trade was building a case to show that the *Waratah* could *not* have sunk, but as well was seeking to contradict witnesses such as Claude Sawyer. He was credited only with evincing "considerable prescience," and trying to be helpful. The court decided he saw a "list" where none existed, in the testimony of others, and that really her "behavior" was no "different from that of other ships of similar size and type in like conditions of sea" and weather. She was perhaps as seaworthy as the reliable *Geelong*.

Indeed, the eminent gentlemen, whose number included two naval officers, who sat in judgment, spoke with some awe of the *Waratah*'s "slow majestic roll."

Similarly, the court disposed of testimony from the *Harlow* and *Tottenham*. Captain Bruce, of the former, by this time had evolved the theory that bunkers of the *Waratah* had overheated and exploded. Rubbish, sniffed the court, in effect. The master had seen brush fires. Had Captain Ilbery been in trouble, he would have fired rockets or other distress signals. And what Captain Cox and others of the *Tottenham* were looking at in the water was undoubtedly "offal" from the whaling station at Durban drifting with the Agulhas Current.

So went the "findings." They were calm, objective, quasi-legal with one partly angry exception.

"No special report...was made by Captain Ilbery as to her behavior on her maiden voyage," although such was "forthcoming from a number of persons." While Lund produced all of his correspondence from the master, "in no one of them is the ship's behavior at sea touched upon. Trivial matters, such as a cow or a little dog being on board were mentioned, emigrants' complaints as to food and attendance...but nowhere was the behavior of his fine new ship mentioned.

"In view of the fact that the *Waratah* was a new departure for this line and that her specification was being used as the basis of the specification of another new ship the Court was quite unable to understand how silence could have been preserved on such an important and interesting subject as the stability and behavior at sea."

The "indifference" with which Lund presented such "trivial" testimony appalled the court, which was "almost compelled to draw an inference unfavorable to the owners as regards their knowledge of the ship's behavior on her maiden voyage."

Too, Lund's was criticized for a lack of fire drills and for allowing lifeboats that were not fully "watertight." However, the court was satisfied that the boats had been repaired and were satisfactory when she left Durban for the last time.

Aware that its jurisdiction was extremely limited, the court nonetheless suggested the possibility of the formation of a committee to study "minimum stability requirements of different types of vessel."

Otherwise, as an amen, it could only "express its regret for the loss of life and its sympathy with the relatives and friends of those lost."

In sum, the inquiry, in setting forth many reasons why the *Waratah* should have remained afloat, only compounded the mystery. Why, surely, did so many ships, older and half her size, manage to ride out this "unprecedented" storm?

Barclay, Curle & Co., the builders, emerged quite unscathed. They would continue to send ships screeching down their Scottish ways. And they had, in great measure, their able counsel, Butler Aspinall, to thank. He was Britain's leading admiralty lawyer.

Nonetheless, the Blue Anchor Line was ruined. Its owners were haunted by the memory of the *Waratah*. They tore to shreds architects' drawings for what was to be an almost exact sister ship and burned them. The remaining Lund's vessels were sold one by one to the Peninsula and Oriental Line.

Lund's, a famous name to travelers and cargo forwarders to South Africa and "Down Under," sailed, along with the queen of her fleet, into oblivion.

But, *what* had happened to *Waratah*, the patron wildflower of Australia? Considering the bafflement admitted by the court of inquiry, Claude Sawyer's nightmare ogre with the bloody sword and/or bloody rag could have risen out of the sea and somehow done in the liner. With such total lack of evidence as to even a probable cause, none really could contradict such a hypothesis, wild and bizarre as it had to be.

The distinctive blue anchor was long gone from steamship funnels. Perhaps no other first-class fare would equal the rich kippers broiled in butter and the tender lamb chops. A void had surely been created in dining at sea. Then a World War came and went. A new generation of travel agents and ocean forwarders could blankly ask, "Lund's who?" or even "Lund's what?"

But the name *Waratah* was not so readily buried, forgotten. In

1932, for example, a sick old seaman, John Noble, surfaced in a hospital in Oshawa, Ontario (directly across the lake from Rochester, New York). He reportedly confided to a nurse that he was a crewman on the *Waratah* when she was struck by a furious storm. This happened, by chance, when some of his "mates" were about to mutiny. Or so he said.

He went on to describe how the liner "suddenly rolled over." Being a powerful swimmer, however, Noble struggled to shore, holding onto "a ten-year-old girl of a wealthy English family." He could have been describing one of the Turner children. That he pinpointed the area as East London indicated that the old salt at least had read something about the Lund's liner.

Noble had no explanation of why he waited twenty-three years to spin this unlikely yarn. Also, what happened to the girl? A check of hospital records in the Oshawa area (by the author) elicited no confirmation that there ever was a patient by the name "John Noble" in the early 1930s. Was it only a newspaper story?

Seven years later, in 1939, timbers were found off the Bashee River which some thought belonged to the missing liner. Then, after another World War intervened, in the early 1950s a South African Air Force pilot believed he had seen the silhouette of what he described as "a large ship" lying on her side atop a reef, but under the surface. This too was in the vicinity of the Bashee River and Cape Hermes.

Patrol vessels used the latitude and longitude given by the pilot to scour the area. Nothing was seen. No echo sounder traced such a wreck.

In 1954, one Frank Price came forward with the story of Jan Pretorius, a Boer, who had been illegally prospecting for diamonds along the banks of the Bashee that last week in July 1909. He saw a ship wallowing inshore during a very bad storm. It was so close that he was sure it broke up on the rocks and shoals. Since he did not want to be arrested in violation of the strict diamond laws, he kept what he saw to himself. Pretorius had sworn Price, an English friend, to secrecy until his demise. This was Price's story.

With the publication, in 1963, of Eric Rosenthal's history of Durban—*Schooners and Skyscrapers*—came a new theory. He quoted a Port Natal pilot, identified as R. H. Sheppard, as reporting that a considerable quantity of surplus dynamite had been discarded off the South African coast in the summer of 1909: "Through some oversight this had not been properly dumped and about half a hundredweight of it was left floating about." The author continued:

"The *Waratah* left Durban and, encountering very bad weather, was driven off her course into a region where there was floating dynamite. She blew up and hardly a soul was saved. Some of the bodies were seen by shipping that passed by."

The author then produced a survivor, "young Staunton," who did not surface until 1915 when he tried to locate his family in Ireland—by means of newspaper ads. "Most probably coming from simple folk, he never thought of giving the matter publicity," rationalized Rosenthal. The chap is, in the same literary breath, disposed of by hustling him off to the Western Front where he "gave his life."

Unwittingly, perhaps, Rosenthal, in his otherwise meticulously researched work, has introduced another basic question mark. One is informed that dynamite is generally stable, detonated by means only of blasting caps.

John Noble, Frank Price, "young Staunton"—if indeed any one of the three existed—would have shared one trait in common. They must have, belatedly, been seized with "the great event syndrome." For example, after the *Titanic* disaster, many persons claimed—with no basis of fact—to have been aboard the doomed White Star superliner. Did Noble, Price, and Staunton want to be identified with a sea tragedy, although considerably down in the statistical casualty scale from the *Titanic?* Certainly, these three entities—wraiths?—were amply qualified to join the imaginative, improbable ranks of J. Habakuk Jephson, Abel Fosdyk, or even Hornibrook's "huge octopus or devilfish," while not altogether dismissing Sawyer's fiend with the dripping sword.

Fact or fiction—the fate of the *Waratah* yet haunts and confounds those who have any interest at all in the sea and who ply its broad pathways. Like a steam-propelled, steel-hulled Flying Dutchman of the twentieth century, does the Lund's liner still steam her ghostly course, perhaps in the distant reaches of the Antarctic?

Or is she in a shallow grave so close to, say, the African coast that even a scuba diver could explore the mysterious caverns that "sea change" has wrought upon her saloons?

Whatever happened in the still impenetrable mystery of it all, not the *Wakool* or the *Woolloomoolloo*, but *Waratah*, queen of Lund's Blue Anchor Line, has become the lost wildflower.

* * *

According to Clive Cussler (identified in the *Scorpion* acknowledgments), his underwater team has found the *Waratah* in about 350 feet of water, which would be at the end of the continental shelf in the area where the liner was last seen. He added, "We don't have a 100 percent identification...yet."

One member of his team, Emlyn Brown, "put divers on the wreck who have confirmed the configuration of the hull (the forward part of the superstructure looked as though it had been badly smashed). The current was so strong that they could only observe what they saw as they were swept over the wreck from stern to bow."

With more sophisticated equipment, including special sonar and radar, the group had plans to return in March 1999.

As a postscript, Cussler declared, "We won't give up until we have an absolute make on the wreck."

Good luck, Clive!

3

RMS *Lusitania*

A midchannel course

SLIGHTLY MORE THAN FOUR years later, on June 15, 1915, a drizzly Tuesday in London, another court was meeting—this within the baroque grandeur of Central Hall, Westminster, *in camera*. The Right Honorable Lord Mersey, wreck commissioner, presided over a solemn little group of two naval and two merchant marine officers—"advisory assessors"—of whom the senior was Admiral Sir F. S. Inglefield KCB. Mersey, in his mid-seventies and newly distinguished for conducting the *Titanic* hearings in 1912, was the patriarch of them all.

There was one other familiar face, Butler Aspinall, who happened to have represented the Board of Trade at the *Titanic* investigation, following his services for Barclay, Curle & Co. during the *Waratah* sessions. Now the veteran admiralty lawyer spoke for another famous client: the Cunard Company. At his side sat a squat, heavyset, glum figure, Captain William Thomas Turner, former master of the 32,000-ton *Lusitania*.

Both Lord Mersey, who also answered to Baron Mersey, and the attorney general, Sir Edward Henry Carson, had much to inquire of the weary, sixty-year-old Cunard master. Carson, a famous trial lawyer who had successfully defended the Marquis of Queensberry in the libel suit brought by Oscar Wilde, shook a piece of paper under Turner's nose. The attorney general was tall, lean, with aquiline nose, piercing eyes—altogether intimidating.

"Look at that paper!" he snapped. "Did you receive a paper like that?"

"Yes."

" 'Section 3, vessels approaching or leaving British or French ports,' " Carson quoted. " 'The danger is greatest in the vicinity of and off prominent headlands on the coast. Important landfalls in this area should be made after dark whenever possible.' Do you remember that?"

"Yes."

"Did you get on May 6 a message saying 'take Liverpool pilot at bar and *avoid headlands*? Pass harbors at full speed....'?"

"I did."

The attorney general seemed dissatisfied as he read from a confidential Admiralty daily voyage notice of April 15:

" 'German submarines appear to be operating chiefly off prominent headlands and landfalls. Ships should give prominent headlands a wide berth.' "

Then he pursued:

"What do you call the Old Head of Kinsale?"

"That is a headland. But I passed ten miles from it and better. My view is that I gave it a wide berth."

"Ten miles...and you thought that a wide berth?"

Carson came closer to the witness as he continued, "What I want to ask you is, why with that information before you did you come so close to Kinsale Head?"

"To get a fix. We were not quite sure what land it was. We were so far off...I do not navigate a ship on guesswork...I wanted to find out where I was."

"Do you *mean* to say you had *no* idea where you were?"

"Yes, I had an approximate idea, but I wanted to be sure."

"Why did you want to go *groping* about to try and find where land was?"

"So that I could get a proper course."

"Did you get a wireless telegram to the effect that submarines were active off the south coast of Ireland?"

"I did."

"Do you remember 'submarines off Fastnet'?"

"Yes."

"Do you remember whereabouts you got that?"

"No. I cannot remember. I cannot say."

"Did you also get on May 6, 'Pass harbors at full speed...steer mid-channel course'?"

"Yes."

Then, the interrogation touched on Brow Head, a medium-sized promontory fifteen miles northwest of the major landfall, Fastnet Rock, almost on the western coast of Ireland:

"What is the width of the channel there?"

"I could not tell you."

"But you could form an idea?" Lord Mersey interjected.

"No, my Lord. I cannot."

Carson added, "You say you were warned specifically to avoid the headlands and to stay in midchannel...."

The wreck commissioner interrupted, "Off Old Kinsale, what is the width of the channel *there?*"

"One hundred forty [miles]," answered Turner.

There was a stunned silence as if the court could not quite believe what it was hearing.

"Then, *how* can you say that ten miles off Old Kinsale is *midchannel?*" asked Lord Mersey, mentally dividing 140 by two.

Before Turner could reply, Carson added, "You really do not think, do you, that you were in midchannel or anywhere near it...you did not think it necessary to be in midchannel?"

"No."

Apparently believing that this line of questioning had been exhausted, with little results, Carson introduced a memo of April 16: " 'War experience has shown that fast steamers can considerably reduce the chance of successful surprise submarine attacks by zigzagging—that is to say, altering the course at short and irregular intervals....' "

The attorney general paused to ask: "Did you zigzag?"

"No."

"Why?"

"Because I did not think it necessary until I saw a submarine."

"Do you mean to say it was not possible for you to follow the Admiralty directions?"

"Yes, it was possible."

"Then, why did you not do it?"

"I considered I followed them as well as I could."

The attorney general persisted. "Then, do you suggest these Admiralty instructions are all wrong?"

"No, I do not suggest that at all."

And so on through six days of hearings, of which two were *in camera.* Turner was not only rumpled in appearance but seemed tired and dazed, even though he had had five weeks in which to recuperate. Was there something the matter with the captain?

Even his counsel, Butler Aspinall, conceded that Turner was "a poor witness," if "an honest man."

To which Lord Mersey generously replied, "He was not a bad witness. I think he means to tell the truth."

But "he was *confused*, my Lord," Aspinall concluded their private little exchange.

Not only did the Mersey inquiry fail to close the books on the torpedoing of the *Lusitania*, but many questions would become ghosts haunting the history of United States-British relations: the actual nature of the Cunarder's cargo (if not as manifested), especially contraband; her routing, escort; the attitudes and intentions, or motives, of the Admiralty and the Foreign Office itself; and, surely, the reason for Captain Turner's admitted disobedience of orders.

Particularly vexing: *Why* had she sunk in a very few minutes when the *Titanic*, similarly compartmented and with a gash one-third the length of her hull, had remained afloat almost three hours? And *why* was the *Lusitania* permitted to enter submarine waters with six of her twenty-five boilers cold?

Are these questions valid, as having basis in fact, or are some or *all* frivolous, the creations of sensation peddlers or the blatantly paranoid?

* * *

When *Lusitania*, fresh from John Brown's teeming yard at Clydebank, Scotland, steamed out on her maiden voyage in 1907, she was furrowing a new wake in maritime history. Her four mighty turbines, thundering out seventy thousand horsepower, drove four huge propellers to produce speeds of up to thirty knots. This was hitherto unheard of in old-fashioned reciprocating engine liners, such as those that the Germans persisted in using and that cost them the Blue Riband. She was the first steamship to cut Atlantic transit time down to four and a half days.

Considering train connection problems, one could not cross the American continent much faster—at best, only by a matter of hours.

She was the largest vessel since the *Great Eastern*, which was classed at some twenty-two thousand tons. But this process of evolution had required the remarkable period of about half a century. She was the first of the modern luxury liners, although her sister *Mauretania*, the yet larger *Aquitania*, then the rivals *Olympic* and *Titanic* followed her off the ways in relatively short order.

Lusitania featured Doric columns in her first-class saloons, arched

Lusitania from a postcard, supplied by survivor Florence Padley.

Sister ship *Mauretania,* from a postcard.

doorways, domed skylights, tapestries, overstuffed damask furniture, potted palms, electric lights, telephones, elevators, candelabra, inlaid mahogany, even—of all incongruities at sea—fireplaces. Her suites rivaled, if not exceeded, the most sumptuous at the world's elegant hotels: the Waldorf or Astor in New York, the Savoy or Grosvenor in London, the Ritz in Paris, Excelsior in Rome, Great Eastern in Calcutta, Grand Oriental in Colombo, and so on.

Company brochures trumpeted as well a nursery, diet kitchens, gymnasium, a hospital, and certainly kennels for those who could not leave Fido or Tabby at home.

Her owners had even boasted initially that she was "unsinkable." But after the fateful spring of 1912, the worldwide horror—and disbelief—over the superliner that struck an iceberg, they no longer discussed this bonus. Nonetheless, *Lusitania*'s double bottom and 175 watertight compartments lent certain logic to the claim.

She and her sister *"Maury"*—dubbed the "lovely sisters"—remained in great favor both with the affluent transatlantic commuting set and also with those immigrating. The two were fast and, for the most part, comfortable. However, *Lusy*'s 762-foot length against an 87-foot beam, giving her a slim-waisted 8.7-to-1 ratio comparable to destroyers or cruisers, resulted in a high-speed roll. Some passengers found this, along with propeller vibrations in stern quarters, quite unpleasant at the least, a certain cause for *mal de mer* at the worst.

By the outbreak of World War I, in August 1914, *Lusitania* had completed about one hundred roundtrip crossings and transported between one-quarter and one-third of a million passengers. She and *"Maury"* manifestly had set new standards of dependability and safety. Now, Cunard, with White Star and all other lines flying the Union Jack, waited on Admiralty orders as to the wartime role for its liners and freighters.

The 19,000-ton *Carmania*, for example, the first major ship to be equipped with steam turbines, was at once converted into an armed merchant cruiser, equipped with 4.7-inch rifles and nests of machine guns. She went into action quickly. On September 14, 1914, off Trinidad Island, a possession of Brazil, *Carmania* sank, after a furious battle, the similar-size German auxiliary cruiser, *Cap Trafalgar*. It remains the only naval engagement between large liners.

But what to do with *Lusitania, Mauretania,* and *Aquitania*, also with the White Star *Olympic*, as well as the *Britannic*, a sister of the *Titanic*, which had not yet debuted in passenger service? Most superliners presented a special and unwieldy problem. All five had been as deliberately and specifically designed for peace as battleships had been forged for war. It was rather beside the point, in reality, academic, that the blue-prints of these liners had routinely indicated where deck plates were or could be of double thickness, suitable for gun mounts.

Olympic and *Aquitania* were at first armed, with the intent of using them as merchant cruisers like the *Carmania.* But they proved too big—too long for maneuverability, to bring port and starboard batteries alternately to bear. They were converted back to use as transports or hospital ships.

Lusitania and *Mauretania* were already registered as "Royal Naval Reserved Merchant Cruisers...at the disposal of His Majesty's Government." They were also permitted to fly the blue ensign, denoting them as naval auxiliaries, contrasted with the white ensign of ships of the battle line. The merchant flag was the familiar "red duster." Which flag he flew in time of war was a matter for the master's discretion. For that matter, most merchant officers were reservists. Some remained aboard their old vessels—as in the case with *Carmania*—others were ordered to warships.

Thus, the "lovely sisters," by international law, were technically legitimate prizes of war. They were naval auxiliaries, whatever "duster" they flew. But neither was desired as a merchant cruiser. After remaining in transatlantic service for most of the autumn, *Mauretania* was withdrawn and readied as a transport or hospital ship, depending on the exigencies of the moment.

Lusitania continued to steam her familiar Liverpool-Southampton "milk run" of the North Atlantic, which she had accomplished so faithfully. By winter she was the only superliner plying between New York and England, even though the sleek, smaller American ships, *St. Louis* and *St. Paul,* were almost as fast. They as well flew a desideratum—the flag of a nonbelligerent.

As other British and neutral lines—such as the Dutch—took their ships out of commercial service, Cunard continued boldly to advertise *Lusitania*'s sailings in prominent display boxes. Some months she sailed from New York twice. It was generally accepted that Kaiser Wilhelm would respect a ship carrying women and children, many if not most of them from nonbelligerent countries, even though she flew the hated Union Jack. And if Kaiser "Bill" did not, certainly this great liner could outrun any submarine that prowled the sea-lanes.

But in early February 1915, a veteran Cunard master, David "Paddy" Dow, then in command of "*Lusy,*" decided that perhaps too much trust was being accorded the Kaiser's attributed humanity. Believing that a submarine was trailing him off the west coast of Ireland, the master broke out the United States flag, which he flew right up to Liverpool Bar and the pilot launch.

Col. Ed House, special adviser to President Wilson who happened to be aboard this crossing, was informed that the captain considered the threat to be so serious that he was making mental plans on how to rescue his passengers. Dow confided to a mutual friend that he thought *Lusitania* could remain afloat "about an hour...if her boilers didn't explode." The somber Ed House gained scant consolation from the assurances.

Unapologetic in the face of ensuing diplomatic protests, "Paddy" claimed his was "a well-established *ruse de guerre.*" Besides, he was carrying "neutral mails and neutral passengers." But his *ruse* would have fooled not even the dullest-witted U-boat captain. What American flagship bore even the slightest resemblance to the four-funneled Cunard giant?

In April, Dow was taken ill, to be replaced by a relief captain. Cunard chose its old trusty, Will Turner. With the line since 1878, he had been to sea as deck boy on sailing ships since before the American Civil War. A great swimmer, he had been shipwrecked at least once and saved others through his own strength. He was that rare canvas salt who was able to switch over to iron and steam. With a feel for huge vessels, he commanded, at various times, the *Aquitania, Mauretania,* and *Lusitania.* King George, on a visit to the *Aquitania,* personally commissioned Turner a commander in the Royal Naval Reserve.

Thus, it was Turner who would take *"Lusy"* out of New York on Saturday, May 1, 1915. She carried 1,257 passengers, about half her capacity, plus a crew of 702, also a reduction from her peacetime complement. As in all her sailings, there were "names" on board: Alfred Gwynne Vanderbilt, at thirty-eight one of the wealthiest young men in the world; Elbert Hubbard, the "Sage of East Aurora" (New York), long-haired, lovable eccentric, author of *A Message to Garcia,* publisher, founder of the Roycrofters community of craftsmen; Charles Frohman, the producer; Justus Forman, author/playwright; Lady Margaret Mackworth, militant suffragette, who had been jailed several times; Marie de Page, working for Belgian relief, the wife of the celebrated surgeon, Dr. Antoine de Page; Theodate Pope, American architect and spiritualist, en route to a psychical meeting called by Sir Oliver Lodge; others....

But this was no routine wartime sailing. That very morning, the German Embassy in Washington had inserted in the shipping sections of New York newspapers this warning:

NOTICE

Travellers intending to embark on the Atlantic voyage are reminded that a state of war exists between Germany and her allies and Great Britain and her allies; that the zone of war includes the waters adjacent to the British Isles; that, in accordance with formal notice given by the Imperial German Government, vessels flying the flag of Great Britain or of any of her allies are liable to destruction in those waters and that travellers sailing in the war zone on ships of Great Britain or her allies do so at their own risk.

Imperial German Embassy
Washington, D.C., April 22, 1915

In the *World* it had been placed directly against the Cunard paid sailing schedule, surmounted with an impressive sketch of the *Lusitania*, "Fastest and Largest Steamer now in Atlantic Service." This in itself had drawn reporters, photographers, even newsreel cameramen down to Pier 54, the foot of 11th Street, Hudson River. What did the passengers have to say to that? Weren't they afraid of being torpedoed?

One of them, the handsome Vanderbilt, who was en route to inspect his stables in London, broke into laughter when questioned. This had been pretty much his same nonchalant reaction when questioned three years ago about his cancellation of booking the night before the *Titanic* sailed.

Photographers had caught him side by side with Turner. The crusty, onetime sailing master who generally thought of passengers as a barely endurable nuisance, rested a hand lightly on the millionaire playboy's shoulder. The captain chuckled:

"...all these people...booking passage on board the *Lusitania* if they thought she could be caught by a German submarine? Why, it's the best joke I've heard in many days, this talk of torpedoing!...I have never heard of one [a submarine] that could make twenty-seven knots...!"

The trouble was—neither could *Lusitania* make that speed on this voyage, and no passenger had been let in on the secret. With six of her twenty-five boilers cold—her vast battery of 192 furnaces only three-quarters fired—she would be lucky to clock twenty knots, fairly slow for a liner that could push thirty knots. There was reason enough: the price and scarcity of coal; the scarcity of stokers, pulled off for that bottomless human pit, the Western Front. Even so, bunkered at one thousand tons below capacity, *Lusitania* carried a mountainous six thousand tons of the precious black stuff.

However, was Captain Turner kidding Mr. Vanderbilt and the gentlemen of the fourth estate, assuming he was quoted correctly? Or, could

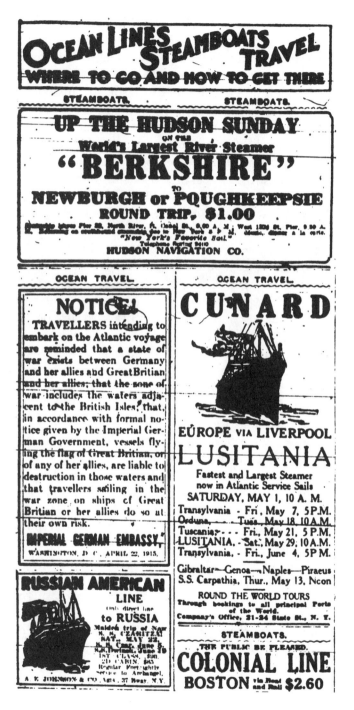

Warning notice in the *World*.

it conceivably have been that he did *not* know the situation below decks? Perhaps he was overendowed with the quality of courage to the point of recklessness. A seaman, Thomas Mahoney, declared the master was "one of the bravest captains I sailed under." He was also one of the loneliest, since his wife had left him to raise their two sons in Australia.

While reporters continued to seek out the better-known passengers, the cargo hatch, located forward, was being battened down. "*Lusy*" was a liner and a fast mail ship, not a freighter. She could not haul nearly so much, for example, as an old tramp like the *Clan McIntyre*. Her manifest this voyage accented foodstuffs. She was bound for an increasingly hungry Island Kingdom. Her largest single item: more than 342,000 pounds of beef, followed by some 185,000 pounds of bacon, 217 pounds of cheese, 205 barrels of Connecticut oysters, and lesser amounts of lard, tongue, beans, pork, and biscuits.

There were as well 4,200 cases of small-caliber rifle ammunition from the Remington Arms Company; 1,250 cases of empty shrapnel shells consigned from Bethlehem Steel; 6 cases of unloaded fuses; a case of air rifles; 200,000 pounds of sheet brass; 11,762 pounds of copper, machine parts, forgings; plus a grab bag of shoelaces, knit goods, woolen samples, leaf tobacco, drugs; muskrat skins; leather sides; dental goods; and—several crates of chickens, mostly likely to be consumed during the voyage.

The total value was manifested with the Collector for the Port of New York for $750,000, which curiously was nearly that paid by the underwriters for cargo aboard the *Waratah*. However, measured by the yardsticks and the dangers of war, none of the cargo, not even the cackling hens, could be considered "safe." Every pound of it, from shoelaces to shell casings, was useful to Germany's enemy. As the Treasury Department observed, "practically all of her cargo was contraband of some kind." A cargo of howitzers or land mines would in no measure have increased a liability to destruction.

Lusitania's sailing was delayed from 10:00 A.M. until 12:30 P.M., partly because of a more or less routine wartime search for bombs or incendiary devices (which German agents were increasingly adept at hiding), and also because passengers from the *Cameronia* had been transferred at the last minute. The Royal Navy had commandeered the latter with orders to Halifax.

Newsreels recording the Cunarder's rapid backing out from her pier plainly showed the friendly extrovert Elbert Hubbard, with his long hair and floppy hat, waving, the gruff Captain Turner grimacing as he looked down from the bridge wings. Most of those on deck were clearly identifiable to their friends. By the same token, the cameras, at an elevation, swept the decks from stem to stern. With all the talk of armed merchantmen flying the flags of both Allied and Central Powers, it was evident that *Lusitania* carried not so much as one old machine gun. She was, to all outward appearances, fully defenseless.

Eloquent from the negative aspect as well was the total absence of smoke from the last of the steamship's four towering funnels. The newsreels recorded it pouring from the first three. Apparently, neither passengers nor onlookers ashore understood the meaning—that the aft furnaces, feeding these great "pipes" with coal smoke, were quite cold. Only an expert or an unfriendly viewer could rationalize the implication of reduced speed.

Even as the *Lusitania* was pounding down Ambrose Channel, the U.S. tanker *Gulflight* was torpedoed without warning by the U-30, off the Scilly Islands in the English Channel. Although she was beached, three American lives, including that of the captain, were lost.

This crossing of the Cunarder's proved typical of the North Atlantic in mid-spring: mostly calm, misty, a definite swell off the Grand Banks, plus patches of fog that set the throaty bass of the liner's horn sounding intermittently. Young Dorothy Conner, a Red Cross volunteer from Medford, Oregon, expressed the sentiments of many when she observed to a fellow passenger, "It's been such a dull, dreary, stupid trip...."

Not until midweek did the skies lift and improve the morale of at least some of those aboard. One, Charles A. Plamondon, machinery company president of Chicago, would write in his diary, "pleasant weather, sunshine all day. Evening concert for sailors' and seamen's homes."

Lusitania. Note that smoke is coming from only three stacks, indicating cold boilers. (U.S. Navy)

Accompanied by his wife, Mary, the rather stocky, mustached executive was a faithful diarist, making sometimes hourly entries. A diary to Plamondon was like a Bible to others. He was devoted to his business, by the same measure, and was a devout Catholic. The reason for this voyage, which he had not really wanted to make at all, was to sell brewery equipment to the Guinness "empire."

But off the southern coasts of the British Isles, lying dead ahead, nothing was "dull," certainly not "pleasant." On Wednesday, May 5, a large schooner, the *Earl of Latham,* was sunk off the Old Head of Kinsale by the U-20. Kapitanleutnant Walther Schwieger, thirty-two, a week out of Emden on his first war patrol, had riddled the broad-beamed craft with gunfire after the crew abandoned.

Proceeding along the shore, U-20 encountered the next morning, Thursday, May 6, the Harrison liner *Candidate,* off the Coningbeg Lightship. This was at the entrance to St. George's Channel leading into the Irish Sea and Liverpool. One torpedo, fired without warning, stopped her. In short order, another Harrison vessel, the *Centurion,* also crossed Schwieger's periscope, and she, too, was struck.

Remarkably, no lives were lost.

Obviously, it was too risky to remain at the scene of two sinkings.

"Since the fog does not abate," Schwieger logged, "I now resolve upon the return journey, in order to push out into the North Channel in case of good weather."

Schwieger reversed course and headed back toward Kinsale. During the night he would surface, take his position from the wink of the friendly Irish lighthouses, recharge his batteries, and let the crew play their gramophones. There were also a couple of pet dogs aboard, which could air on deck and generally disport themselves.

It wasn't just luck that enabled German submarines to relax in these waters and operate with seeming impunity. A total of twenty-three merchantmen, for example, had been sunk off the British Isles since the *Lusitania*'s sailing from New York. There wasn't much to stop the U-boats, only the tatterdemalion Irish Coast Patrol along the approaches to the English Channel and the Irish Sea.

Under Rear Admiral H. L. A. Hood, this unit was comprised of four obsolete cruisers, some old destroyers, and a scattering of armed yachts and trawlers, capable of barely adequate speeds. They were responsible for a formidable area—No. 21, in war plans—the entire south Irish coast. Hood was demoralized enough when he arrived at Queenstown since his new assignment was a demotion, for a "not wholly effective" job in organizing the Dover patrol, aimed at keeping submarines out of the English channel from the east.

He hoisted his flag on the twenty-year-old, 5,000-ton cruiser *Juno*, of about the same size and vintage as the three other cruisers. Cumbersome, bag-loading, six-inch naval "rifles" were the main battery. They were worthless against a fast, maneuverable target.

Carelessness or, certainly, lack of incentive, however, in guarding this "lifeline of empire" was not responsible for the lamentable inadequacy of the Irish patrol. The Royal Navy was fragmented. Its best units were divided between the Dardanelles, supporting the bloody assaults on Gallipoli and guarding home waters against the Kaiser's mighty High Seas Fleet, just across the North Sea.

The Grand Fleet had, at the same time, to protect its vast anchorage at Scapa Flow and coastal areas such as East Anglia against fast German cruiser raids. Only in January had there been action of the two opposing fleets off the extensive North Sea shoals known as Dogger Bank. This resulted primarily in the loss of the battle cruiser *Blücher*. A dramatic photograph of the German crew clambering desperately over her keel and exposed starboard side imbued the British public with a not-wholly warranted sense of confidence in the Royal Navy's ability to sink enemy warships on sight.

Since his departure from Liverpool, Turner had been in possession of confidential Admiralty notices. The two principal ones dealt with avoiding "headlands and landfalls" because of German U-boat activity and the advisability of zigzagging "when cruising in an area known to be infested by submarines." Thursday at 7:50 P.M. the captain heard from the Admiralty again, a brief warning: "Submarines active off south coast of Ireland."

It came from the Naval Center in Queenstown, relayed by the powerful wireless station at Valentia Island on the west coast of Ireland. But it appeared incomplete. Turner ordered Marconi operator Stewart Hutchinson to ask for a repeat. It flashed back the same.

Before 8:30 the Morse, in simple merchant code, was tapping it again from Admiralty wireless: "To all British ships 0005 (Greenwich):

"Between South Foreland and Folkestone keep within two miles of shore, and pass between the two light vessels. Take Liverpool pilot at bar and avoid headlands. Pass harbors at full speed. Steer midchannel course. Submarines off Fastnet."

Fastnet Rock, off the southwest tip of Ireland, had long been a prominent navigation point for mariners. As the liner neared this rock, Turner was convinced that he had taken all possible precautions.

The lifeboats had been swung out that morning. Many of the watertight bulkheads had been closed. Steam pressure was close to maximum: 195 pounds per square inch. The *Lusitania* should be making 21 knots. He apparently did not or could not consider firing up the cold boilers. It was, nonetheless, a possibility for a period of a few hours, even with the shortage of stokers.

Through the night the same "0005" message was repeated at intervals, seven times in all.

Friday, May 7, dawned foggy, disturbing to submarine and merchantmen alike. Turner ordered speed reduced to eighteen knots. By 8:00 A.M. the dank, opaque blanket was even thicker. He cut back the liner's speed to fifteen knots—almost half her peacetime rate. The great ship felt her way eastward, on a course of eighty-seven degrees, blowing her hoarse, throaty horn for friend or foe alike.

This reduction was all too obvious to those on board. According to Michael Byrne, of New York, "You could hear whenever you passed a group of passengers, 'Well, why are we not making full speed of twenty-five knots? As Captain Turner told us at our concert, "we could run away from any submarine." ' "

Mrs. Theodore Naish of Kansas City sniffed, "I thought we could row a boat faster than we were moving."

Byrne felt an additional sense of insecurity since he had concluded that the big vessel was defenseless. The first day out of New York, he methodically had prowled every deck, even looking under winches and wherever there seemed to be an overhang.

"I took particular notice to see if they had any guns mounted or unmounted. There were none...I inspected every deck above the waterline."

In mid-morning, the mates figured *Lusitania* must be passing twenty miles to seaward of Fastnet Rock. Then, shortly after 11:00 A.M., the fog rolled off, leaving the weather warm and clear, the sea flat with a slight, pleasant groundswell.

"A lovelier day cannot be imagined," noted Mrs. Naish. "The air was warm, no wind, bright sun, smooth sea." The relatively slow speed now did not seem to bother her as it had.

The master ordered speed returned to eighteen knots, rather than the previous twenty-one. At 11:25, a new Admiralty wireless:

"Submarine active in southern part of Irish Channel, last heard of twenty miles south of Coningbeg Light Vessel. Make certain *Lusitania* gets this."

Greatly disturbed by the news of the *Candidate* and the *Centurion*,

Alfred A. Booth, chairman of the board of Cunard, had hurried in person to "the admiral or senior naval officer in Liverpool and asked him to send a message...to convey the fact that these ships had been sunk," only hours earlier.

But the message omitted this crucial intelligence.

About noon a hint of land appeared off the port beam, slowly growing in size. Since Turner thought he saw a tower, he at first "assumed" the promontory to be Brow Head, which was about ten miles northwest of the Fastnet Rock: But how could this be, since he should have passed Fastnet in mid-morning? Anyhow, there were "several towers in the area."

At 12:40 P.M., still another warning: "Submarine five miles south of Cape Clear, proceeding west when sighted at 10 A.M."

Lusitania, Captain Turner would rationalize, must be well past that submarine since Cape Clear was just to the east of Fastnet. He "thought," as he would recall, "we were a long way clear of it; we were going away from it all the time." The submarine dead ahead, south of Coningbeg Light Vessel, was another matter.

Then, twenty minutes later, at exactly 1:00 P.M., the bridge watch recognized a good landfall: Galley Head. But Galley Head was some thirty-five miles east of Brow Head, which Turner had mentally logged only an hour ago. The liner was making just half that figure—eighteen knots.

Turner would admit he simply did *not* know *where* he was. Almost as a mariner's reflex action, he altered course radically by twenty degrees toward land. *Now* he would come inshore close enough to find out just where he was—and end the confusion.

By 1:30 the Irish coastline was sharply in view even to those with indifferent eyesight—trees, rooftops, a church steeple, green hills. Ten minutes later, Turner picked up a landmark as familiar as the rose gardens of his cottage in Great Crosby, a suburb of Liverpool—a spectacular, loaflike, 245-foot-high promontory, the Old Head of Kinsale. Its candy-striped lighthouse was a beckoning Lorelei. On his present course, he could be entering busy Cork Harbor in two hours.

"Give prominent headlands a wide berth...fast steamers can considerably reduce the chance of successful surprise submarine attacks by zigzagging...pass harbors at full speed...steer midchannel course..."

Turner was complying with not a single one of these Admiralty instructions. Had he already forgotten them? This was William Thomas Turner, trusted officer of the Cunard Steamship Company for three decades, one of their outstanding ship-handling masters since 1903.

The Old Head of Kinsale, with lighthouse at far right. (Photo by author)

What was in his mind?

For at least simple expediency, to avoid running hard aground, there had to be another course change. At 1:45, the helmsman swung *Lusitania* back to the former eighty-seven degrees east. This was rather a disappointment to the passengers who wanted to see still more of the verdant, friendly looking land. They put away their Kodak Brownies.

Howsoever, although the master knew, belatedly enough, *where* he was, he did not know how far away he was. He made a decision—based largely on habit. He would institute a four-point bearing. It would require forty minutes. Speed must not be altered, even by fractions, course must be held undeviating. But when he was finished, Turner would know his distance from the Old Head of Kinsale virtually within feet. To him, this was as routine as his kippers and tea at breakfast.

At 1:50 P.M. Albert A. Bestic, junior third officer, commenced the tedious, traditional mariner's navigational procedure. It was one generally reserved, and for obvious reasons, for peacetime conditions.

About one o'clock, meanwhile, aboard a surfaced U-20, Kapitanleutnant Schwieger had spotted something. He logged:

"Right ahead appear four funnels and two masts of a steamer with course vertical to us," and five minutes later, "Submerged to eleven meters and traveled with high speed on course converging…hoping she would change course to starboard along Irish coast," then at 1:50, even as the four-point bearing was being started, "The steamer turns to starboard, directs her course toward Queenstown, and makes possible an approach for a shot. Ran at high speed…in order to gain position directly ahead."

About 2:09, the submarine commander received confirmation from his armament officer: "Torpedo ready!"

"Fire!"

In the ornate first-class dining saloon on the *Lusitania*, C. T. Hill, a tobacco man from Richmond, looked at his watch and decided, "I must hustle for I'm late."

He had an appointment to dictate letters to Miss Gale, the ship stenographer. He went into a lift, but alighted on "B" deck first, which was where his own cabin—110—was located. At an entrance to the deck he saw Jones, the chief steward, who at that instant turned to him and called out "Good God, Mr. Hill, here comes a torpedo!"

Both men saw the wake. The two leaned over the railing and watched it stop at the side of the liner.

A number on board spotted it at the same time.

"Torpedoes coming on the starboard side!" shouted the fo'c'sle head lookout, eighteen-year-old Leslie Morton, a seaman.

"Torpedo!" chorused James H. "Jay" Brooks, a tall, young tire chain salesman from Bridgeport, Connecticut. He had been sunning on the Marconi deck, the highest part of the superstructure.

Though on the port side of the lower bridge, Captain Turner thought he saw the wake: "I tried to change our course but was unable to maneuver out of its way…."

Two watched the speeding missile and could swear it was a "porpoise." These included Mrs. Florence Padley, of Vancouver, relaxing in her deck chair, and Michael Byrne, contemplatively smoking a cigar under the captain's bridge.

The latter was certain it smashed in between the second and third stacks and "made a noise like a million-ton hammer hitting a steel boiler." Turner thought it went into the side between the third and fourth funnels where he saw "a big volume of smoke," while yet others placed the entry forward, below the first and second stacks.

Mrs. Maude Thompson, of Seymour, Indiana, was setting her watch by the ship's clock, "and I remember that it was just 2:05." Then "the impact of the torpedo against the ship could be plainly felt; the noise of the impact, however, was not like that of an explosion, but made a 'jamming noise' like a heavy boat will make in rubbing against piling, for example.

"There was no noise at any time like an explosion, and no further sound following the striking of the torpedo."

C. T. Hill, interrupted en route to dictating, likened the sound to "that made by the slamming of a door," then "a dull, muffled explosion."

Lady Margaret Mackworth, the suffragette, mentally catalogued, "dull, thudlike, not very loud." And Charles Lauriat, Boston bookseller, agreed it was a "rather muffled sound," if as well "heavy."

Very specifically, A. J. Mitchell, a Raleigh Cycle representative from West Bridgford, England, in his cabin packing, believed it to be like "an iron safe falling onto iron from a height of thirty or forty feet."

Charles T. Jeffrey, auto manufacturer from Kenosha, Wisconsin, "thought it might be a mine or that we had run on a rock. It shook the whole ship just as a train would shake if the locomotive suddenly stopped and backed into it."

All, including Captain Turner, were in agreement with Mrs. Jessie Taft Smith, of Chicago, that "the ship seemed to lift...." The decks "rose" underfoot, then settled.

None, including the Cunarder's officers, was fully certain whether one or two torpedoes had struck. Ogden Hammond, of Bernardsville, New Jersey, American businessman, was in the lounge on "A," the boat deck: "The first [torpedo] caused the ship to tremble...and the second caused a somewhat louder report. The boat trembled more violently and immediately began to list starboard...the headway was noticeably checked."

His wife, Mary, dropped her purse but was able to laugh as she retrieved it, observing, "I guess I won't need this where we'll be going!"

Others, too, curiously, were impelled to wry comments. Edwin Friend, an authority on psychic research traveling with Theodate Pope, struck his fist in his hand and exclaimed, "By Jove, they've got us!"

Though on the covered promenade deck, he and Theodate narrowly missed a shower of soot and debris. Jay Brooks had been close to the eruption, which came—obviously from the engine room—out of a ventilator by No. 1 funnel: a geyser of steam, water, coal, and smoke. Knocked to the deck, he had the sensation that the steam would choke him.

At 2:10, Schwieger continued his log:

"Shot hits starboard side right behind bridge. An unusually heavy detonation follows with a very strong explosion cloud (high in the air over first smokestack). Added to the explosion of the torpedo there must have been a second explosion (boiler, coal, or powder). The superstructure over point struck and the high bridge are rent asunder and fire breaks out and envelops the high bridge. The ship stops immediately and quickly heels to starboard. At the same time diving deeper at the bow…"

Like most aboard, seeking life belts, valuables, or loved ones, Mrs. Jessie Smith, of Chicago, "went toward my stateroom. I was told not to hurry as there was no danger."

Other passengers were treated to the same servings of optimism. At least one woman, being helped up the sharply tilted stairs, was encouraged by Robert Wiemann, first-class saloon waiter, "Take your time, she's not going down." The circumspect, however, could detect a ring of doubt in his voice.

As Ogden Hammond gained the deck he heard the order, "Don't lower the boats!" Then, a second order given by the officer of the deck, "There is no danger. Go back, keep off the deck!"

The ever-curious Michael Byrne asked the first officer, Arthur R. Jones, "Are we badly damaged?" to which the latter confidently responded, "We'll beach her."

"How can you when your engines are gone dead?"

Although Byrne heard the third officer, J. I. Lewis, second Jones with "It is all right now!" others knew better. Turner himself was aware from the first that *Lusitania* would not answer the helm, or the engine telegraph. The huge liner, listing at thirty-five degrees, was drifting ahead in a wide, slow arc from her own momentum.

"Jay" Brooks was but one who watched the captain hold up his hands and shout, "Lower no more boats! Everything is going to be all right!"

The stricken vessel had much too much way on her to permit the lowering of boats without swamping. Turner, however, had to know that "everything" was *not* going to be "all right."

Even so, as Ogden Hammond continued, "Sailors started to lower the boats. My wife was with me all the time. I started to return to my stateroom on "D" deck to get life belts, but my wife refused to let me leave her. We therefore walked toward the stern of the ship on the port side.

"When opposite the last boat which was being lowered we were told to get in. The boat was only half full, about thirty-five passengers, men and women being equally divided. The sailor in charge of the rope at the bow of the lifeboat lost his head and let the rope slip. The boat fell down and all the passengers fell into the sea, from sixty feet.

"There were no boats successfully launched on the port side."

Meanwhile, Marconi Operator Robert Leith, high in his tilting radio shack, was hanging on to the transmitter and tapping out, over and over in plain Morse: "Come at once. Big list. Ten miles south Old Head Kinsale. MSU."

"MSU," the signature, happened to be *Lusitania*'s merchant call letters. Power was failing. Leith was preparing to switch over to an emergency dynamo.

The message was picked up by several ships, none of which was any closer than two to three hours' steaming. All, nonetheless, changed course and started for the Old Head of Kinsale.

Rear Admiral Sir Charles Coke, commanding the naval station at Queenstown, dispatched a motley assortment of tugs, tenders, and sail fishing boats out of the harbor. Admiral Hood ordered lines cast off from his flagship *Juno* and the other three cruisers to get underway as soon as their boilers were hot.

All of these patrol craft were tatterdemalion, perhaps reminiscent of a Gilbert and Sullivan comic opera navy. Even so, there were many who wondered at the time: Why were they, all of them, in port, at their docks or moorings, with no steam up? Conceivable conservation of coal measured against the exigencies of war hardly seemed a valid explanation.

If the Royal Navy in Queenstown was unaware of the Cunarder's timetable, others in the area did not share this ignorance. The Coast Guard and the lighthouse keepers, certainly, awaited her—and with misgivings since they were fully aware of recent U-boat activities. The keeper of the Kinsale light from his lofty vantage point had *seen* the *Earl of Latham* sink on Wednesday.

There were those on the Old Head this Friday, as if in anticipation. They watched the big, imposing liner appear; they heard her torpedoed.

"It was a sort of heavy rumble like a distant foghorn," recalled a fifteen-year-old, John J. Murphy. And a young girl, biking away from the Head, remarked to herself, "The *Lusitania*'s been torpedoed...."

At the very throne of empire, in London, the liner's arrival seemed to have been anticipated as well. Colonel House was leaving a noontime luncheon with King George V.

"We fell to talking, strangely enough," wrote Wilson's confidant in his meticulous diary, "of the probability of Germany sinking a transatlantic liner. He said, 'Suppose they should sink the *Lusitania* with American passengers on board?' "

Perhaps the young, hotheaded Kapitanleutnant, eager to please the Kaiser on his first cruise, had himself not considered the political consequences of Americans or other neutrals being on board. Minutes after he had loosed the only torpedo he claimed to have fired, Schwieger logged, with at least a hint of surprise:

"She has the appearance of being about to capsize. Great confusion on board, boats being cleared and some of them lowered to the water. They must have lost their heads. Many boats crowded come down bow first in the water...it seems as if the vessel will be afloat only a short time. Submerge to twenty-four meters and go to sea. I could not have fired a second torpedo into this throng of humanity attempting to save themselves...."

The starboard decks were awash as Marconi Operator Leith transmitted: "Send help quickly. Am listing badly!"

At this point, George Hutchinson, the chief electrician, came to the door of the radio shack to ask, "What about it, Bob?"

Before the radioman could reply, an engineer ran across the decks, balancing himself against the great list, calling out, "The watertight doors are all right, quite all right, don't worry!"

Bob Leith smiled faintly as he commenced to unlace his shoes.

Hugh Johnston, the quartermaster at the helm, who had been watching the brass inclinometer, now sang out, "Twenty-five degrees!..."

The degree of list was accelerating. But even as he spoke Turner was beside him, ordering, "Save yourself!"

In moments, a wave caught Johnston and swept him across the deck. The bow of the Cunarder had struck bottom, only three hundred feet below the surface here, while the stern rose high in the air, and the ship "quivered her whole length," it seemed to the captain. Standing knee-deep in green water, Turner pulled his cap tightly around his head, then climbed a ladder leading to the signal halyards. He kept going, up.

It was 2:28 P.M., no more than eighteen minutes, perhaps less, after the torpedo had struck. For moments the liner hung at this precipitous angle, her four great propellers exposed and turning slowly. Added to her momentum, with what steam was left, they had driven her some two to three miles in that short period. In fact, according to Turner, "she had headway."

For those still clinging to the fantail, the sight before them was incredible, the stuff of nightmares—the swarms of men, women, and children, projected onto the water, some just below the surface, perhaps alive, others in the few boats that were launched, yet others struggling to unlimber what were called collapsible boats, in reality more like rafts than anything else.

Captain Turner ashore in Kinsale. Note his shrunken cap and uniform. (National Archives)

Lusitania survivors. (National Archives)

To the Thompsons, Maude and her husband, E. Blish, the "plunge" was "entirely without preliminary warning." They had remained on "A" deck since the explosion, although he had gone briefly to his cabin for a life belt, which he had at once given to a lady.

"It [the *Lusitania*] stood up almost perpendicular and thereby swept everyone overboard in a mass," Maude would recall, "and we were swept half the length of the ship."

The couple went under together. It was the last time she would ever see her husband.

The stricken liner somewhat righted, then went down sideways, her stern pointing shoreward, snagging many in her rigging as she went. At least two were sucked into her funnels and as quickly expelled in a rush of water and steam.

In spite of the Cunarder's contortions and death agonies, her disappearance came as a strange kind of shock.

"My God! The *Lusitania*'s gone!"

This was the startled amen of George Kessler, New York wine merchant—the "champagne king"—from the relative security of a lifeboat.

In mere minutes the Cunarder had been destroyed as completely as some waterborne Carthage. Nothing remained but a clutter of boats, debris, and human beings. Those who beat the seemingly overwhelming odds against survival often did so in unusual ways. Theodate Pope, after successfully fighting off a large man who kept attempting to climb onto her shoulders, managed to clutch, then straddle an oar. Lady Mackworth, abandoning temporary salvation atop a hen coop, shifted to a large wicker chair.

A group of men found finger space on a buoyant keg. Someone else got a death grip on a half-awash piano. Boards provided a shaky haven for many, while Turner himself clutched a small chair. He kept flailing at seagulls that, curiously, had picked him as a handy target.

All lost track of time. It was perhaps two hours before the first rescue vessels arrived, the naval auxiliary *Indian Prince* and the trawler *Peel 12*. These were followed during the long afternoon by the ancient tug *Stormcock*, the trawler *Bluebell*, the Greek coaster *Katarina*, and a harbor sidewheeler, *Flying Fish*—even, at long last, Admiral Hood's flagship *Juno*.

It was the *Bluebell*, without power as most fishing boats, that happened to save the captain, after he had been immersed for three hours. Quite by chance, a sharp-eyed sailor saw the glint of gold braid on Turner's sodden sleeve. But daylight had almost faded. It would be dusk before the survivors began coming ashore from Kinsale to Queenstown. And they were, in eloquent understatement, "wholly unmarshalled." So wrote Wesley Frost, U.S. consul at Queenstown, who continued:

"We saw the ghastly procession of these rescue ships as they landed the living and the dead...under the flaring gas torches along the Queenstown waterfront. The arrivals began soon after eight o'clock and continued at close intervals until about eleven o'clock. Ship after ship would come up out of the darkness and sometimes two or three would be just described awaiting their turns in the cloudy night to discharge bruised and shuddering women, crippled and half-clothed men, and a few wide-eyed little children...every voice in that great mixed assemblage was pitched in unconscious undertones, broken now and then by painful coughing fits or suppressed hysteria."

And, continuing on through this night, "piles of corpses like cordwood began to appear among the paint kegs and coils of rope on the shadowy old wharves."

The famous along with the unknowns had perished: the Elbert Hubbards; Vanderbilt; Charles Frohman; Justus Forman; Marie de Page; the Plamondons; an entire family from Philadelphia, the Paul

Cromptons, their six children, and even their nurse, were all lost...Lady Marguerite Allan, from Montreal, had survived, also her two nannies, but her beautiful twin daughters were missing...wives were left without husbands, such as Maude Thompson, of Indiana, and husbands without wives, such as Ogden Hammond, of New Jersey...children who had suddenly become orphans, such as Virginia and Bruce Loney, of New York.

On the wharves, still wearing his very shrunken uniform and even his hat, which somehow he had clung onto in the water, Turner blurted out to a correspondent from the *New York World:*

"I tried to change our course but was unable to maneuver out of its way. I tried to turn the *Lusitania* shoreward hoping to beach her. There was no rushing for the boats, no struggling for places; everything was being done with perfect calmness and orderliness." Then, as a sort of amen:

"I followed the instructions of the Admiralty and kept well to the middle channel."

He shrugged with certain detachment, "It is the fortune of war."

This was in much the same mood of his recent comment to lawyers in New York questioning him, relative to the *Titanic*, about marine architecture: "I don't bother about their construction as long as they float. If they sink I get out."

Perhaps Will Turner still did not comprehend the enormity of the tragedy: 1,198 dead, passengers and crew, out of 1,959 who had been aboard. However, of this number, 785 were passengers. The percentage of passengers to crew lost was surprisingly comparable, 61 percent and 58 percent, respectively. The toll of children was especially shocking: 94 drowned out of 129. Included in this pathetic total were 35 infants of whom all but four were lost.

None of the dead had been buried; bodies were still washing ashore when John J. Horgan, the coroner of Kinsale, convened his inquest on Saturday. It was held in the little town's historic Market House/Town Hall, before a jury of twelve fishermen and shopkeepers, "humble, honest citizens."

Of all the hastily gathered witnesses, the master of the *Lusitania* made the most lasting impression on Horgan: "Clad in a badly fitting old suit and still suffering from the strain of his experience, he looked, and was, a broken man. As he finished his evidence, which disclosed that he had gone down with his ship, I expressed our appreciation of the courage which he had shown...worthy of the traditions of the service to which he belonged. Bowing his head, he burst into tears."

The architecture of the waterfront street in Cobh (Queenstown) is little changed since the coffins of the *Lusitania* dead were borne past in 1915 (Top photo, from *Illustrated London News;* bottom photo by author)

In the middle, right behind the pedestrian, is the monument in Cobh to the seamen who aided in the rescue of *Lusitania* survivors. Immediately behind the monument are the old U.S. consular offices. To the far right is the old town hall, which was used as a morgue. (Photo by author)

Not every coroner and lawyer—in a community of several hundred habitants—is given the opportunity to pass judgment on history. Horgan savored the challenge...with ill-concealed pride, he delivered his verdict: "We find that this appalling crime was contrary to international law and the conventions of all civilized nations, and we therefore charge the officers of the said submarine and the Emperor and Government of Germany under whose orders they acted, with the crime of willful and wholesale murder."

Wearing his coroner's hat, as it were, he concluded that "the deceased died from prolonged immersion and exhaustion...."

The Crown Solicitor for Cork arrived too late with instructions from the Admiralty to stop Captain Turner from testifying.

A very few of the *Lusitania* victims were buried in or near Kinsale. Three were laid to rest up the hill from the Market House in the churchyard of historic Anglican St. Multose, whose stone belfry long had dominated the fishing village.

New York World headline, Sunday, May 8, 1915.

The marker over one grave would read, "Unknown Victim (Woman) of the *Lusitania* Outrage, 7th May 1915." The other two were identified males.

A mass funeral—for 120—was solemnized at the Old Church Cemetery, outside of Queenstown. The cortege wound past the city's main shopping district—the waterfront esplanade—up the precipitous hill past towering St. Colman's Cathedral and on out to the gravesite in pasturelands. There a military guard was present to accord honors appropriate for civilian war dead.

Others who had perished ultimately found their resting places in Ireland, in England, in France, in America—they had at last come home.

Only thirty-six witnesses had been called up by Lord Mersey's formal inquiry in London. They were passengers, crewmen, and those, such as Alfred Booth, harboring more than casual interest in the *Lusitania*. Neither Admiral Hood nor any other naval officers were summoned. On July 17, the court delivered itself of conclusions comparable in depth and shock to Coroner Horgan's:

"The Court...finds...that the loss of the said ship and lives was due to damage caused to the said ship by torpedoes fired by a submarine of German nationality whereby the ship sank. In the opinion of the Court the act was done not merely with the intention of sinking the ship, but also with the intention of destroying the lives of the people on board."

More remarkable yet were the accolades tossed by Lord Mersey almost matter-of-factly in the direction of the torpedoed liner's master: "Blame ought not to be imputed to the Captain. The advice given to him, although meant for his most serious and careful consideration, was not intended to deprive him of the right to exercise his skilled judgment in the difficult questions that might arise from time to time in the navigation of his ship. His omission to follow the advice in all respects cannot fairly be attributed either to negligence or incompetence.

"He exercised his judgment for the best. It was the judgment of a skilled and experienced man, and although others might have acted

Crumbling graves of 120 *Lusitania* victims in the otherwise abandoned Old Church Cemetery in Cobh (formerly Queenstown), Ireland. (Photo by author)

differently and perhaps more successfully he ought not, in my opinion, to be blamed."

The pronouncement read as though it were alluding to some other captain, on another ship, in some wholly different episode, in a never-never time frame. But what else had this "skilled and experienced man" testified *in camera* to merit His Lordship's rather effusive endorsement?

Further excerpts of the examination follow:

"You know that was not midchannel or anything like…never mind. Take this from me; you were able for two hours to see the land."

"Yes."

"I put it to you, whether it was right or wrong, you thought it was sufficient to be that ten miles off?"

"Yes."

"And therefore you did not think it necessary to be in midchannel?"

"No."

"Now, *why* did you disobey the Admiralty instructions? You did not try to get to midchannel: that was not your aim."

"My aim was to find the land."

"What I am putting to you is that you never for a moment tried to carry out what the Admiralty had laid down."

"I thought I was trying my best anyhow."

"Now I want to ask you another question. You knew that was a dangerous zone?"

"Yes."

"And you had these telegrams, we know. Why were you only going at eighteen knots?"

"Because I was getting up to the Bar, and did not want to have to stop at the Bar."

"What I want to ask you about is this—you see, you told me you had plenty of time in hand."

"Yes."

"What was there to prevent you keeping well away until it became necessary for you to come up and cross over to Liverpool to the Bar? You see you were trying to waste your time by going slowly near the land—eighteen knots."

"There was plenty of time."

"You could have kept out?"

"We could have kept out, but when we were up here, there was a submarine reported off Fastnet, due west, and we had passed that."

"You had all this time in hand, and you were purposely going slow."

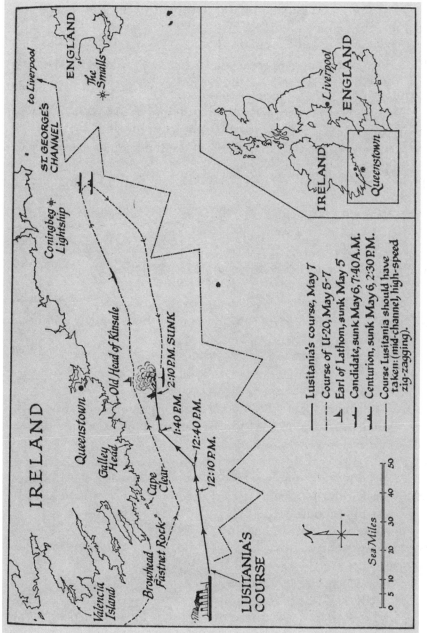

Map of *Lusitania's* course. (Courtesy of Thomas A. Bailey and Paul B. Ryan)

"Not slow—eighteen knots."

"Well, not your best speed, passing ten miles from a headland instead of going at full speed up the channel."

"Yes."

"Did you do that deliberately?"

"I did."

"Was that not against your instructions?"

"Well, yes."

Lord Mersey interrupted the questioning to ask, "When did you reduce your speed from twenty-one knots to eighteen?"

"When we made the land...I forget the time, ten or eleven o'clock probably, as near as I can remember."

Attorney General: "That morning there was a lot of fog and you reduced speed?"

"Yes, to fifteen knots."

"And then you got up to eighteen knots?"

"Yes."

"You had plenty of coal aboard, had you not, to go to twenty-one knots?"

"Yes."

"The distance from where you were, you have already told me, to Liverpool was about 250 miles."

"Yes."

"Do you know at that time up to what hour you could have crossed the Bar?"

"About four o'clock [A.M.], 6:53 was high water."

"Could you have crossed the Bar at any time between 4:00 A.M. and 9:30?"

"Yes."

"I am putting it that you had so much time that it was not necessary for you at this particular period to have come near land at all but to have stood well out?"

"I could have gone out again."

"You could have stood out. Why did you go this long way out at Fastnet?"

"To keep clear of submarines."

"Exactly, and why did you not stay out to keep clear?"

"I wanted to find out where the ship was for the purpose of navigating her safely."

"Then there was nothing to prevent you, on the facts I have elicited, keeping in midchannel and still arriving in proper time at Liverpool?"

"No."

Mersey again spoke, "I want him to do justice to himself. I do not understand what you mean when you say you were coming in because you wanted to navigate the ship safely. What danger was there in mid-channel?"

"Well, my Lord, it might have come on a thick fog, and I did not know exactly the proper position of the ship, and two or three miles one way or the other might put me ashore on either side of the channel. Therefore, I wanted to know my proper position."

"And they (the Admiralty) gave you directions to do something which may send you ashore if you do it?"

"No, I am not speaking in that sense."

Attorney General: "It is not an impossible instruction, is it, to go up midchannel?"

"None whatever providing you know the position of your ship."

Aspinall interjected: "Now at the time you got this thick weather and you reduced your speed, did you know with any certainty where your ship was?"

"No."

A silence, then, "You mean that?"

"Yes, I mean it."

Aspinall then continued, "You had hauled in somewhat but nothing like far enough to take you into midchannel?"

"No."

"Now, what I want you to tell me is this: why it was when you altered course, you did not alter out more so as to bring you up to midchannel?"

"Because I wanted in the first place to make Coningbeg, seeing that we were twenty miles south of it. Then I thought it was safer close to the land in case we did get a submarine."

"You did not tell us that before?"

"I did not think of it."

Cunard's veteran attorney showed manifest frustration as he pursued:

"You must apply your mind, if you will, and do not answer questions hurriedly or hastily. Just *think*. You remember after you had altered back your course to S. 87E?"

"Yes. I cannot give the times. I cannot remember the times."

"Now, if this trouble had not happened at all, how long would you have continued on that course of S. 87...up to what spot on the Irish coast?"

"I could not have gone closer than within half a mile of Coningbeg Lightship."

"Would that have been giving effect to the Admiralty letter of instructions to keep midchannel?"

"No, it would not."

"Why did you, having a knowledge of what the Admiralty instructions were, steer a course which you had intended should take your ship so close to the Coningbeg and not out into midchannel?"

"Because there was a submarine in midchannel as I understood it, and I wanted to keep clear of him."

Twice Mersey interrupted to say, "I do not understand that answer—I do not understand it at all," when Turner indicated if he had set course farther to sea he might have encountered an additional number of submarines. The Commissioner persisted:

"When you go out far away from the land, do you expect to meet more submarines than when you are close to the headlands?"

"I expect to find them any distance within one hundred miles or so of the land in those times."

"I understand you just now to say that the further you get out the more submarines you expect to meet, which seems to me to be odd."

"No, what I meant to say was that by going out further round and wasting time I might have met others."

"I should have thought it was getting into safety to get away from the land...." Mersey, manifesting a sense of despair, now turned to Aspinall, requesting, "Will you tell me...what you understand this gentleman to have wished to convey to us?"

The Cunard attorney, as an answer, reviewed the course of the doomed liner from Brow Head to Kinsale, concluding, "...and he did give us that proof."

"What proof?" snapped the Commissioner.

Aspinall, who had alluded to a previous affidavit of the captain, was embarrassed. Belatedly, he realized he had been putting words into the confused master's mouth.

"I am afraid I was wrong in saying that. He did not make the statement in the fullness I have just made it to your Lordship."

Mersey looked at both men, asked a few more general questions, then adjourned for the day. It must have seemed the wisest course at the moment.

Recalled, Turner was queried on another tangent by Admiral Inglefield:

"At any time on the forenoon of the seventh, did you or your officers take any observations of the sun for fixing your position, either by latitude or longitude?"

"No."

"Why?"

"Because the officers were particularly looking out for submarines and periscopes."

"But you could have got them?"

"Yes, decidedly. The weather was quite clear."

"Anyway, you did not?"

"No, I did not. It is quite true."

The Solicitor General, Sir Frederick Smith, representing the British Government, who had left most of the questioning to Carson or Aspinall, then asked, "When you stopped because of the fog, did you sound your foghorn?"

Apparently forgetting that he had not "stopped" the liner at any time, Turner replied, "Yes, certainly."

"All the time?"

"All the time, automatically. Every minute."

"Did it occur to you that might be very dangerous, having regard to the submarines?"

"No."

"Would it not have been audible for a long way?"

"No doubt."

Captain Turner, by any measure, had not given a very good accounting of himself or his actions.

Omitted, quite deliberately, from the inquiry were the other considerations: cargo, severity of the explosion, lack of escort by the Admiralty. As to the cargo, the manifest as presented was accepted without question. It might as well have been since every positioning of the torpedo (assuming only one had been fired, as Schwieger logged) placed the entry point at least 150 feet astern of the limited cargo hold. High explosives could have been stowed without detonation.

Besides, no passenger or crewman ever reported seeing or smelling anything that hinted of gunpowder or other explosives. [The many survivors still alive in the 1950s also confirmed in conversations or in correspondence with this author such an absence. This was during research of *The Last Voyage of the Lusitania,* in collaboration with Mary Hoehling.]

It could be theorized, too, that steam and coal dust could somehow have built up in the double bottom to create an explosion, like contained dynamite, or the effect of gunpowder in an artillery shell. Thus, the safety engineered into a double bottom would prove paradoxical peril. The passenger, Jay Brooks, was among those speculating on such a possibility.

All witnesses to the torpedoing agreed on seeing steam and other debris coming up through at least one forward ventilator on the boat deck.

An armed merchant vessel? The abashed German Foreign Office much wished the world to believe that, if not necessarily bristling with guns, the Cunarder carried a number of naval rifles either "mounted under decks or masked." None was seen in the newsreels of her sailing, nor by those crewmen or passengers who went out of their various ways to seek such out.

Anyhow, actual presence of armament scarcely made a naval auxiliary any more legitimate a wartime target. It was just that sticky matter of civilians: women and children, men beyond draft age, and, especially, those from neutral countries.

What about the reduced speed, those six cold boilers? Cunard was offering *Lusitania*'s monthly turnarounds as "a service," and Alfred Booth explained quite candidly, "We did not hope to make any profit and as a matter of fact we did not make any profit."

To the court's satisfaction, he reiterated that the company could not afford to operate the liner at all under full steam.

Why did *Lusitania* sink so quickly? With 195 pounds per square inch of steam pressure in her boilers, the force of the explosion augmenting that of the torpedo could readily have opened a yawning hole in her side or keel or both. (The dimensions of which, however, have eluded several divers over the years, as have other "mysteries" locked in the encrusted, broken old hull. Was there gold bullion aboard? Or guns? The wreck holds whatever secrets there may be.)

Where was the Irish Coast Patrol? Its absence from the western sea-lanes to England has caused the most intense, and sometimes fanciful, speculation on the sinking.

Manifestly, Admiral Hood had proven no more efficient than in the Dover Patrol, for which he had been mildly reprimanded. No explanation was offered either by him or the Admiralty for keeping his old cruisers and other units in port during the submarine alerts.

Admiral Coke, the Queenstown naval commandant, however, had the impertinence to criticize Turner for not following orders.

The question of the absent escort did not arise during the inquiry. Its presence, better than nothing at all, might not have repelled the U-boats, but their operations could have been rendered more difficult. That is, Schwieger, ducking an adversary, even if somewhat obsolete, might have been sufficiently distracted to miss or to strike a glancing blow.

The Royal Navy, as represented by the Irish patrol, was impartial in its ineptitude and lack of a sense of urgency. If it had neglected the great *Lusitania*, it had also accorded no succor to the smaller *Candidate* and *Centurion* or the sailing ship *Earl of Latham.*

That the warships might have been deliberately kept in port in the hopes the *Lusitania* would be sunk is almost too frivolous to discuss. This rather mindless theory is predicated on the equally hollow belief that Britain's leaders, presumably from Prime Minister Herbert Asquith on down, sought an "incident" that would propel the United States into the war. The moralities aside, England in early 1915 did not need the services of her cousins across the Atlantic.

France, Russia, and Germany, in that order of attrition, were hurting badly. The British Expeditionary Force had, surely, been bloodied at Mons and Ypres. But the wasting charnel house of the Somme had yet to take place. Nor had the Dardanelles effort attained disaster proportions. Plenty of men were volunteering for the forces. When the British nurse Edith Cavell was executed by the Germans, in Belgium in October 1915, tens of thousands of young Englishmen would sign up at monstrous rallies throughout the United Kingdom to "avenge Nurse Cavell."

[Specifically, the British Expeditionary Force had lost about thirty-seven thousand officers and men killed and in deaths from wounds by May 1, 1915. By comparison, France alone had already counted more than one million casualties, in excess of one-third of which were deaths. As a measure of the conflict's acceleration, by the end of September of the following year, 1916—after the Somme, Dardanelles, and other actions—Great Britain had sustained since August 1914 approximately 1,150,000 casualties (killed, died of wounds, missing, prisoners, disease), one-quarter of which represented the dead.]

Britons were eating in the spring of 1915. The war machine was kept supplied, in part through mounting orders for armaments placed with American factories. London well knew that the United States possessed nothing it could call an army, certainly not an air force.

The Navy was largely obsolete, basking in its easy victories of the Spanish-American War and memories of the Great White Fleet that Teddy Roosevelt dispatched pugnaciously "round the world."

From the German perspective:

In assessing the legitimacy of his target, the U-boat Kapitanleutnant had necessarily to be ignorant of many factors: the liner's cargo; armament or lack of it; and, as Berlin kept charging in lame defense, the alleged presence of troops on board. For all Walther Schwieger knew, several regiments of uniformed, fully armed territorials could have been marching within the mostly covered decks. And by the same token, the passenger complement could have been composed solely of several orders of cloistered nuns, as well as very old women and men returning to Britain to live with their children.

* * *

Exonerated by both Coroner Horgan and Lord Mersey, Captain Turner went back to sea. In early January 1917, commanding the 14,000-ton *Ivernia*, he was torpedoed off Cape Matapan, Greece. A total of 153 soldiers and crewmen perished. Once more Turner swam away from his bridge and hung onto a chair as a life preserver.

Concerned, conceivably, that the onetime master of the *Lusitania* might ultimately exhaust his supply of ships—if not as well of chairs— Cunard beached him. When Turner retired in 1920, Alfred Booth decorated his veteran employee with the Order of the British Empire. Turner retired to Great Crosby to take care of his dog and, in turn, be solaced by his housekeeper, Mrs. Mabel Every.

An abstemious man, by the appraisal of his longtime friend, George Ball, Turner limited himself to but one pipeful of tobacco a day. As for the *Lusitania*, he "always had an intense reluctance to discuss the matter." Necessarily defensive, he was once quoted as blaming an "error in transmission or decoding" of Admiralty messages for the *Lusitania*'s being "nineteen miles from course stated." Howsoever, by his own testimony, he was much farther than that from "midchannel"— nearly fifty miles farther.

The realities of the tragedy were not easy to live with.

William Turner survived until 1933, when he succumbed to what was diagnosed as cancer of the liver. Subsequently, following World War II, some historians took a look at the captain of the Cunarder and came up with conclusions far less compassionate than the official inquiries. He was a "blunderer...unable to understand the King's English." He was "stupid" and guilty of "clear culpability." And this wasn't all.

But was this oversimplification true? Did such an assessment take into account the fact that to graduate from sailing ships to a handler— and tamer—of such a giant as the *Aquitania*, a third again the size of *Lusitania* or *Mauretania*, implied not only intelligence and imagination but also the ability to learn? The superliners were scientific wonders. No master could blandly take the word of his chief engineer, his chief electrician, his chief radio operator, etc. He had to possess at least an appreciation of the workings of these monsters of steam, steel, and electricity.

Cunard was perhaps at its zenith in the early years of the twentieth century. No company of its size and prestige would appoint a "stupid" man, a "blunderer" to a position of utmost trust and responsibility—the management of its most valuable properties. Even as Lord Mersey had, the line must have thought Turner a "skilled and experienced man."

But that was yesterday. The present had commenced April 30, 1915, when the *Lusitania* departed New York on her last voyage.

"Why, it's the best joke I've heard...this talk of torpedoing...I have never heard of [a submarine] that could make twenty-seven knots...."

"Did you know with any certainty where your ship was?"

"No."

"Do you *mean* to say you had *no* idea where you were?"

"Was that not against your instructions?"

"Well, yes."

"I wanted to find out where the ship was...."

"You did not tell us that before?"

"I did not think of it."

"You must apply your mind, if you will...."

"You really do not think, do you, that you were in midchannel or anywhere near it?"

Neither, as quoted at departure or in testimony, was William Thomas Turner, a historically competent master, making a great deal of sense. What had happened to this competent man? Honored by his company, by the King. A favorite of the affluent transatlantic set, such as Vanderbilt, or Frohman....

In submarine-infested waters, as repeatedly warned, *what* had impelled the captain to hold his ship, against all orders and common sense, on a steady course for a four-point bearing, requiring forty minutes of undeviating direction?

It was as though Turner had taken at least partial, temporary leave of his reason. Elevation of blood pressure? A small stroke? Hallucination?

Therein could lie the heart of the mystery of the *Lusitania*. Since no medical records exist (in the unlikely event they ever did), mystery it must remain...and one which mightily influenced the course of history.

* * *

Successive salvage expeditions retrieved three of the liner's four huge brass propellers, two of the bow anchors, a ship's bell, the raised brass lettering *Lusitania* from her bow, silver and chinaware (by cutting a hole in the stern for access), and other objects. Some are on display in a small museum in Kinsale.

As one might have foreseen, Robert D. Ballard, of the Woods Hole Oceanographic Institute, discoverer of the *Titanic*, led the most scientific exploration in 1993. His cameras found the wreck lying on its starboard side, badly crushed, cracked open amidships, resembling "a junkyard more than a luxury liner."

The strong currents of the Celtic Sea and cloudy waters make both exploration and photography difficult. Speculating on what might have compounded the damage from the torpedo and hastened the *Lusitania*'s destruction, Ballard wrote: "...a coal dust explosion. The German torpedo struck the liner's starboard side almost ten feet below the waterline, rupturing one of the long coal bunkers that stretched along both sides." (*National Geographic*, April 1994)

Ballard estimated that the bunker was almost empty at the end of the voyage, with inflammable dust remaining. This would be readily ignited by a bursting torpedo.

And so Ballard put to rest the long-persistent beliefs that the great liner carried ammunition.

4

HMS *Hampshire*

Who killed Lord Kitchener?

ALMOST A YEAR TO the day after the torpedoing of the *Lusitania*, on May 8, 1916, Walther Schwieger locked the 13,000-ton *Cymeric* in U-20's periscopic crosshairs. The White Star liner was carrying only cargo as she approached Fastnet Rock. But the Kapitanleutnant did not know that, any more than he had known what or who was aboard the big Cunarder.

Schwieger, who now wore the medal *Pour le Merite*, was about to score his latest kill. As the liner, carrying several crew members with her, vanished beneath the cold Atlantic, Schwieger's total sunk on this cruise soared to 23,000 tons. He was already Imperial Germany's seventh-ranking submarine ace, with upwards of 190,000 tons, representing some ten cruises, to his credit. "Sink-on-Sight Schwieger" was the sobriquet he had earned among the elite of the underwater fleet as Germany's unrestricted submarine warfare mounted—even as it increasingly angered and alienated the United States.

Not quite two weeks later, on May 20, Kapitanleutnant Kurt Beitzen piloted U-75 into the North Sea. His was one of several boats under orders, ostensibly, for reconnaissance around the Orkneys, especially the Great Scapa Flow naval anchorage. They were to attack units of the Grand Fleet, if encountered, and, in the case of U-75, sow mines. The U-75 carried twenty-two mines. This left no space for torpedoes.

However, Beitzen's orders, unlike those repeatedly issued Schwieger, were ambivalent as to merchantmen: "If time and circumstances permit, trade war will be carried on during proceedings." He had only his deck gun for such attacks.

So U-75, pregnant with her cargo of death, wallowed northward. She was one of a singularly named class of minelayers, "Sisters of Sorrow." It was, at least, apt.

The growing submarine fleet, by 1916, was operating out of bases that included the original U-boat lair in the small sandstone island, Helgoland, rising 160 feet out of the North Sea; the big ports of Emden, Wilhelmshaven, and Kiel; also Zeebrugge, Belgium, where the German conquerors had constructed elaborate, protected pens. U-75, like others, could have left from and returned to any one of these.

As this second spring of Armageddon wore on, the war at sea was stirring beyond submarine operations alone. Some forty-eight hours before U-75 had departed Emden, Admiral Reinhard Scheer, dynamic new commander in chief of the High Seas Fleet, had issued an order for "a bombardment of the fortifications and works of the harbor at Sunderland...about the middle of the east coast of England...to call out a display of English fighting forces." He elaborated:

"The bombardment of Sunderland by our cruisers is intended to compel the enemy to send out forces against us. For the attack on the advancing enemy the High Seas Fleet forces to be south of the Dogger Bank, and the U-boats to be stationed for attack off the east coast of England. The enemy's ports of sortie will be closed by mines."

However, as the weather "continued to be unfavorable" for the scouting zeppelins on which Scheer placed much reliance, the operation was postponed from day to day. The "eyes" of Germany's rather magnificent fleet, these hydrogen-filled rigid airships, which had already terrorized London and other cities with night bombing raids, could cruise far ahead of the warships while flying at altitudes out of range of opposing gunfire.

Aggressive and smart, Scheer was also prudent. He knew he could not possibly take on the entire Grand Fleet since his own was outgunned by something like 344 to 244 heavy naval rifles. Britain's very newest class of battleships (or dreadnoughts) mounted giant fifteen-inch guns compared to the German 13.5 and to most of the older Royal Navy dreadnoughts and battle cruisers, for that matter.

The total firepower Britain could bring to bear was overwhelming, even though the Germans had every reason to be proud of their own gunnery. Scheer planned to pick at isolated units of the foe. His

Zeppelins could provide vital intelligence as to the whereabouts of the Royal Navy's "heavies."

Coincidentally, perhaps, the Admiralty was plotting along rather parallel lines. Residents of areas such as Lowestoft on the Norfolk coast, which had been bombarded by German battle cruisers, were putting pressure on the government to go after the High Seas Fleet and destroy it if possible. Architects of this counterplan were two dissimilar admirals, Sir John Jellicoe, commanding the Grand Fleet, and Sir David Beatty, commander of the Battle Cruiser Fleet. Rather diminutive in stature, Jellicoe was cautious, plodding. Beatty—tall, handsome, daring—was much a swashbuckling British admiral out of a cinema matinee.

The admirals resolved to dispatch light units toward the Danish and Dutch coasts in a familiar cat-and-mouse ploy. The "heavies"—battleships and battle cruisers—would wait just over the horizon to pounce if the High Seas Fleet were lured from base. London wished passionately to demolish the enemy to the last torpedo boat. Berlin could aspire only to nibble away piecemeal at the mighty Grand Fleet.

Thus did the two gambits differ in objectives.

While final touches were being applied to these scenarios on opposite shores of the North Sea, an entr'acte, though of no secondary import, was quietly—it was hoped—unfolding. Horatio Herbert, Lord Kitchener, Earl of Khartoum, was preparing to leave for Russia. The Czar's armies were bled white, in excess of two million casualties already (though statistics were exceptionally unreliable). There was a shortage of munitions, guns, food, clothing, finances—everything.

The specter of a separate peace loomed.

The tall, austere Secretary of War had received a personal invitation on May 13 from Czar Nicholas II. Known to every Briton as the stern, if not intimidating, face on the recruiting posters—Your Country Needs You!—Kitchener seemed an obvious choice. He was sufficiently knowledgeable to ascertain the true state of affairs in Russia as well as that dangerously sagging ally's most immediate needs. As the Admiralty's official chroniclers, Sir Julian Corbett and Henry Newbolt, would write:

"Lord Kitchener seemed to be more fitted than any other member of the Government for such a Mission. His prestige and status in foreign countries were almost as great as at home; he could speak with full authority upon the campaign to be undertaken during the year, and upon the best way of giving cohesion and force to the Allied effort."

David Lloyd George, then Minister of Munitions, no friend of Kitchener, had to concede that he "was one of the first to realize the magnitude of the war...I doubt whether any other man could at that

It was a formidable Lord Kitchener who glared out from this famous recruiting poster. (Author's collection)

moment have attracted the hundreds of thousands who rallied to the flag at his appearance."

At the same time, the British statesman who would become prime minister postscripted that "Kitchener is one of the unsolved mysteries of the war. He was like one of those revolving lighthouses which radiate momentary gleams of revealing light far out into the surrounding gloom and then suddenly relapse into complete darkness."

Lloyd George, who as a young man happened to visit the United States at the close of the Civil War, quoted a sharp-tongued woman friend who had observed of Kitchener, "not a great man, but a great poster."

He was in likelihood better appreciated in Russia than at home, where his blunt, stubborn approach had brought forth many enemies. In the House of Lords, for example, an irate Member had suggested the War Secretary's salary be reduced by a token $500. In fact, the opinions prevalent in the Court of St. James found some voice in the correspondence of Walter Hines Page, the United States Ambassador to England:

"There was a hope and feeling that he [Kitchener] might not come back till after the war…he was in many ways a hindrance in the cabinet…an impossible man to work with." There were those who would "induce him to go away for a long time."

On May 26, the War Secretary expressed his readiness to go "at the head of a military and financial Mission." Those accompanying him included: Colonel Oswald A. C. Fitzgerald, his personal military secretary and longtime constant companion; H. J. O'Beirne, counselor at the British Embassy at Petrograd; two technical advisers; two military aides; a cipher clerk; a detective assigned by Scotland Yard, Sergeant McLaughlin; and three servants—eleven in all. The number appeared ample to serve his Lordship's military, professional, and personal needs.

The Admiralty thereupon dispatched what it earnestly hoped to be a top secret message to Admiral Jellicoe, conveying the intelligence that Kitchener's party would leave London on Monday, June 5, for Scapa Flow to board a designated "cruiser" for the White Sea port of Archangel, a journey of more than two thousand miles through cold, stormy, and peril-fraught seas.

The next day, May 27, the fleet commander proposed HMS *Hampshire*, an eleven-year-old cruiser of 10,850 tons, with a six-inch armor belt and a main battery of 7.5-inch naval rifles. Early in the war she had joined in the hunt for the elusive German raider *Emden* in Far Eastern waters. With a top speed of twenty-one knots, her cruising speed was, nonetheless, seventeen knots, meaning it would require more than five days for the voyage to Archangel. A rather obvious choice for such a mission, *Hampshire* was equipped with comfortable cabins for high-ranking passengers.

* * *

Arriving off the rocky, windswept west coast of the Orkneys on May 28, U-75 consumed two days laying her twenty-two mines. This she accomplished "in several detached groups about seven meters below high water" (according to official German records). She chose this channel out of Scapa Flow rather than the east on the supposedly mistaken intelligence that it was "a route used by warships." Actually, the course, up past Black Craig, the Bay of Skaill, Marwick Head, and the Brough of Birsay, was designated for smaller fleet auxiliaries, and that only "infrequently."

Kapitanleutnant Beitzen concentrated on the five-mile stretch between Marwick Head, to the south, and Birsay, about two miles off-shore. The water was deep here, about 180 feet, and even the big battle cruisers, the 30,000-tonners, could, if desired, easily navigate the west channel. To anchor his contact mines at some twenty-one feet below the surface meant that Beitzen must attach each of these mighty explosive packages by some 160 feet of chain or cable.

It was a curious setting for the mines. Most of the auxiliaries would have steamed above them. Given tidal action, there would have been a tendency for the mines to "dip" yet lower below the surface, allowing

HMS *Hampshire*—she carried Lord Kitchener on his last voyage. (U.S. Navy)

even cruisers to pass over them. The *Hampshire*, however, listed a "maximum draft" of twenty-five feet. Even if lightly loaded and fueled, she would be in danger from the twenty-one-foot mine setting in slack water or if she were pitching heavily in a head wind. Otherwise, there was a reasonable gamble she could steam above the minefield.

Beitzen's was a tedious operation, requiring much skill and familiarity, as well as an extremely dangerous one. An accident and twenty-two or so mines would erupt like Vesuvius. However, Beitzen was lucky in several respects, including—remarkably—"no interference whatever from the enemy's patrols." The crew cranked up the U-boat's ever-present gramophones and headed for home.

Then, on May 30—the signal! Secret radio direction-finding stations dotting the eastern English coasts southward from the Orkneys had been monitoring transmissions from the High Seas Fleet. These sensitive wireless snoopers had been zeroing in on the new 28,000-ton battleship *Bayern*, the principal and very powerful transmitter for the whole Fleet. Overnight, *Bayern*, as well as those responding to her, had changed position one and a half degrees—readily translated into several significant miles.

"This movement," First Sea Lord Henry Jackson would recall, "decided me to send our Grand Fleet to sea…to try to meet the German Fleet and bring it to action."

The electrifying order flashed to all units of the Grand Fleet, at Scapa Flow, at the Firth of Forth, at Cromarty in Moray Firth, and other lesser anchorages: "Fire boilers…raise steam at once!"

All that day and into the night crews were tumbling back aboard their ships, which as hurriedly upped anchor and pounded out into the North Sea. Across that confined, fateful body of water, the Germans were already underway. By dawn Wednesday, May 31, the juggernauts and their somewhat smaller, more graceful escorts, cruisers, and destroyers would be out into their arena: 149 major British men o'war, 116 German.

Radio surveillance of the foe was, however, but one facet of intelligence in this first "modern" global conflict. Verdun, Ypres, the Russo-Austrian front eloquently illustrated the slaughter and the stalemate of opposing armies of comparable size. Another dimension had to be explored, and this proved to be the battle of wits: the struggle, if not necessarily to influence or control men's minds, at least to probe them and snatch highly guarded, precious secrets.

Would this provide for one side the slight, but needed, winning edge?

The British had not stopped with monitoring German naval transmissions. They had broken codes. Thus were Royal Marines waiting on

Good Friday 1916 in Ireland for Sir Roger Casement when he was landed from a U-boat off the coast from Tralee to help foment an uprising against the English. So precise was British intelligence that a German freighter, lying well offshore with semiobsolete, captured Russian weapons, had been at the same time sunk by Royal Navy units. Convicted of high treason, Casement would be hanged in August. (Since he was a member of the nobility, he was accorded a silken noose.)

Nonetheless, the Irish Republicans, the Irish Volunteers, and other nationalist groups did lead the Easter Rebellion on Monday, April 24, in Dublin, in which 450 were killed and 2,500 wounded. In consequence, 15 leaders were hastily tried and shot in early May.

A fresh crop of martyrs resulted. Ireland's struggle for independence was now fueled anew. Britain had to contend with enemies at least as formidable in their hate as the Central Powers. They too would seek an edge through wits.

German intelligence, under the veteran colonel Walther Nicolai, had been equally active in England, France, and Russia since the outbreak of hostilities. Against the professionalism of Scotland Yard and its military counterparts, the head of what Nicolai called the *Nachtrichtendienst* found counterintelligence in Great Britain the most adept of the three countries. In fact, one of his seemingly more experienced operatives, Karl Lody, was captured and shot in the Tower of London before the end of 1914. He was but the first of a significant number of German spies to die there.

Unquestionably Nicolai's most celebrated agent, Mata Hari, through her acquaintance with Allied officers, predominantly French, was accused of being indirectly responsible for the deaths of at least fifty thousand soldiers fighting under the flags of the Entente. In the face of apparently overwhelming evidence, she was convicted by a military court and executed in a suburb of Paris in October 1917.

Russia was a different matter. It seemed, sometimes as though Nicolai had as many operatives in that beleaguered country as the Kaiser's generals counted their soldiers. They penetrated at all levels, starting with the Czarist court. The *Nachtrichtendienst*, in fact, became so cocky that it played games on Rasputin, the heavily bearded, self-proclaimed "monk" with the sunken, magnetic eyes. Mysterious healing powers were attributed to him, especially of the dread hemophilia that afflicted the Czarist family.

When German agents learned of one of this mystic's frequent visits to army hospitals, they would thereupon disguise one of their own (or a paid Russian) as a wounded soldier. This "patient" would gesture so pathetically that Rasputin would come over to the cot and launch into his "healing" rites in word, chant, and gesture. At the conclusion, the "plant" would sit up, throw back the covers, and proclaim himself "cured."

This was satisfying to all, especially to Rasputin.

That this strange personage was in some way linked to the *Nachtrich-tendienst* was rumored, but not established. Like so many others of the Czar's circle, Rasputin's guilt in this respect probably was indiscretion. The royal court did not know how to keep secrets or even how to whisper.

As there had been historically, double agents operated during and even before the Great War. Certainly the most notorious was Colonel Alfred Redl, of the General Staff of the Imperial Austrian Army. Confronted in the Klomser Hotel, Vienna, with evidence that he had been in the pay of the Russians, Redl was permitted a "gentleman's" way out. He was presented with a loaded revolver and a handshake.

Intelligence, by the late spring of 1916, had failed to tip the scales in favor of either Entente or Central Powers, but it was not for lack of trying on the part of any of the combatants. The movements of ships, armies, or high personages could not necessarily be kept secret, even though pertinent communications were so stamped.

The wireless monitoring of the High Seas Fleet had enabled Jellicoe to hurry his ships out of port. But this genre of electronic intelligence could not per se guarantee victory.

On Wednesday, May 31, the fleets met head-on, rather by chance as to time and position. German intelligence as provided by the zeppelin scouts had been hampered by bad weather. Scheer, therefore, had imperfect advance information on the positioning of the Grand Fleet, especially the battleships.

The opposing navies slugged it out into the night, the battle cruisers suffering from the late arrival of Jellicoe's battle fleet. By the next dawn, the Royal Navy could count fourteen warships sunk, totaling 114,000 tons, including three battle cruisers with almost their entire crews. The Germans lost eleven ships, representing 63,000 tons. The 6,000 British dead were twice the foe's losses.

The English called it "Jutland," the Germans, "Skaggerak." By any name, for the brave but luckless Britons it spelled something quite short of victory. When he was First Lord of the Admiralty, Winston Churchill, in one of his periodic visionary utterances, had observed that the war could be lost "in an afternoon." All too aware of this possibility, Jellicoe wished to keep the Grand Fleet "in being." In this he had succeeded—if at a sobering price. As well, the High Seas Fleet was back in base (and would never again sortie in force).

Although the litters of the wounded began to be borne ashore in many ports as early as the following forenoon, Thursday, the Admiralty did not issue its terse announcement until Friday evening. Thus, most Britons were not aware of the magnitude of the engagement until Saturday morning, already June 3—three days after the fact.

"It is clear," wrote the London *Times,* "that we have suffered the heaviest damage at sea that we have met during the war."

If the people generally were not prepared for so stunning a loss, neither was Fleet Street. Easily the most frivolous, if not the most lunatic, headline read:

GLORIOUS END OF OUR CRUISERS

Surely, there was nothing "glorious" in the total, almost instantaneous fragmentation of the battle cruisers *Queen Mary, Invincible,* and *Indefatigable,* where the majority of the 6,000 had perished. *Queen Mary,* at 32,000 tons, was among the largest capital warships afloat and, capable of thirty-two knots, perhaps the fastest. In the cynicism and conceivable futility of it all, she and most Royal Navy ships of the line were girdled with the finest steel armor plate obtainable from Imperial Germany's famed Krupp works. It was, as well, touted as virtually "impenetrable."

Lost with the *Invincible* was her captain, Admiral Hood, who traced his sea-dog lineage back to the time of Nelson. After the *Lusitania* debacle, he had considered himself very fortunate to be given such a fine command in the Grand Fleet.

Kitchener, the rather unlikeable miracle man who could persuade or shame five million men to "volunteer," presumably was informed of Jutland. Whether he understood its various implications was something else. Nonetheless, he spent a quiet Saturday, the third, and part of Sunday at his beloved Broome Park, near Canterbury. Unquestionably, Colonel Fitzgerald was with him.

The War Minister used to say he wanted to retire to Broome to tend his art collection and his roses. He also owned a stable. Yet Kitchener was not a cavalryman, but an engineer, an infantry leader famed for his fighting in the Sudan. Khartoum, as the capital, was the inspiration for his recent earldom. He knew little of the war at sea or even of the hazards of ocean transport in such times. To the stubborn, opinionated war minister, embarking on a cruiser or a naval transport for distant shores through imperiled waters meant nothing vastly more complex—or adventurous—than boarding a tram at Trafalgar.

Thus, on Sunday evening, as fog rolled up from the Thames,

Kitchener arrived at King's Cross Station, on the north side of London. With his small entourage, he stood briefly on the platform, gaunt, tired, but with the sort of nonchalance of one anticipating a grouse shoot on the moors. He was easily identifiable by anyone. Those—and there were a number—who saw the tall figure with the furious walrus mustache could wonder if he had not just stepped out of the poster.

Then, characteristically, he lit a cigarette—and started for his car. Close by the famed personage was Detective McLaughlin, as recognizable in "the Yard's" traditional bowler for whom he was as Kitchener. It seemed modest enough a guard.

Sir George Arthur, one of the earl's aides, had come to see his superior off. Concerned with administrative details, he must remain behind. Then Arthur was aware that "some confusion occurred, as Mr. O'Beirne's [the counselor at Petrograd] servant had misdirected himself to the wrong station and left his master cipherless."

No one, certainly not McLaughlin of Scotland Yard, appeared to question the chance nature of so singular a "misdirection" when this mission had been under preparation for at least ten days. However, O'Beirne was dispatched to retrieve his errant servant and follow by another train which was being hastily assembled in the King's Cross yards.

Then, Arthur continued, "something unusual happened." Kitchener, who had now "entered the carriage to escape more observation than was necessary," returned "to the platform and said very quietly—and a little sadly—to his friend [Arthur], 'Look after things while I am away.'

"Thereupon, as if unable to explain to himself the impulse which had prompted him to have a last word, he quickly regained his seat and looked away out of the window until the train started."

Kitchener's four-coach special chugged out of King's Cross at 5:45 P.M. and through the density and sprawl of London, darkened against recurrent zeppelin raids. For the seven-hundred-mile run to Thurso, across Pentland Firth from Scapa Flow, the train would speed over the tracks of four different rail lines and change locomotives five times. No. 552, a "small boiler type," would haul the cars from King's Cross to Grantham, over the right-of-way of the Great Northern.

The special made the 105-mile run to Grantham in just three minutes under two hours. There, with increasing grades ahead, engine no. 284, of the "large boiler" class, replaced the smaller one. Boiler volume was in direct ratio to power since Britain's railways were not using super-heated steam. Both engines, however, employed the standard two drive wheels on each side.

At 9:34, or not quite four hours out of King's Cross, the train ground into York, where it waited approximately three-quarters of an hour for the extra section, carrying O'Beirne, his cipher book, and in likelihood other confidential papers. This train, consisting of only two coaches, was "worked through" in but three hours, twenty minutes, sometimes pounding ahead at more than seventy-three miles per hour.

Typical of England's network of different rail lines, Kitchener's train would move over three more track systems before reaching Thurso: the North Eastern, the North British, and the Highland Lines.

As the train hammered ahead toward Edinburgh, Perth, and the Scottish Highlands, the weather worsened mile by mile until, shortly before midnight, the train was being rocked by gale winds and slanting rain. Kitchener, however, had drawn the shades of his compartment and submerged himself in paperwork. He paused only to make occasional requests of his official party, or to ring for the porter to bring him tea and various light edibles.

A big man—almost six feet, four inches—the hero of the Sudan had to maintain his nourishment. But his tastes were simple. For breakfast, fried sole or kippers, toast, and coffee. A generous serving of mutton was a favorite dinner entree. Temperate, he might have a whiskey and soda at lunchtime, a glass of wine in the evening. Instead of the more fashionable cigars, Kitchener preferred cigarettes, possibly his only vice. He smoked many when under tension.

And while the locomotive wailed through the Highlands there was unremitting activity aboard the *Hampshire*. Jellicoe, when advised of the Russian mission, had been curtly reminded that "only five or six persons" at the Admiralty knew anything at all about it. Thus, the commanding admiral had not alerted Captain Herbert Savill to his ship's special orders until Sunday afternoon, in fact shortly after worship services.

Like other units of the Grand Fleet, the cruiser was being swabbed down after Jutland as the crew endeavored to make her "smart and tidy." She had served during the great clash in a liaison capacity between the cruisers and battleships, doing little firing, although it was believed the *Hampshire* had rammed a submarine. All five hundred-some aboard her agreed the cruiser was indeed a lucky ship. She had not sustained even one hit.

Savill, good-looking onetime commander of the Royal Naval College at Greenwich, had been as much a rationale for Jellicoe's choice as the ship herself. He could be depended on to follow orders with a devoted exactness. Nor was the cruiser unfamiliar to Kitchener. When consul general to Egypt four years previously, he had traveled aboard her from Alexandria to Malta.

Early Monday, on schedule, the train rasped into the pier-side depot at bleak little Thurso. The stationmaster observed that today's was "the foulest weather ever known." There the destroyer *Oak* met the official party for transportation across seething Pentland Firth to Scapa Flow where Jellicoe and his flagship *Iron Duke* were waiting.

The War Minister, dressed in a field marshal's great coat of visibly enormous weight, was piped aboard *Iron Duke* before noon. His presence evoked considerable surprise even among the admiral's immediate staff, so close had the secret orders been kept.

Jellicoe, however, with a sense of history, had ordered one of the Grand Fleet's official photographers to record the event. This he succeeded in doing, eloquently mirroring the drenched quality of those wearing "foul-weather gear" surrounding the tall, commanding figure.

After a tour around the impressive, 26,000-ton battleship (or "dreadnought"), the Earl of Khartoum lunched with the admiral and his Flag officers. It caused at least raised eyebrows when Kitchener declared he was "looking forward" to his trip "as a real holiday." Jellicoe would recall, further:

"The strain of the last two years, he confessed, had been very great, adding that he felt that he could not have gone on without this break, which he welcomed very much." On the other hand, he was not "very sanguine that he could achieve much in Russia."

The Grand Fleet commander felt a certain fellowship with Kitchener when he alluded to the "difficulty" he experienced in dealing with the Cabinet. Jellicoe observed that military men were accustomed "to carry out their ideas without having first to bring conviction to the minds of men who, although possessing great general knowledge and administrative experience, have naturally but little acquaintance with naval and military affairs, which in themselves form a lifelong study."

When conversation, inevitably, turned to Jutland, Kitchener "evinced much interest in the tactics and the general story of the action." In likelihood, the admiral did not dwell on the question that was already being asked: Why had he not pursued the retreating High Seas Fleet, allowing even its crippled units to return to base?

Whether or not the field marshal anticipated this voyage as a "holiday," he impressed his host "strongly" that he was "working to a timetable, and that he felt that he had not a day to lose. He mentioned three weeks as the limit of his absence, and I expressed astonishment at the program which he had planned...he was most anxious not to lose a

Lord Kitchener (light coat, back to camera) with Admiral Jellicoe aboard the *Iron Duke,* presumably the last photograph of the War Minister. (Imperial War Museum)

moment on the sea trip and asked me more than once what I thought was the shortest time in which the passage could be made."

Even as the two very senior officers had lunched and chatted, the storm picked up its intensity. The sea smashed against the thick steel plates of the *Iron Duke* and rocked her measurably as she tugged at her buoy. The wind, butting in from the northeast with growing menace, howled through the mighty vessel's twin funnels, masts, turrets—anything that jutted above deck. The direction of the storm as well dictated that the east channel from Scapa Flow was impossible to sweep, also that light destroyers could not keep up with the *Hampshire.* Yet her orders had specified this route.

What was the answer?

Jellicoe excused himself to confer with his chief of staff, Admiral John Madden; with his navigator; and with other senior lieutenants. There appeared general agreement on the weather and its effect upon the east exit. A deciding factor was the report that at least one submarine had been sighted in that same area in the last twenty-four or forty-eight hours.

The decision: *Hampshire* should follow the west channel, past lonely Sule Skerry Light and into a relative lee from the storm. Thus, the destroyers could keep up with the cruiser's challenging speed. And, as a clincher, the admiral reasoned:

"It was practically impossible that this route could have been mined by any surface minelayer owing to the dark period in northern latitudes being confined to a couple of hours, during which no ship could expect to approach the shore for mine-laying without having first been sighted. The route was one used by Fleet auxiliaries, and was, therefore, under frequent observation...mine-laying by enemy submarines had been confined to water well to the southward of the Firth of Forth...danger from this source was, therefore, considered to be very remote."

While Jellicoe believed "the weather itself" constituted its own "protection" against submarine attack, "more to be feared than...mines," he was aware that the furious seas had kept minesweepers in port for the last "three or four days."

The Grand Fleet admiral had adopted a defeatist view toward persuading the War Minister to delay his departure pending a sweep of the channels—"two or three days' " time, assuming the vessels would have to wait for the seas to moderate. "Such a decision...would never have been agreed to by Lord Kitchener." Besides, through Jellicoe's rationale:

"With the knowledge...at my disposal as to enemy mine-laying possibilities, I did not consider the delay necessary...I should not have hesitated...to take the Grand Fleet to sea on the same night and by the same route" as resolved upon for *Hampshire.*

Shortly after 4:00 P.M. Lord Kitchener was taken from the *Iron Duke* in the admiral's "barge" through the choppy waters to the nearby *Hampshire.* There the sudden appearance of the august personage occasioned the same sort of surprise as on the flagship. On the other hand, it was Detective McLaughlin who persisted in the memory of Chief Shipwright William C. Phillips:

"One of the staff impressed me very much. He was dressed in khaki and his personality struck me as unusual...."

The cruiser slipped her buoy at 4:45 P.M. In a few minutes she was joined by the destroyers *Unity* and *Victor.* Neither possessed the size or the speed for such an escort in a storm of this violence. Both captains had mentally questioned the decision. However, they dutifully tagged along, rounding Tor Ness headlands, then butting into the open seas. When they should be benefiting from a lee, all three were pitching wildly, as the Admiralty bluntly put it, "in the teeth of the gale."

Savill knew the worst had happened. The winds had backed around to the northwest and were howling at fifty knots, producing mountainous seas—"the most terrific gale in my experience," according to Petty Officer Wilfred Wesson. Phillips, like most of his shipmates, "hung on like grim death."

Hampshire's lee course now would have been on the east channel, as originally ordered. After 6:00 P.M. *Victor* signaled that she could not keep up with the cruiser's eighteen knots. She was almost submerged in the raging seas. Savill signaled *Victor* to return to base. Even as he did so, *Unity* advised that she was down to twelve knots. This was too slow in submarine waters. By 6:30, the captain of the *Hampshire* had ordered both escorts to return.

They might as well have remained, since soon the cruiser herself was able to make only thirteen and a half knots.

"Chow time" wasn't much this turbulent night. Kitchener and his party were served in the captain's suite. The old soldier, however, had no appetite. Not much of a sailor, he was observed to be "rather green" from the violent contortions of his "holiday" vessel.

"With stout hearts and a good ship we battled against the elements," Phillips would recall. "It was now about 7:30 P.M., dusk was slowly creeping over, and we had just finished supper. Myself and some messmates were preparing to have a hand of cards when I was sent for by my superior officer...as I had charge of certain stores...was told to get the key of our storeroom and issue bedding, etc. for the use of Lord Kitchener.

"All the storerooms, magazines, etc. were guarded day and night by sentries, and in order to carry out my duty I went to the sentry for the key..."

Hampshire was now, noted the Admiralty, offshore between the Brough of Birsay and Marwick Head, turning to the east to round the northern extremities of the islands. Somewhat inside the normal course steered by the auxiliaries, she nonetheless had deep water—180 feet. But there was no relief since the gale roared offshore and "she was taking heavy seas all over her."

On the other hand, it seemed that "everything...on board was proceeding normally. The captain was on the bridge. The routine order, 'Stand by Hammocks!' had just been piped."

The sentry was at that moment in the act of opening the key case when "a terrific blast went through the ship, shaking her from stem to stern." According to Phillips, "we reeled against each other and the key case fell and smashed to pieces at our feet...the fumes which began to spread gave evidence that we had probably struck a mine...the force of the explosion had extinguished all the lights."

Others heard it as "a rumbling explosion," like "an electric globe bursting," or "not a loud explosion," perhaps "a double explosion," and "pretty loud." It all depended upon where one was in relation to the blast.

Petty Officer Wesson, for example, was impressed by the "terrible draft of air" which "came rushing along the mess deck, blowing all the men's caps off." He figured a hatch had blown away and he went racing off to locate it.

The stricken cruiser's bow submerged as waves foamed over the fo'c'sle. The Admiralty would describe:

"The explosion seems to have occurred under the forward half of the ship and probably near the keel...the ship at once began to settle down...the explosion seemed to tear the center part of her right out...she was unable to steer; the electric power failed; all lights went out; and no wireless communication was possible."

Orders were passed by mouth, "Abandon ship!" It wasn't necessary, since all hands who could were automatically taking their emergency stations.

In spite of the rain, mist, and overall gloom, *Hampshire*, only about a mile and a half offshore, was visible. The twilight in this latitude in June should last until about 11:00 P.M. A lookout with the Orkney Royal Garrison Artillery, stationed at the pinpoint village of Birsay, was among those who observed the explosion and the cruiser "immediately...go down by the head."

He raced to his billet to report breathlessly to the duty corporal, James Drever. The latter took a quick look for himself and then ran down the path to the Birsay post office. The tiny garrison boasted neither telephone nor telegraph of its own.

At the post office, which did have a telegraph but no telephone, the corporal found a highly agitated postmistress, Miss Jessie Comloquoy, who had witnessed the explosion from her own residence nearby. He scribbled a message, which he handed to her.

"Battle cruiser seems in distress between Marwick Head and the Brough of Birsay...."

It was addressed in duplicate to Commander, Western Patrol, Stromness, about twenty miles down the coast, and to the artillery command at Kirkwall, the same distance on the eastern shores.

Although the *Hampshire* was going fast, Shipwright Phillips observed "no panic whatever." He would record:

"Some of the poor chaps who had been in the vicinity of the explosion were reaching the deck in a terribly mutilated condition, but everyone was cool and calm...without any loss of time the boats were turned out and lowered, but during the lowering operations they were smashed by the heavy seas.

"The dynamo [generator] was out of action and could not be worked, and consequently five of our largest boats could not be launched and they remained in their crutches...." [That is, they needed electric power to be launched.]

The more phlegmatic—and optimistic—crew members clambered into these big and now immovable boats, waiting for the sea to float them free. The less sanguine were reacting quite differently.

"Anything with floating capacity was thrown overboard," Phillips continued. "A few others and myself picked up our carpenter's bench and threw it overboard, meaning to jump over after it and use for buoyancy, but it came back into the ship partly smashed, whilst I saw two officers jump overboard with a small drawer from their cabin under each arm."

But—*where* was Lord Kitchener?

In the "gunroom flat," according to one. This apparently was a sort of ready room for the gunners.

Petty Officer Wesson was certain he saw the War Minister arrive erect and monolithic on the quarter-deck as the gunnery officer, Lieutenant Humphrey Matthew, barked out:

"Make way for Lord Kitchener!"

If he remained the stolid soldier, the field marshal nonetheless, "looked very ill," it appeared to Wesson.

Leading Seaman Charles W. Rogerson thought he heard Captain Savill "calling to Lord Kitchener to go to the boat." But it was also obvious that he could not hear the commanding officer because of the wind's roar.

Yet others were sure the captain was urging his illustrious passenger to go below to the warmth of the galley. And there was as well a report that "four military officers" were walking on the quarter-deck, perhaps unable to find a boat.

At any rate, Phillips's first concern was not to look for Kitchener. Worrying about a boiler explosion and noting that "the ship's first funnel was...almost submerged, I with my boots off, but otherwise fully clad, jumped, and with a last good-bye plunged into the seething waters."

Wesson jumped at the same time and struck out for a Carley float. This was a large, oval raft, made of cork and wood slats, or grating for a base, with rope inside and out for handgrips. Nearly paralyzed at once from the cold, he looked back and thought he saw the War Minister "still on the starboard side of the quarter-deck, talking to his officers," as though making no effort to save himself.

Now the propellers were out of the water, motionless as *Hampshire*, like the *Lusitania*, poked her prow deep into the sea. To Rogerson, one of some several dozen clinging to a float, it seemed as though the stricken cruiser suddenly executed "a somersault forward," projecting all still on her decks into the raging waters.

On shore, Corporal Drever watched in disbelief the cruiser vanish before his eyes. He rushed back to the postmistress to ask if this fact could be added to the telegram. In her agitated state, Miss Comloquoy signaled to Kirkwall: "Oh, the ship has sunk. Can that be added to the telegram?"

She understood the operator at Kirkwall to reply, "That is all right!"

Hampshire, like the *Lusitania*, was utterly destroyed in about fifteen minutes, leaving scant debris and very little to hint that seconds earlier a cruiser of approximately eleven thousand tons, carrying more than five hundred souls, had been afloat upon these very waters.

After the initial shock, if not near hysteria of the moment, Miss Comloquoy, now somewhat calmer, decided she had better communicate again. At 8:20 she tapped out, "Vessel down." Fifteen minutes later, she was amplifying, "Four-funnel cruiser sunk twenty minutes ago. No assistance arrived yet." Then, as a gloomy postscript, "Send ships to pick up bodies."

This was addressed not only to Kirkwall, but to commands at Stromness and Longhope. It seemed that *one* of the recipients would surely be reacting. Actually, the response in the Western Patrol headquarters, Stromness, was much more instantaneous than either the postmistress or the corporal had any reason to expect. Without really appreciating what the telegraphist was talking about, Captain F. M. Walker, R.N., had the feeling that something very serious had happened. The skippers of the small patrol yacht *Jason II* and of the armed trawler *Cambodia* happened to be in a back room, warming up over a cup of tea.

"Be ready to put to sea at once!" Walker, commander of Western Patrol, ordered the two officers.

At the same time, Walker contacted his superior, Vice Admiral Sir F. E. Brock, who had been among those lunching on the *Iron Duke* at noon. With the receipt of the second and third telegrams, "Vessel down" and "four-funnel cruiser," there was no doubt what ship was involved. Brock ordered, in effect, every vessel through the size of a destroyer to sea, with Walker himself in personal command. The army was alerted to send motor lorries and shore parties to the Brough of Birsay area.

By "8:31 P.M.," according to the Admiralty, the rescue fleet, as it were, was actually putting into the stormy night, led by *Jason II* and *Cambodia*. Walker swung aboard the ocean-going tug *Flying Kestrel*, flanked by two more trawlers, *Northward* and *Renzo*.

Unity and *Victor*, thankful to be mooring, were ordered to return at once to the wild coasts they had just quit. Two more destroyers would follow, also the yacht *Zaza* and trawler *City of Selby*. Five more destroyers reported they could get up steam and be ready to depart after 2:00 A.M.

Phillips had gained a float, but far in excess of the forty-five men for which it was designed were aboard it or clinging to the sides. The lifejackets worn by many produced a buoyancy that tended to defeat their purpose, making it hard to hang onto the raft "and practically hopeless for those who clung to the sides." He continued:

"It was decided to lighten the raft, and volunteers from among those wearing life belts were asked to leave, and so bring it up to a proper floating capacity. Thereupon, living up to the traditions of the 'True British Sailor,' with a few smiling remarks such as 'We shall be there first,' some eighteen answered the call and plunged into the billows, thus sacrificing themselves to give their shipmates their only possible chance of reaching the shore.

"We stood now in some four feet of icy cold water, with waves engulfing us every instant; our four paddles which we had used for a short time were now unmanageable, and we were at the mercy of the wind and sea."

If not before, exposure now was having its effect. A man next to Phillips, whom he thought was a servant with Kitchener, asked him "in a very pitiful way" if he thought the group would ever reach the cliffs of this exceptionally rocky shore. When Phillips attempted to reassure him, his companion replied, "I don't think so, mate." With that, he slumped to the bottom of the raft. Phillips believed he had died.

"The night was drawing on and men were dying very swiftly now; some simply gave in exhausted and dropped off as if going to sleep; others fought very hard...but eventually succumbed to the cold and exposure...some poor fellows lost their reason."

It was much the same on the other rafts that had floated away from the sunken cruiser. Numbed from "the fearful cold," as another survivor put it, the sailors lost their grips and vanished into the black, frothing waters. "An almost overpowering desire to sleep came upon us, and to overcome this we thumped each other on the back, for no man who went to sleep ever woke again."

Some tried to sing familiar songs such as "Tipperary" to keep up their spirits and circulation. But it was too cold. The words seemed to congeal in their throats.

"They were clustered round you, dying as you looked at them."

Phillips estimated he had been on the raft about two hours. "Darkness had almost overwhelmed us and the cliffs were entirely lost to view. The gulls had already spotted us and came hovering round with their shrill cries." He was "lying across" he did not know how many dead bodies in the raft.

Unknown to the rugged shipwright, however, two destroyers, the yacht *Jason II* and trawler *Cambodia,* had arrived shortly after ten o'clock at the position indicated by the postmistress. Considering the continuing gale and the fact that *Unity* and *Victor* had turned back once, this was a rather remarkable record. Using searchlights, at their own peril, in a time of blackout, the vessels discovered wreckage and a number of bodies, which were brought aboard—but no survivors.

Lifeboat stations along the coast were not specifically alerted. But well before midnight, with the grinding of lorries along the back roads and sheep paths behind the cliffs added to the shouts of foot parties, the word of some major offshore disaster had been spread. However, the small, forty-foot auxiliary motor lifeboat berthed at Stromness was a good example of what was available as well as of the hopelessness of anything so light challenging the night's storm.

It was, as a matter of fact, a hastily assembled ground party that had found Phillips: a naval surgeon, a few Territorial soldiers, Marines, and some farm laborers.

"All at once I became aware of the old familiar sound of breakers beating on a rocky coast, and the awful thought that I should be smashed on the rocks, or perhaps hurled and killed against the cliffs passed through my mind...the sound of breakers warned me that the critical moment was approaching...At last one large wave swooped us against a very high cliff, only to recede on the crest of the wave...."

Capriciously, almost, the sea had saved Phillips and five other survivors by depositing their raft on some low, accessible rocks, in what the Orcadians (Orkneys residents) called "geos," or inlets between the cliffs.

"Our feet and hands were rubbed, and we were rushed off to the farmhouse, stripped, and laid before a huge fire, given a nip of spirits, dressed in Scotch flannels, then carefully wrapped in warm blankets and put to bed."

Not many were so fortunate. *In toto* but twelve men survived, being borne to land in two other floats besides Phillips's. Not one cruiser officer lived, although among the dozens of dead washed ashore was the body of Kitchener's aide and friend, Colonel Fitzgerald.

By dawn, the fury of the gale had subsided. Sea birds took flight once more. An intermittent, cold rain fell from leaden skies, creating a dismal, if not morbid, backdrop for the spirits of the Royal Navy.

"My own sorrow...was overwhelming," Jellicoe would admit. "Everyone in the Grand Fleet felt the magnitude of the disaster that had fallen upon the nation, and it can well be imagined that the feelings of the Fleet generally were intensified in me on whom lay the main responsibility for his safe passage to Archangel."

The commanding admiral would continue to speculate "whether anything could have been done that was not done short of postponing the departure of the *Hampshire* altogether..."

It "positively made" his chief of staff, Admiral Madden, "feel sick, and I can't get it out of my head. Seeing the ships blow up on the thirty-first had no such effect as that was all in the day's work."

Fleet Street received the news at precisely 1:40 P.M. this Tuesday, June 6. The Admiralty merely quoted a telegram from "the Commander-in-Chief of the Grand Fleet."

"I have to report with deep regret that His Majesty's ship *Hampshire* (Captain Herbert J. Savill, R.N.) with Lord Kitchener and his Staff on board, was sunk last night about 8:00 P.M. to the west of the Orkneys, either by a mine or torpedo. Four boats were seen by observers on shore to leave the ship. The wind was N.N.W. and heavy seas were running...I greatly fear that there is little hope of there being any survivors...."

The bulletin hit the streets almost at once, along with posters carried by the newsies. The *Star*, for example, had printed a poster, seemingly with the speed of light, proclaiming in huge type:

KITCHENER DROWNED
(Official)

It was a bombshell of disbelief to Londoners returning to their offices from lunch. Lloyd George himself put the mass reaction this way:

"A pall of dismay descended on the spirit of the people. Men and women spoke of the event in hushed tones of terror. The news of a defeat would not have produced such a sense of irreparable disaster."

Flags were abruptly half-staffed, curtains drawn in Whitehall's baroque warrens of Empire. Performances in the West End, the theater district, were canceled. The Corn Exchange in Liverpool and the

Glasgow Stock Exchange halted trading, then locked their doors. Even many of those last bastions of solace, the common pubs, shut their taps. The bartenders hurried home.

The motivating impulse would be rationalized by Henry Newbolt: "Kitchener too long had been a legendary hero of the people, and in their time of need he had by the mere sound of his voice called armies into being."

With a well-honed sense of expediency, the *Daily Mirror* hustled on the streets Wednesday a special "Memorial Number," depicting Kitchener's life in pictures. The *Daily Mail* ran a speculation piece under the heading:

WHO SPIED ON LORD KITCHENER?

The *Morning Post* stated unequivocally, "Circumstances point at espionage or treachery." Other papers posed much the same proposition. At Edinburgh, a correspondent reported on tightened security in the Orkneys, with closer checks on those newly arriving. But it seemed a bit tardy.

One writer thumped out an all-inclusive warning:

LONDON HUNS AT LARGE!

The journalist, unfortunately, had exhausted most of his ammunition in the scare heading. It was much in the substance of the fable that appeared earlier in the war of the Russian "troop trains" rattling through the British Isles. How did observers know they carried the Czar's armies? Why, because there was snow on the cars' roofs, of course.

Nonetheless, these were especially chancy times again for butcher shops owned by those of German ancestry and, indeed, even for unsuspecting dachshunds. As had happened after the *Lusitania* torpedoing, for one instance, angry citizens called for a boycott of such small businesses, if not actual closings. Cries for "deportation!" rumbled as irrational hate surged anew.

With canary feathers undisguised, the *Leipzig Neueste Nachrichten*, in publishing Kitchener's career, boasted that the obituary had been written several days previously, "on receipt of information that Kitchener was going to Russia."

The claim occasioned no raised eyebrows at the Berne, Switzerland, office of the Wireless Press Service, which filed, "It is possible that the information reached Germany via Petrograd where the Russians still complain that enemy espionage is rife."

On Saturday, Colonel Fitzgerald was buried at his home, Eastbourne, on the Channel.

A week after he had been lost, on Tuesday, June 13, a memorial service for Lord Kitchener was solemnized in St. Paul's. The list of mourners, led by the King and Queen, read like a Who's Who of Allied civilian and military leaders. A sea of "black and khaki," it looked to the London *Times*, stretched out from Sir Christopher Wren's cathedral in all directions—such a multitude, according to the reporter, that it could have filled St. Paul's three times.

The "fragile pallor of women in black" appeared altogether in harmony with the playing of "Chopin's Funeral March" by the Irish Guards (of which the deceased was a member). But the final notes of "Last Post" had not long faded into silence before rumors arose to haunt an Island Empire still gripped in a life-and-death struggle for existence.

These were "foolishly encouraged by his [Kitchener' s] sister, Mrs. [Millie] Parker," wrote Sir Phillip Magnus, a primary biographer of the War Secretary, "and it was said that Kitchener had been betrayed to the Germans; that he was a prisoner; or that he had been spirited away to a cave in some remote island of the Hebrides where he lay plunged, like King Arthur or Barbarossa, into an enchanted sleep from which he would presently awake.

"The subconscious minds of a surprisingly large section of the semieducated masses recoiled, irrationally, from the need to accept the fact that their deified hero could share the common lot of death without jeopardizing the cause which he symbolically embodied."

These thoughts, by coincidence perhaps, had previously been expressed in much the same words by John Gilbert Lockhart.

There were those who remained sturdily confident that Kitchener, in all his trappings, medals untarnished, would come marching down the gangplank of one of the prisoner repatriation ships. In likelihood he would be puffing detachedly on a cigarette, as some returning matinee idol.

When he did not, despair only deepened.

Incredulity persisted at the catastrophic loss of life—about 98 percent of the *Hampshire*'s crew. Charges were heard that not only was the navy slow in responding but that it actually discouraged offers of local assistance. Such accusations were, not surprisingly, denied sharply by the Admiralty. Certainly, the rapidity of the sinking, the bitter cold, and the continuing violence of the storm were quite sufficient to thwart rescue efforts even in the unlikely event that they could have been anticipated, then carefully organized.

Too, important minutes had been irretrievably lost since no wireless message had been received from the cruiser. Why was that? What had happened to the auxiliary, or emergency power for the *Hampshire's* transmitter? All capital ships of the Grand Fleet had used their wireless extensively at Jutland.

Had her transmitter been tampered with?

The war ended. A Kitchener Memorial Tower, square and squat, was erected atop the bleak promontory, Brough Head, to stand as severe and unyielding as the man himself. Nearby, a mound of earth is said to be the tomb of some pagan warrior, the ruler of a long-forgotten tribe which "raised vast monoliths to the sun and moon."

But neither the ghost of the *Hampshire* nor that of her illustrious passenger could long be put to rest. Two years after the Armistice, in 1920, George Arthur published a definitive biography of his friend and hero. One line in particular caught the eye of the curious:

"By an unhappy error of judgment an unswept channel was chosen for the passage of the cruiser; and Kitchener—the secret of whose journey had been betrayed—was to fall into the machinations of England's enemies, and to die swiftly at their hands."

How had that secret been "betrayed"? By whom? Just what "machinations" specifically? Sir George had presented a riddle that for some reason he did not, would not, or could not clarify. Six years later he only added to this sense of mystery. On February 10, 1926, the London *Times* published a letter from him:

"There is so much loose talk and so many questions are addressed to me with regard to the death of Lord Kitchener that I would ask you to let me say that early in 1920 the First Lord of the Admiralty (the late Lord Long) asked me to read the secret or unpublished report on the sinking of the *Hampshire* on the understanding that I would not divulge a word to anybody.

"I declined to read the document under these conditions as my object was to give in my *Life of Lord Kitchener* the correct version of the tragedy, and this I could not do if the material were in my hands which I was not allowed to use. I told the First Lord that I should submit that neglect, or at any rate carelessness, must be charged to the Admiralty or the Commander of the Grand Fleet in the arrangements made for Lord Kitchener's voyage. The reply of the First Lord was: 'I do not think you could say otherwise.' "

What "secret report"? And, ten years after the sinking, *Why* was it still "secret"? *What* was the Admiralty hiding, and why?

This necessarily peaked the curiosity of the House of Commons. The First Lord of the Admiralty, W. C. Bridgeman, was called to clarify the matter. In no way apologetic, he was quoted as testifying, "It was never stated that the full report of the Naval Court of Inquiry was published." He insisted there remained "valid objections to the publication of such a report."

When questioned subsequently on whether he would reopen the Court of Inquiry on the *Hampshire*, the First Lord was adamant that he would not unless "some *prima facie* evidence [were] produced which would justify that course."

The next month, on March 12, there was a singular mass meeting at the London Opera House. At least twenty-five hundred persons turned out to view a short motion picture, *The Tragedy of the Hampshire*, and to sign a petition. As reported by the *Manchester Guardian*, the event had been promoted by a journalist going under the name of Frank Power, who for the past four years had been writing articles in the *Sunday Referee*, of London, on the circumstances surrounding the loss of the ill-fated cruiser. The thrust of them splashed a canvas of suspicion, double-dealing, old-fashioned espionage, and overriding official negligence and incompetence. In 1921 Power's vivid imagination had inspired another film, *How Kitchener Was Betrayed*, which, however, was legally suppressed, partly at the behest of the Kitchener family.

In view of "the new evidence brought before the public by Mr. Frank Power," the *Guardian* quoted the petition, "the report (on the *Hampshire*) should be published and a further public inquiry held." Further, he told the multitude that he possessed "written sworn testimony that there was an internal tragedy in the *Hampshire*...there were three explosions and it was an internal explosion which sounded the death-knell of Kitchener."

In an effort to lend weight to this charge, Power pointed out but did not otherwise identify six men with him who he claimed were "survivors" from the *Hampshire*. The *Guardian* did not indicate that any one of them had addressed the audience.

Power, by implication, linked the arrest of "two spies" he said were caught on the cruiser with this "internal explosion." They were then "shot in the barracks."

He alleged there had been "a policy of hush-hush all along...something to hide which the Admiralty was afraid to face."

The *Guardian* reported that the short film presentation, while mildly interesting, had little to do with its title. It was a montage, mostly of film clips of Kitchener's career and of Orkneys scenics. It did bring home the austerity of this rocky, cliff-dominated coast and the awesome challenge faced by castaways in coming ashore.

Nonetheless, Power had drawn a very large crowd and induced most present to sign a petition. Capitalizing on this obvious success, he next announced that Kitchener's body had been washed ashore in Norway and buried. Further, he was going in person to fetch the remains back. And London, for a time, would hear no more of Frank Power.

But this year, 1926, Lord Kitchener and the *Hampshire* persisted in the news. On the tenth anniversary, June 5, the *Times* wrote nostalgically of seeing the headline boards, "Kitchener Drowned!" and continued:

"The impression was and remains so vivid that every feeling and thought it provoked can be revived...a slight impatience with the sunlight which was doubtless playing tricks with one's vision. Next, a sense of the absurdity of such news...to report him drowned was to insult the common intelligence. Then, a bewildered groping after any shadow of possible meaning...."

On July 20, the First Lord of the Admiralty again said there would be no inquiry. But he hurried back into Commons to announce that the Admiralty was about to publish a "white paper" on the whole *Hampshire* episode. The members, though necessarily taken off guard, applauded the decision. And on August 10 this paper was indeed released—some twenty-eight pages in length, single-spaced and available at His Majesty's Stationery Office for a modest six pence.

The *Times*, in separate editorial comment, applauded, and wished "sensation mongers will seek some other field."

But the white paper, as many had feared, left much to be desired, much unanswered. It was a credible and reasonably detailed review of the actual voyage, the sinking, and of what some of the survivors endured. But its thrust was defensive, if not apologetic, nor did it even claim to be the *full* exposition of a major naval inquiry a decade past.

Undoubtedly projected into print by the continuing barrage of Frank Power, the paper was found to be obsessed with denying reports of spies or that the *Hampshire* was not fully seaworthy: "There is not the slightest ground for attributing to her either bad condition or a 'bad record' in the matter of spies, though fables...have been numerous and persistent."

Further, "There is not the slightest ground for believing that any spy or ill-affected person was on board the *Hampshire* at any stage in her history, and that anyone who tries to persuade the public to the contrary belief is either imposing upon them, or has himself been imposed upon."

And continuing the same rationale, "the evidence confirming the conclusion that the *Hampshire* struck one or more German moored mines is so complete, that it is scarcely credible that any intelligent person can still venture to advance the hypothesis of an internal explosion caused by spies on board."

The Admiralty relied heavily on the "definite opinion" of eight of the twelve survivors that the cruiser had struck a mine "... explosion seemed to tear the center part of her right out." But no weight was accorded the fact that none of these was an officer, with the professional training to be a witness in such rather technical matters.

Three days after the sinking, the report continued, "a group of moored German mines" was spotted in the same area. Perhaps it was sheer good fortune that spared the considerable rescue fleet that morning and following day, since the trough of the waves in such a storm would have brought the destroyers at least in proximity to the moored mines. The paper offered in substantiation reports from Admiral Scheer and excerpts from *Der Krieg zur See*, the German official history of the naval war on the activities around the Orkneys of U-75.

In any event, the white paper was adamant that only "one or more German moored mines" could have been responsible for the destruction of the *Hampshire.*

That "the secret of Lord Kitchener's Mission" could have been "strictly guarded at the Admiralty" or "carefully preserved by the navy" was necessarily more hope than proven fact. It was known in ruling circles both in London and Petrograd from the inception of talks before the middle of May. Without question, Fleet Street was aware of the trip, but because of the Official Secrets Act or ethics, or both, "newspaper row" conveyed nothing into type.

Far from criticizing the commander in chief of the Grand Fleet, the report found that Jellicoe's "decision" to change routes was "a prudent one in the difficult circumstances of the moment." It took no exception to the admiral's airy assumption that "it was practically impossible that this route could have been mined...." [Shades of Lord Mersey!]

Close to half of the white paper was devoted to a justification of the rescue efforts and the communications attendant thereto. It was clear, the document maintained, "in the actual circumstances in which the accident occurred, any such differences in time [in reaching the scene] could have had no practical result in enabling lives to be saved at sea...."

Garbled, it was nonetheless as reasonable as any statement in this naval apologia. Considering the fury of the seas, the bitter cold, and the rapidity of the sinking, it was miracle only that twelve had survived.

In an almost wistful aside, contrasting with the "narrative" as a whole, the Admiralty observed, "One of the most tragical features...is the fact that the information upon the strength of which the fatal mines were laid in this locality was inaccurate information [resulting] in the German belief that it was used by warships...unconnected coincidences of exactly similar type occur...in the experience of almost every human being, but are apt to be overlooked except when, as in the case of the *Hampshire*, their consequences are momentous."

The final bit of testimony in attempted refutation concerned Frank Power's allegation that Kitchener's body had been washed ashore in Norway and buried there. The remains recovered and interred in Scandinavia, it was noted, "were those of officers and men who lost their lives in the Battle of Jutland a few days previously."

Most were in agreement that the sea currents were unlikely to have carried bodies such a distance and in a long easterly arc.

In the meanwhile, Frank Power had actually brought a coffin into London. On August 17, 1926, it was removed from its packing case and opened at a funeral home in the presence of the Lambeth coroner, one Ingleby Oddie. The coffin was empty. Of yet more significance to Coroner Oddie was the obvious newness of the casket and the fact that it had "*never* contained a body."

"Nobody," sniffed one reporter, "in this country imagined for a moment that Mr. Power's claim would be substantiated."

The writer seemed on rather firm ground, the firmer by September 9 when the Home Office announced that Scotland Yard had determined the coffin had been bought by Power in Kirkwall and shipped to London. However, the report added, Frank Power had indeed promoted the charade of a mock funeral service in Stavangar, Norway, using another coffin.

Why had this man gone to such lengths to perpetrate his macabre and shameless hoax? None would ever know the answer, since Frank Power disappeared, never to surface again. Nonetheless, the aura of suspicion—was it sabotage?—he had augmented, if not necessarily created, would persist in spite of the Admiralty's most earnest efforts.

For six years, the mystery of the *Hampshire* lay dormant, while the West became preoccupied with depression, with Hitler and Mussolini—and with Josef Stalin's accelerating extermination of the kulaks and others who opposed him. Then, in 1932, a prolific and imaginative writer, Clement Wood, published, in New York, *The Man Who Killed Kitchener*. This *enfant terrible*, as revealed by the author, was a Boer Huguenot and "Europe's best swordsman," the dashing "Master Spy," Frederick "Fritz" Joubert Duquesne. His overriding obsession in life was a pathological hatred of the English. Correctly or not, he believed their troops had hanged an uncle and raped his mother during the Boer War.

As described—conjured?—by Wood, Duquesne, masquerading as a Russian naval officer, "Count Zakrevsky," came aboard the *Hampshire* as an observer. At the crucial moment, Duquesne supposedly opened a port and signaled by flare to a waiting U-boat which thereupon torpedoed the *Hampshire*. Wood explained to his readers that the spurious count was picked up by the submarine to become the mysterious "thirteenth" survivor.

On the other hand, there *was* a Fritz (or Frederick) Duquesne, although British intelligence located him in the United States at the time of the loss of the *Hampshire*. In fact, he was most sincerely wanted in England for allegedly placing a bomb aboard the Lamport & Holt freighter *Tennyson* before it sailed from either Rio or Bahia, Brazil, in February 1916. Three British crewmen died in the blast. Brazil had become a nest of the Kaiser's spies and saboteurs.

Between the wars, Duquesne became a nationalized U.S. citizen, earning his livelihood, it was said, as a lecturer and writer. But he made news again in mid-1941 when he was arrested and charged with leading a ring of German agents bent on obtaining information on bomb sights and other classified military hardware. Much of their activities had been in Schenectady and other New York State manufacturing areas. Pearl Harbor intervened, and a federal judge threw the book at the hapless Duquesne.

Sentenced to eighteen years, he was not paroled until 1954. He died of a stroke two years later, a lonely, shrunken man of seventy-eight, with no known next of kin. His remains were laid to rest in some now-forgotten potter's field, and with them the mystery of what connection, if any, the man had with the *Hampshire*.

In 1933, yet another "master spy" came forth to take credit for destroying the *Hampshire* and Britain's War Minister. Ernst Carl, one of Colonel Nicolai's spies in England, claimed in his freshly published *One Against England*, that he had teamed up with the Irish Sinn Feiners to smuggle two time bombs, wrapped in blankets, aboard the cruiser. He then repaired to his room in the "White Horse Inn," Kirkwall, from which he watched the warship explode in "two pillars of flame." The distance and the storm clouds combined to make this latter statement absurd. And Baedeker's travel guide of that period listed no White Horse Inn at Kirkwall.

In that same year, 1933, the one aspect of the *Hampshire* that had not yet been probed splashed into the news, if in back pages, on both sides of the Atlantic. This concerned purported divers who reached the wreck and retrieved gold bars—perhaps as valuable as half a million dollars.

It all added up to another formal denial by the Admiralty, which knew of no salvage operations whatsoever. None had sought permission to dive for the *Hampshire*. The Royal Navy still claimed ownership. And, as for the bullion—*what* gold bars?

However, between 1948 and 1951 a Canadian company negotiated to conduct salvage operations, but was finally refused by the Admiralty. Anyhow, the lost cruiser was officially listed as a "gravesite."

Also in 1951 a New York locksmith published his *Unlocking Adventure* in which he wrote in detail of how he had allegedly reached the wreck in 1933. Charles Courtney indicated that a German salvage vessel had been chartered by—of all people—Sir Basil Zaharoff, the shadowy figure of international munitions.

"Every gun on the cruiser was loaded and beside it was a mound of skeletons and earphones on their heads, lying by shells that were never fired...."

Fully uniformed officers floated off like watery apparitions when he touched them, Courtney added to his lurid description. He opened safes, he claimed, containing the equivalent of $100,000 in bullion.

The locksmith was a professional in this specialized field, if not diving. He was said to have done some work for Zaharoff, but all else was clearly the product of a vivid imagination. He even put the *Hampshire* wreck depth at 385 feet, or 205 feet greater than the assumed position.

To the best of topographers' knowledge, the cruiser lies exactly where she sank—plainly marked on nautical charts three miles off Birsay Bay near Brough Head and the Kitchener Memorial Tower.

To this very day, more than four score years after *Hampshire* sank in gale-wracked waters, doubt persists whether the Admiralty yet holds a secret report, or indeed if there ever had been one. In 1967 a small group of papers bearing on the cruiser and other ships was released to the Public Records Office, in keeping with the fifty-year declassification rule. The contents were inconsequential.

But the damage had been done. The Admiralty's handling of the disaster and the release of a defensive, well-censored white paper ten years after the event served effectively to perpetuate a mystery.

What *did* occur that night somewhere off the rugged promontory, Marwick Head?

All evidence points to a mine. A torpedo in such weather is unlikely. Nor did the German Navy ever claim a U-boat was there on that date.

On the other hand, there *could* have been a bomb, although most likely not placed either by the flamboyant Fritz Duquesne or garrulous Ernst Carl. There were enemies aplenty in the British Isles—the Irish and Colonel Nicolai's agents—capable of introducing such a device on board. Security was loose in the Orkneys, as admitted afterwards by the announcement that visitors' credentials would be more carefully inspected.

That the cloak of secrecy with which the Admiralty and the War Ministry sought to wrap the mission to Petrograd had been compromised was first attested to by Sir George Arthur. There is scant doubt that confidences could not long endure in the corrupt and loose-tongued Czarist court. It was of no great consequence whether Rasputin, as many continued to believe, was in effect an informer for the Kaiser's forces. There were scores of others equally qualified.

Perhaps the question of most significance in the whole mystery of the *Hampshire*—why has not the Admiralty sent a diver down to examine the wreck?

Major units of the German High Seas Fleet, scuttled following their internment in Scapa Flow, were salvaged. Waters in this anchorage are as deep as 100 feet. The *Hampshire* lies in only 180 feet of water. Granted, Scapa is sheltered, ideal for underwater operations, and currents swirl around the wild, west Orkney shores, but exploratory diving in the latter area is quite possible. The *Lusitania*, in some 300 feet and also washed by currents, has been reached by scuba and more traditionally suited divers.

Yet, the Admiralty, so far as is known, has not attempted to reach the *Hampshire* and has even refused permission to those firms that made formal application to do so.

Why?

What, at this late date, might the Royal Navy be guarding? Is gravesite the only reason?

The Admiralty had every reason to be haunted by a guilt complex after its mortal carelessness in sending the Empire's War Minister out over unswept channels. "It was practically impossible that this route could have been mined...such a decision [to delay] would never have been agreed to by Lord Kitchener..."

Admiral Jellicoe must still have been suffering from post-Jutland syndrome. For nearly two years the Germans had been demonstrating their deadly skills with mines and torpedoes. They had been employing both weapons virtually at will. (By war's end, Great Britain would have lost a staggering eight million tons of her merchant marine.)

As for the commander of the Grand Fleet having to obey the War Secretary—the Earl of Khartoum had no authority whatsoever over the Royal Navy. He would have had no choice but to "agree."

"One of the most tragical features," as the Admiralty rationalized, was the supposedly mistaken mining of a route not used by warships. Or, was it "mistake"? Could not the Germans be *making sure* of this exit only as a pre-Jutland sowing, but for Kitchener's voyage, assuming that the latter was already known?

And why was at least one submarine—later identified as the U-47— prowling off the east channel from Scapa Flow *after* Jutland and as the *Hampshire* was being groomed for an ill-starred voyage to Archangel?

Among the unanswered questions: What about the servant with the cipher book who supposedly had "misdirected himself to the wrong station," necessitating an extra section for the special train? What might have been the implication of this, against the ever-present wartime by-play of espionage?

What sank the *Hampshire*? Who, if anyone, betrayed her mission?

Within reasonable bounds, one can continue to speculate the answers to these questions. Only the Admiralty may have the capability of settling them once and for all.

*   *   *

Was the *Hampshire* carrying gold bullion to Russia along with Lord Kitchener?

Neither the Royal Navy nor the Foreign Ministry has ever confirmed this tantalizing conjecture, but salvagers have been fascinated by the possibility ever since the cruiser was sunk.

Neither the 180-foot depth of icy water nor the strong currents are a particular frustration to experienced scuba divers, and some undoubtedly have seen the encrusted *Hampshire* in her stony crypt. But the "Gravesite—no trespassing!" edict prevails.

Enforcement is something else in these remote waters. Most recently, a Dutch salvage group was spotted by a naval vessel happening past, and ordered away.

Others may have been more fortunate.

5

The *Cyclops*

Spurlos versenkt

FRITZ DUQUESNE WAS FAR from being the only German agent or fevered sympathizer on the loose in Brazil.

Waterfronts in Rio, Bahia, and lesser ports were in effect crawling with them. In Bahia, for example, the crew of the gunboat *Eber*, interned early in the war—more than one hundred crewmen and their officers—had preempted the local German Club and a number of cafes, which soon sounded and smelled like the *Bierstubes* of Hamburg. It was the same story in Rio at its German Club, plus the roistering Highlife (pronounced "Heegie-Liffey") Club.

They noisily prosited the Kaiser and shouted *Deutschland uber Alles* until the morning's early hours. When they should have been sleeping off their hangovers, they plotted dark deeds against the enemy England until Brazilian counterintelligence experienced all the nervous symptoms of acute frustration.

Even though local authorities thought of them as "riffraff," "troublemakers," and such, these were naval personnel under the Imperial Eagle, the "elite" leaders. In their number were the crews of forty-five interned German merchant vessels—an increasingly ragged little band—as well as "tourists" being slipped in regularly from Spanish liners. They swelled the permanent German colony of some several thousand and, especially in the southern part of the vast country, formed paramilitary groups known as "rifle societies." They goose-stepped and banged away almost every afternoon.

In Brazil there was no shortage of German nationals. And as if to ensure this Teutonic presence, other Germans kept crossing the borders from Argentina, Uruguay, and Paraguay. Many, if not most, were armed with the latest Mausers, the heavy military rifle that had proven so deadly on the Western front.

Even as relations between the two nations deteriorated, Berlin had the unmitigated arrogance, in late January 1917, to request that a wireless station or even a submarine base be permitted somewhere on the Brazilian coast. When Rio refused, it was rumored that some kind of a shore operation had been established by a U-boat, or raider, anyway, at Santos.

Although this was subsequently denied by both governments, there was other activity that seemed to compromise a country's neutrality. The majority of the interned *Eber*'s crew escaped on the Swedish steamer *St. Croix*, supposedly to be transferred at sea to a raider. Those left behind had other plans.

Early in April 1917, almost coincident with the United States's declaration of war on Good Friday, the sixth, the 4,461-ton Brazilian

USS *Cyclops*. (U.S. Navy)

steamer *Parana* was torpedoed and sunk off Cherbourg. Three crewmen were lost. (Cuba and Panama entered the conflict the next day, April 7.)

On May 22, a second ship flying the Brazilian flag, the *Tijuca*, also identified as the *Lapa*, was torpedoed off Brest, France. This inspired the formation of special patrols by the Brazilian Navy. As well, the United States Navy created the small Pacific Fleet, the primary purpose of which was to cooperate with the Brazilians in intercepting raiders and also German agents moving to South America on neutral steamers.

Admiral William R. Caperton showed his flag for the fleet on the armored cruiser *Pittsburgh,* which in turn was commanded by Captain George B. Bradshaw, Annapolis, '89. He was tall, mustached, a disciplinarian long feared by all who had ever served under him.

A short item on August 27 in the Reuter's wire service out of Rio announced the arrest of a German identified only as Kopschitz, a rifle club member, for "tampering with certain military correspondence." He was turned over to the Brazilian military and never heard from again.

In September, Count Karl von Luxburg, German charge d'affaires in Buenos Aires, was expelled following the discovery that he was transmitting merchant shipping intelligence via the Swedish Legation's own diplomatic code to Berlin. It was assumed that he had masterminded a thriving espionage/sabotage ring from Argentina, with an even larger German population than Brazil's.

Luxburg would be credited by some with dramatizing, if not necessarily originating, the heady phrase/threat *spurlos versenkt,* or "sunk without trace." This was employed, understandably, in the context of Allied shipping but was to prove a double-edged sword in hastening American participation in the conflict.

Late the next month, the Brazilian freighter *Macuo* was torpedoed. It was believed to be the fourth vessel flying that country's flag to be lost in the war. Rio's patience was at an end. This latest sinking coupled with apparent widespread clandestine operations was too much.

On October 26, Brazil declared war on the Kaiser's Germany, vowing to take "extreme measures to stamp out Prussianism in Brazil forever!" All interned German merchantmen were seized, but not before much of their machinery had been damaged. Scuttled, the *Eber* burned to the waterline. Remaining crewmen were arrested. German businesses were placed under government control. Portuguese was decreed the language in schools predominantly German. The German Clubs were padlocked.

On November 17, the Brazilian freighter *Acary* was torpedoed off the Cape Verde Islands. Emotions in the South American nation heated further, but not to the point where an expeditionary force to France was contemplated. However, there were those remaining in Brazil this winter of 1917–18 who continued, in their own ways, to fight for the glory of the Fatherland and were aided in their movements by the fact that Brazil was surrounded by "neutral" countries.

One, conceivably, of this group did not fit the pattern at all. His persuasions should have been far different. He was Alfred Louis Moreau Gottschalk, forty-five-year-old American consul general in Rio and a descendant of the famed pianist of the same name.

Though New York-born and a second-generation American citizen, Gottschalk had shown himself to be sympathetic with the Kaiser. Before his country's declaration, he had cooperated with German firms supposedly in excess of diplomatic demands. He had dispatched funds through various foreign banks to the Red Cross. In prewar years he spent his vacations in Berlin. With his finely trimmed mustache, top hat, cane, and pearl vest, he cut a true dandy's figure in the sidewalk restaurants of Unter den Linden.

Perhaps all this, belatedly, had something to do with his being recalled by the State Department to Washington for "talks" early in 1918. There appeared to be a fertile field for earnest conversations. But not many passenger liners plied between the two hemispheric continents. How to bring the consul home?

The Department phoned "Main Navy," a new, many-winged temporary cement structure a few blocks down 17th Street. The duty officer in Operations looked at a secret wall chart and found the answer. The big collier *Cyclops*, a naval auxiliary in its overseas transport service, was scheduled to sail Saturday, February 16th, from Rio for Baltimore with a cargo of manganese ore. She had accommodations—dormitories, to be sure—for almost a hundred passengers.

Not the newest, *Cyclops* nonetheless was one of the largest in the Naval Overseas Transport Service: 10,000 tons, 542 feet long. Her twin steam engines (vertical, triple expansion) could push her great bulk of more than 20,000 tons when fully loaded through the waters at fourteen knots. Since the U.S. Navy had virtually nothing to compare with the sleek new British capital ships, *Cyclops* could easily keep up with the American fleet, especially in convoy with slower merchant vessels.

The mammoth collier, with fourteen towering king posts, was launched at Cramp's shipyard, Philadelphia, in May 1910. Mrs. Walter H. Groves, daughter-in-law of the builder's president, Henry S. Groves, wielded her champagne bottle like a bludgeon against the *Cyclops*'s ample starboard bow. It shattered into seemingly thousands of minute sparkling fragments. But the ship would not budge.

Skilled shipwrights and helpers further down in the scale of proficiency hastily cranked up additional jacks under the broad keel and smashed with huge sledge hammers at the restraining timbers in the ways. A lovely woman, Mrs. Groves nervously fingered the orchid on her coat and looked as though she were about to cry. Was it *her* fault?

Finally, after long minutes that seemed hours, the collier groaned, then slid with a rasping screech into the muddy waters of the Delaware River. But the old salts who had been present walked away shaking their heads. The ship's consummate reluctance to take to the water, like some hesitant prehistoric monster, could bode only ill. Of that belief they could in no way be disabused.

As an auxiliary, this was not a "reg" ship of the line. Her crew, civilians all, would be subject only to such discipline as the captain—and possibly a few other senior officers—could enforce. Too, as a collier, she would be calling at ports where no ships of the fleet would be available for assistance. And considering the *Cyclops*'s ponderous size, former experience with harbor tugs or even destroyers would hardly be regarded as a qualifier.

But the Navy, still flushed with victory after the Spanish-American War, was ebulliently confident that it had its man. He had been an officer on a transport in that war and more recently had been strong-arming colliers for the Navy. His name was Georg Worley, about fifty years old, nee John Frederick Georg Wichmann, in Bremen, Germany, before migrating to San Francisco following the Civil War.

Worley, husky, mustached, a drinker and a brawler, was scarcely in the tradition of Nelson, Drake, John Paul Jones, or even Davy Farragut. But neither was he supposed to sail into battle aboard a prestigious flagship. He had skippered several private yachts off the Pacific coast and for a time managed a saloon, which he claimed to have won in a poker game.

The Navy had no especial occasion to question the conduct of its ham-fisted collier master until 1908, when the third mate of the *Abarenda*, under Worley's command, was murdered by the ship's carpenter. While Worley was absolved of any blame in the homicide, the court of inquiry did speculate why the auxiliary's master did not run a tighter, better-disciplined ship. But this manifestly did not stand in the way of command of the big *Cyclops*.

The choice seemed to be a good one. *Cyclops* soon won the coaling record for the fleet: 574 tons to the battleship *Arkansas* in one hour. It was pointed out at the same time that the collier was capable of coaling a squadron of dreadnoughts plus ten torpedo destroyers for a cruise of four thousand miles.

But if *Cyclops* were an efficient and a useful ship, this did not necessarily imply she was either a smart or a happy one. Some crewmen complained that Worley chased them about the decks in alcoholic rages, at times brandishing a wrench. Nor did the master evince much patience toward panicky coal heavers in rough seas when the *Cyclops* demonstrated a tendency toward disquieting snap rolls. This in spite of the fact that she had been designed with "self-trimming" holds and an improved system of water ballast tanks.

But burly, gruff Georg Worley (family and close friends called him Fred) boasted that he treated his men "like a father," and there were those who agreed. They attested he lent them money or clothing if they were in need, and surely he was good almost any time for a bottle of beer or a slug of whiskey.

As he had on the Pacific coast, Worley became a legend along the Atlantic's waterfront taverns where he was often known as "Old Dutch" or "Dutchman," especially after 1914, by the crews of the interned German ships. Indeed, there were many who said he was much too friendly with them. For example, he was seen as a frequent visitor aboard the erstwhile raider *Prinz Eitel Friedrich*, warped near the *Cyclops* in the Portsmouth Navy Yard. But, then, Worley loved to speak his native tongue and to drink beer, certainly to sing the old familiar Lieder.

Unappreciated by a literal-minded Navy Department was Worley's sometimes diabolical sense of humor. It attained its own curious apogee after he had spread the rumor that he kept a tame lion, the gift of an African chieftain. This finally elicited a curt "OPNAV" from the Chief of Naval Operations, soberly quoting regulations—chapter and verse—against "pets on board naval vessels." For days afterward, Worley's deep, raucous laughter boomed in Norfolk saloons as he affirmed that he harbored "no Goddamn pussy cat on my ship!"

Pleased with this little charade, the *Cyclops*'s master next boasted that the Kaiser himself had come aboard in Kiel to admire, in particular, the engines. He had lavishly praised Worley, the latter insisted, for operating a "smart ship." This time the Navy Department ignored the commanding officer, knowing well that the collier had never dropped anchor anywhere near that major German naval base.

With America's entry into the Great War, Georg Worley could no longer *prosit!* with his German friends, certainly not in public. In June 1917 *Cyclops* was in the convoy that escorted the famed First Division to France, arriving in St. Nazaire. But with the collier's return in late July—serious charges.

Led, apparently, by the assistant surgeon, Dr. Burt Asper, of Gettysburg, Pennsylvania, a delegation of the ship's complement formally charged the commanding officer with a series of offenses. These included drunkenness, insulting language, chasing at least one sailor "at gunpoint," showing a "suspicious" masthead light, and even threatening to pilot his ship into Rotterdam and turn it over to the enemy.

In his defense, Worley wrote to the Navy Department that "the evidence in this case is not sufficient to send a stray dog to the pound." And a counter-group that included the paymaster, Ens. Carroll G. Page, of Vermont, claimed to have "gotten along well" with the captain. Page added that the collier bore "one of the toughest crews" and "a very hard-boiled captain" was essential to manage them.

The inquiry concluded that Worley obviously did drink more than he should while at sea, and quite likely showed "favoritism" in granting shore liberty. But the Navy graybeards rejected out of hand all serious complaints, including allegedly chasing a sailor with a revolver, or the insinuations that he might have been signaling to U-boats or wanting to guide the collier into Rotterdam.

And if too many summary courts and confinements on bread and water appeared in the logbook, this was not in discord with wartime discipline on other naval auxiliaries, and surely not aboard ships of the line. For example, the very name "Black Jack" Bradshaw, down in South American waters on the *Pittsburgh*, could cause a seaman's heart to miss a beat.

Thus cleared, for the most part, Worley kept command of his big collier. On the other hand, *Cyclops* was removed from the "Atlantic Train" and assigned to duty coaling the fleet along the East Coast. Some speculated this was to keep her in proximity to the many naval bases from Maine south to Florida.

After the explosion of the ammunition ship *Mont Blanc* in Halifax harbor on December 6, 1917, devastating much of the city, the *Cyclops* was ordered north under full steam, bearing coal, medical supplies, and food. While there Worley fell, aggravating an old hernia so severely that he had to use a cane. Even so, he limped badly and was in obvious pain.

When he returned to Norfolk, Worley confided to his wife, Selma, and his eleven-year-old daughter, Virginia, that he would undergo an operation after his next voyage. The hard-bitten master, who boasted that he had never been sick in his life, evinced "real panic" at the thought of surgery. Or so it seemed to little Virginia, who admitted to being "a real daddy's girl."

This Christmas, Georg Worley hobbled clumsily about on his cane, occasionally uttering melancholy predictions about the future—"if any." However, he wanted to take a long rest—maybe a whole year—after his operation and go back to Port Orchard to recuperate.

He even talked of buying a car and motoring across the country. This surprised his small family no end, since the commander of one of the world's largest cargo vessels could neither drive an automobile nor lead a team of horses.

And as winter snow and sleet beat against *Cyclops*'s king posts at her Norfolk berth, new orders were being written in New York. They were complex. She would carry coal to Brazil and return with a cargo of manganese ore. Under charter to the United States and Brazil Steamship Company, the collier would be delivering the ore to the United States Steel Corporation at its Fairfield plant in Baltimore. Thus she would be steaming more as an ordinary merchantman than a naval auxiliary.

Arranging this voyage was the South American Shipping Company, 78 Broad Street, in Manhattan's financial district. However, in doing so, the company represented the E. G. Fontes Company, of Rio de Janeiro, which in turn owned the Morre de Mina Mines, source of the manganese.

It so happened that the employee of the South American Shipping Company who signed the agreement for the cargo was a German alien, Franz Hohenblatt, who had taken out only his first citizenship papers. Apparently, he was regretting that simple, preliminary step. This was *Weihnachten*, the Christmas period. There was traditional partying in spite of the war. One afternoon, Hohenblatt returned to the office to blurt out, in his thick accent, in the hearing of a fellow employee, Harry Lambert, "Damn every one of them! They should be shot, ja—!"

Lambert, conservative, quiet, was not at all certain of the specific objects of his coworker's intemperate remarks: Were there others in the shipping office, representatives in Brazil, or even the crew of the collier to which the ore was being consigned?

"They are fools for fighting for this country!" Hohenblatt added, expressing regret that America's declaration of war had made it impossible for him to return to fight for the fatherland.

Lambert chose to ignore this hotheaded, tipsy German. He really did not take him very seriously.

The *Cyclops* sailed from Lynnhaven Roads, the vast Norfolk/Chesapeake Bay anchorage, on January 7, an unusually somber Worley at the helm. In fact, he had confided gloomily to a friend, "This may be the last time you will see me. I may be buried at sea."

His hernia still troubled him. In addition, he left little Virginia at home sick with measles. These factors combined with another wartime voyage and that into a mounting winter storm could be considered enough to depress a man.

But the passage turned out to be for the most part calm, unchallenged by U-boats or raiders. Arriving at Bahia after just two weeks at sea, the collier took on bunker coal and continued to Rio, where she docked on January 28. Her arrival was not, however, without incident; the cylinder of the starboard engine had blown out even as the big vessel steamed into the harbor.

Painfully, Worley took cane in hand to report the accident to Captain Bradshaw on the *Pittsburgh*. He did not make much of an impression, unshaven, dejected, limping about the relatively smart decks of the naval cruiser. But then Bradshaw didn't hold fleet auxiliaries in any higher esteem than he did the rustiest old tramp steamer out of the back slips of Hong Kong. Besides, Bradshaw, himself a semi-reformed alcoholic, was certain that his caller had been drinking.

Howsoever, the captain wanted to get this seaworn collier loaded and out of his jurisdiction, along with her slovenly master, who, in a word, "wasn't Annapolis!" He dispatched a board of engineers to determine the seriousness of the disabled engine.

The board quickly threw up its collective hands. Neither engine was considered in "satisfactory condition," both were guilty of "lost motion," and the whole greasy, steamy area was a deafening discord of grinding "noises." The board nonetheless advised the Bureau of Construction and Repair in the Navy Department that the *Cyclops* would have to plod home on one engine. There was no yard in South America which could maintenance the vessel.

The engineer lieutenant on watch at the time the cylinder burst, Louis J. Fingleton, of Portsmouth, New Hampshire, was blamed for not stopping the offending machinery at the first sign of trouble. Whether he should face at least a board of inquiry was left to the brass in Norfolk.

And while the cargo of coal was being unloaded and that of manganese dumped aboard, Worley wrote home:

"I am in hopes to get back safe and then go to the Norfolk hospital...I feel I am sick...our trip down here was rather pleasant, but it gets tiresome this running without lights...."

Not all on board, however, were in agreement that the voyage had been "pleasant" in the least. For one, Dr. Asper, was penning to his family in Chambersburg, "*If* I get back, I'll ask to get off *this* ship...."

Two sailors from the *Cyclops* succeeded in that goal. One crashed a full wine bottle onto the skull of his shipmate during a "misunderstanding" in the sweltering Highlife Club. The latter was killed as certainly and as quickly as if his assailant had clutched a machete. Thus, the bottle wielder was left behind in Rio to await Brazilian or U.S. Navy justice.

On February 16, approximately two weeks after her arrival, the collier thumped out of Rio Harbor, on one engine. She carried 10,800 tons of manganese ore (insured for $500,000), plus 1,000 additional tons of bunker coal, which added up to a gross of more than 20,000 tons. *Cyclops* now drew fifteen inches over her Plimsoll line, thirty-one feet down in the water—which seemed to ensure exceptional stability.

Aboard, too, was passenger Consul Gottschalk.

Four days later, the naval auxiliary stopped at Bahia. There she embarked seventy-two service passengers from the cruiser USS *Raleigh*. Most of them were on rotation duty, on leave, or mustering out. A few were brig cases, facing disciplinary action. When the deeply laden ship cleared Point San Antonio, at the entrance to Bahia Harbor, on February 21, she carried 309 persons, crew, service personnel, and Consul Gottschalk.

The *Raleigh* duty officer, via shore cable, advised Naval Operations of the collier's departure, noting she was due in Baltimore on March 7. This was transmitted in plain English.

The South Atlantic proved in a beguiling mood—flat, blue, calm. On one engine, *Cyclops* pounded ahead at ten knots. She made Barbados on March 3—practically home. The morale of all, especially Dr. Asper, was noticeably elevated.

Commander Worley's actions and behavior, however, were no less strange than they had been. For example, he ordered an additional eight hundred tons of bunker coal, although with one engine "compounded" (shut down), the vessel was consuming less than forty tons a day. There was quite enough on board already to make Cape Henry or, in the event of unexpected head winds, to put in to a more southerly port such as Savannah. Worley also signed for 180 tons of provisions, at least twice as much as needed.

"Why don't you wait for Baltimore or any East Coast port?" suggested the American consul, Brockholst Livingston. "The rates are much cheaper."

Worley paid him no heed whatsoever. He also ignored protocol in not calling on the British port officer at this West Indian possession of empire. The latter, Lieutenant Harold Holdsworth, returned the snub by refusing to go on board the *Cyclops* for customary amenities and offers of assistance. Worley, who could care less, upped anchor on March 4 after leaving a message to Naval Operations with Consul Livingston:

"Arrived Barbados, West Indies, 17303 for bunker coal. Arrive Baltimore, Md., 12013. Notify Director Naval Auxiliaries. Comdr. Train (Atl.) 07004. USS *Cyclops.*"

The big collier put Bridgetown astern, continuing northward through seas as serene as she had traversed coming up from Bahia.

Nine days later, March 13, the ensign on watch in Naval Operations pulled Worley's Barbados dispatch off the peg marked "Due" on the big fleet and auxiliaries movements board. Routinely, he started to transfer it to another peg, "Arrived," paused, scratched his head, and then asked his radioman to "call up" the signal stations at Cape Henry and Cape Charles. When did the *Cyclops* pass this entrance to Chesapeake Bay?

Very quickly, the reply: She had *not* come through.

The duty ensign shrugged. The collier could have slipped past the capes in the fog, or she might still be a few miles out at sea. He prepared a query addressed to the *Cyclops* herself to be transmitted from the powerful naval wireless towers, "NAA" in nearby Arlington, Virginia: "S. C. Cipher #1 Report probable date arrival in Baltimore, Md. 1013."

And having thus delivered itself, the Navy again forgot all about the collier—for five whole days. Then on March 18, operations belatedly realized the *Cyclops* had not answered its question of March 13. The *Pittsburgh*, still at anchor off Rio, was asked how much coal was aboard when the auxiliary quit South American waters. Since Bradshaw hadn't the fuzziest idea—or interest—he in turn queried the *Raleigh*, at Bahia. Two days later, March 20, the Pacific Fleet commander conveyed the doubtful intelligence that "so far as he knew" the captain of the *Raleigh* thought *Cyclops* "intended proceeding Baltimore direct ..."

Thus, he was answering a question which had not even been asked.

Cape Henry and Cape Charles signal stations watched in vain for the familiar silhouette of many king posts. Then, on March 23—*ten* days past the *Cyclops*'s estimated arrival date—Naval Operations ordered the Sixth Naval District, at Charleston, to keep radioing the collier until she might answer. The next morning, Sunday, March 24, Charleston replied:

"Have been unable to communicate with USS *Cyclops* by radio from 11:00 A.M. Saturday to 10:00 A.M. Sunday. Shall I continue?"

The Navy Department snapped that Charleston certainly should keep trying to "converse." This same Sunday three patrol vessels were ordered on the search out of Guantanamo, Cuba. All naval stations south of Norfolk and into the Caribbean, including the Virgin Islands, were also ordered to try to raise the missing ship by radio.

For the next week, the Navy, like a guilty person talking frantically to himself, kept flashing earlier queries to Rio, to the Pacific Fleet, to Barbados. These elicited, in addition to the repetitious fact that *Cyclops* had departed Barbados on March 4, assorted minutiae, including:

The Brazilian Coaling Company, which had stowed the manganese, advised that the collier could have carried two thousand more tons "without being overloaded." This was seconded by the shipping representative, William Lowry, who asserted the *Cyclops* was "well trimmed" when she sailed.

At the same time, the consul passed along the "theory locally" that the boilers had exploded. However, the *Pittsburgh*'s survey board had reported nothing amiss other than the one disabled engine. The easy passage to Barbados seemed to bear out that her propulsion machinery was operating satisfactorily otherwise.

Brockholst Livingston revealed not only an inherent distaste for Worley but that he himself was an imaginative gossip peddler, luridly advising the Navy and State Departments:

"Master alluded to by others as a damned Dutchman apparently disliked by other officers. Rumor trouble en route here, men confined, one executed, also conspiracies. Some prisoners from fleet in Brazilian waters, one with life sentence…have names of crew but not of all officers and passengers. Many German names appear…."

The Chief of Naval Operations, Admiral William S. Benson, suggested "scrutinizing," as he darkly added, "while not having definite grounds, I fear fate worse than sinking though possibly based on instinctive dislike felt towards master."

Not until early April were the families of those on board advised— and interrogated. The word came as far more of a shock than if they had been told the *Cyclops* had been torpedoed and sunk with all hands. What last letters had they received? Any German sympathy apparent? Mutinous sentiments? What about Worley? Could he have rendezvoused with some enemy submarine or other vessel and sailed to a remote port?

The offices of the South American Shipping Company in lower Manhattan were paid a routine visit by intelligence officers. Might they speak to Franz Hohenblatt who had written orders for the ore?

Harry Lambert was embarrassed. Hohenblatt was gone. Lambert had never voiced his suspicions to the authorities, and now it was too late. Before he left, said his fellow employee, Hohenblatt had burned some seven hundred letters he had received from Germany, with the curt observation, "They won't get anything on me!"

And that was the last ever seen of Franz Hohenblatt.

On April 15, the Navy officially announced that the collier was missing: "No well-founded reason can be given to explain the *Cyclops* being overdue, as no radio communication with, or trace of her has been had since leaving the West Indian port...the Navy Department feels extremely anxious for her safety."

A list of those on board accompanied the terse bulletin. Curiously, since the Navy had studiously avoided any public speculation, newspapers at once focused suspicion on Worley. His name and German birth were seemingly enough to convict him without trial—or even cursory thought. In some wholly unproven fashion, the captain *must* have delivered the big collier into enemy hands.

These suggestions were, at the very least, disturbing to the master's family.

"Do you think," Selma Worley told reporters, "my husband would prove traitor to his wife and little daughter? My husband was an American through and through."

She then explained how "Fred," as she knew Georg Worley, had, before sailing, purchased a $500 Liberty Loan bond. When she protested that $100 was quite enough, he replied that his "patriotism" dictated he contribute five times that amount. Selma also recalled that Virginia had even donated her "pet polly" to the Red Cross, which sold the bird for $40 at a rally.

She also read portions of the letter he had posted in Rio, especially the concluding lines:

"I have no news regarding the war to write. Only hope that the German people will soon see their error and hang the Kaiser and his whole followers and then have peace."

Mrs. Worley professed to believe that both he and his ship were safe. How or where she could not explain. However, she would not wait in Norfolk for his return. She packed up and, with her daughter, set out for Port Orchard—and a new life.

On June 1, Assistant Secretary of the Navy Franklin D. Roosevelt formally declared the *Cyclops* lost and all aboard legally dead. But even with the doomsday finality of this official obituary, Naval Intelligence was not quite ready to close the books on its missing collier. As late as June 29 it prepared a confidential memorandum on the leading possibilities relating to her disappearance.

1. Mutiny, then was navigated "off track."

2. Gottschalk somehow took command and "handed over" the *Cyclops* to the Germans at some "remote port."

3. Torpedoed or hit a mine.

4. Manganese dioxide mixed with coal dust and exploded.

5. Foundered.

6. Worley himself effected a rendezvous with a submarine.

7. The remaining engine failed, and she drifted [*Waratah*like]—down toward the South Pole.

Intelligence officers could ask, but without any physical evidence, they could not directly answer any of their own questions. Numbers 1, 2, and 6 appeared particularly gossamerlike. And as for Gottschalk, all of the Navy's previous suspicions were tied into knots when friends in New York revealed he was going to apply for a commission in "the National Army" upon his return, whatever the State Department's reasons for recalling him. He had written them that he did not believe he was "doing enough" for his country as consul.

If *Cyclops* had been torpedoed or had struck a mine, in all likelihood she would have had time to flash a radio distress. But, as in the case of the *Hampshire*, there had been no wireless communication from the collier.

There *could* have been an explosion of the gases and dust from the cargo and from her bunkers. But who could prove it, especially with no wreckage?

Foundering presupposed violent weather or a sudden, inexplicable cargo shift. The testimony of those who had loaded her in Rio seemed to preclude the latter. The Weather Service went at length to check conditions along the *Cyclops*'s projected route to Norfolk, including the querying of six ships. One, the Lamport and Holt Liner, *Vestris*, en route from New York to Buenos Aires for hides and beef, reported exceptionally calm seas that March. Others had logged "Force 1" winds—one to three knots—the first two weeks in March. Only the transport *General Goethals* had recorded winds as high as twenty-five knots, and that was on March 7, near Nassau.

Meteorologists added, "It is a safe statement to make that there were no storms in that area in March." Regardless of the seas, the Bureau of Construction and Repair volunteered its own amen, "The vessel has proved staunch and seaworthy through years of service."

Further, engine failure was particularly unlikely in light of her successful passage to Barbados. Also, the collier could have radioed for help, in that event.

Meanwhile, throughout the spring and into the summer Brazil attempted, rather desultorily, to do something about "all those Germans." The government cleaned out the Lloyd Brasiliero steamship office and ordered German banks to "liquidate" without delay. Other businesses, such as importers owing allegiance to the fatherland, were ordered to cut back the count of nationals to a minimum. But it was like swatting at flies. As one was eliminated, yet another and another would appear elsewhere.

The Pacific Fleet kept stopping neutral Spanish ships, sometimes removing German citizens. But how many spies, bearing forged passports—say, of Britain or the United States—actually landed in Rio and other ports?

A nation which, unlike its European counterparts, did not contemplate standing armies as a way of life, Brazil roughed out plans for its own brand of draft: the designation of some one million young men as "subject to recruiting" in "first and second lines." Its "shooting societies" had already been increased to 564, embracing more than fifty-six thousand persons.

And as the war in Europe slowly wound down, in great measure from mutual exhaustion and numerical depletion, the rumors as to the *Cyclops*'s fate whispered on. She had been torpedoed by a Brazilian destroyer (perhaps in error). She was variously at Kiel, Emden, Antwerp, somewhere in the Adriatic, in Antarctica (presumably provisioned and bunkered for a cruise of interminable duration)...bottles containing messages allegedly from the missing collier washed ashore along the East, Gulf, and West coasts. Their scribbled names proved invariably not to match anyone who had been on board the big ship. Planking and life preservers, even a barnacled wreck on a remote Bahamian key were reported. But no identifying names, much less markings, could ever be established.

Those who had smugly maintained, over any attempts at contradiction, that *Cyclops* had been torpedoed or had struck a mine were sobered into silence a few weeks after the Armistice, November 11, when Admiral William H. Sims, personal emissary in London of the Secretary of the Navy, cabled, following a report from his counterpart in Berlin on the Allied Naval Armistice commission: "It is definite that neither German U-boats nor German mines come into the question...."

It didn't matter. Letters from relatives, friends, and simply the morbidly curious—asking questions or volunteering "explanations"—kept pouring into the Navy Department month after month as the Great War itself receded into history. Among the more bizarre profferings was that

Worley had become a sole survivor after a mine had cut *Cyclops* in two. He made his way to Houston—of all places—where he shortly died under an assumed name, according to one Frank Sefrit, of Bellingham, Washington.

In 1920 the Navy actually dispatched a destroyer to Riding Rock Key, in the Bahamas, to investigate what was reportedly the hull of the lost collier. All manner of flotsam was encountered, but nothing that looked like it had ever been a part of the naval auxiliary.

If not stranded, possibly she had been blown out of the water by a disappearing submarine fortress, located somewhere near Barbados, or such was the reconstruction of a writer in Hearst's *American Weekly*. The gunners inside this deadly Jules Verne-like creation had fired on the *Cyclops* when spotted in company with the raider *Karlsruhe*. Among the many flaws in this journalistic *bouillabaisse* was the signal one that the *Karlsruhe* had sunk early in the war. She *was*, however, off Barbados at that time.

What was labeled as the diary of a German saboteur turned up in the Navy Department. The writer claimed to have gone aboard the *Cyclops* with three others, in order to secrete a dynamite charge in the engine room. Shortly before it was due to detonate, they left in a small boat.

Or "gargantuan squids...monster cuttlefish," mused one George Noble, in the *National Marine*, "helped themselves to the ship's people as delicately and effectually as one plucks gooseberries" before "crushing the structure to matchwood." It was *Mary Celeste* revisited.

In far more sober vein, Commander Mahlon S. Tisdale, who had himself served briefly on the collier, wrote in the U.S Naval Institute Proceedings that a sudden cargo shift may have turned the *Cyclops* turtle. One who did not think much of the ship's stability, he theorized that a contributing factor might have been open manholes. He pointed out that manganese was a most undesirable cargo, since it was disproportionately heavy in relation to its bulk.

Unquestionably an experienced and thoughtful naval officer, Tisdale, not long before his death, reaffirmed his views to this author. However, he somehow had neglected to take into consideration, among other factors, the *Cyclops*'s vaunted self-trimming holds and new stabilizing tanks.

The Bureau of Construction and Repair stuck to its original assessment of the stability of the collier. Nor did it profess much concern over the possibility that a sudden jamming of the steering mechanism combined with the fact she was running on one engine, one propeller, could have heeled her over, causing the manganese to tumble to one side, thus quickly capsizing her.

As to propulsion, Naval Intelligence did not comment one way or the other on the hypothesis that the engine breakdown could have been sabotage. No imagination whatsoever was required of any member of the "black gang," wielding a wrench, quickly to incapacitate one or both cylinders.

In an otherwise careful investigation, relatively little weight was accorded sabotage. This could be considered ostrichlike in light of what German operatives had done or been credited with doing during the war.

1. From the very inception of hostilities, a "factory" for the production of cigar-shaped incendiary devices had been working overtime inside the interned liner *Friedrich der Grosse* at Hoboken. These small time bombs had caused fires, some fatal, on forty outbound Allied merchantmen. Captain Franz von Papen, military attaché at the German Embassy, Frank von Rintelen ("the dark invader"), Dr. Walter Scheele, and Wolf von Igel were among the German agents responsible.

2. In the summer of 1916, Black Tom Pier, in New York harbor, a mile long, packed with warehouses, trains, barges, and ships all loaded with ammunition, blew to bits. The rubble burned for days, sending billowing clouds of oily, black smoke over Manhattan and into Westchester County and Connecticut.

3. A plot to dynamite ship-building ways at Hog Island, in Delaware, was uncovered at the last minute and hundreds of pounds of bombs seized.

4. Two major Italian warships, the *Leonardo da Vinci* and the *Benedetto Brin*, burned mysteriously at their moorings. The armored British cruiser *Natal* caught fire at her Scapa Flow anchorage a few days after Christmas 1915 and sank with heavy loss of life. The Admiralty later blamed improper stowage of cordite, but this was only speculation. And, what about the *Hampshire?*

5. Brazil had been a nest for German agents throughout the war. How many, besides the flamboyant Fritz Duquesne, had placed or attempted to place bombs on outgoing Allied ships? Indeed, countering such "vipers" had been the principal motivation for creating the U.S. Pacific Fleet.

6. An untold number of German agents taking passage aboard U-boats had been lost to depth chargings and minefields. If such an operative had placed a bomb on the *Cyclops*, he did not necessarily survive the war to boast of his accomplishment.

7. Furthermore, would the postwar German government necessarily admit if she had torpedoed or sabotaged the collier? With war
reparations already mounting to astronomic proportions, why assume
responsibility for a loss that seemed truly *spurlos versenkt?* After all, this
was the nation that had tossed nonaggression treaties aside as "scraps of
paper." Secretary of the Navy Josephus Daniels had pronounced his
official amen: "There is no more baffling mystery in the annals of the
Navy than the disappearance of the *Cyclops.*"

"Personally," wrote Dr. H. D. Stailey, of Santa Rosa, California (in a
letter to the author), "I cling to the theory of an internal explosion
from a bomb as the most likely cause...no radio messages re trouble
were received by anyone; hence her radio was either out or there was
no time to use.... my best conjecture would be an internal explosion—
a bomb or boiler—and a rapid sinking."

The then Lieutenant Stailey was aboard the *Raleigh* at Bahia in
1918. He was one of scores with some intimate knowledge of the *Cyclops*
whom the author either interviewed, corresponded with, or both, for
chapters in two previous books. The number included especially next
of kin, notably Mrs. Donald (Virginia Worley) Stott, of Port Orchard,
Washington. He has reopened old files, his own and those in the
National Archives, and put out fresh "feelers."

But the entire disappearance and the circumstances, climate, and
innuendo persist in much the mood of Churchill's characterization of
Russia, "a riddle wrapped in a mystery inside an enigma." *Cyclops*, all
20,000-plus tons of her, ship, cargo, bunkered coal, and the 309 souls
aboard vanished as completely as though, like the *Waratah*, she and
those she carried had never existed at all except in the minds of those
left behind.

With no deathbed confessions, secret files belatedly opened, or
telltale wreckage washed ashore—anywhere, remote or otherwise—
the mystery remains as profound today as it did that long-ago spring
of 1918.

This author leans to war-related sabotage. But he can't prove it,
any more than Commander Tisdale could prove his theory of the collier's capsizing.

One may still ask: What happened to the *Cyclops?*

6

Morro Castle

A case of the "human equation"?

THE GREAT WAR BECAME no more than an unfortunate interruption to transatlantic travel. As a matter of fact, only three of the superliners, notably the *Lusitania*, had been lost. Old favorites, such as the *Mauretania*, *Aquitania*, and *Olympic*, were scrubbed up, repainted, and hurried back into passenger service. There were new names, too, on old hulls: the *Majestic*, *Berengeria*, and *Leviathan*, in particular, through war reparations. They had, respectively, been the *Bismarck*, *Imperator*, and *Vaterland*.

Still greater ships appeared on the ways or on drawing boards in the 1920s, like the *Bremen* and *Europa*, *Rex* (pride of the Italian Line), *Queen Mary*, and the fabulous, ornate *Normandie*. At nearly eighty-three thousand tons, France's pride was the world's largest superliner and, at a top potential speed of nearly thirty-five knots, the fastest at that time.

In this decade there appeared a new fashion, a new objective, a novel *raison d'etre* in ocean voyaging—the cruise ship. Prior to the war there had been excursion boats aplenty, especially on the Hudson, the Mississippi, and the Great Lakes. Their voyages usually spanned no more than a few daylight hours, overnight at the most. Early in the century, the existence of excursion vessels was ferociously dramatized with the burning of the *General Slocum* in the East River in 1904 and the capsizing of the *Eastland* at her Chicago pier in 1915. The loss of life, mostly women and children, in both was worse than appalling, approaching two thousand in total.

In the easy twenties, with a desire for fun and escape, but with no firm reason for any particular destination, the cruise ship suddenly seemed a heaven-provided answer to ennui and a vacation to nearby latitudes that need not consume a month or more—or even too much cash. Congress itself served up a big boost to American shippers—and travelers—by passing, in 1928, the Jones-White merchant marine bill. It authorized $250 million to aid ship construction through low-interest loans and by making available long-term mail contracts.

Among the first to take advantage of this nautical largesse was the New York and Cuba Mail Steamship Company, better known as the Ward Line. Its liners and freighters—mostly the latter—had been familiar sights for nearly three decades passing into Havana Harbor under historic Morro Castle. Their eight vessels were as small as the *Antilla*, 3,432 tons, built in 1904, but no larger than the *Orizaba*, 7,000 tons, vintage 1918. All were relatively slow—twelve knots might be a mean speed—and some were actually coal burners. Considering the new look in the international merchant marine, the Ward Line had to modernize fast to stay in business.

Ward contracted for two beautiful cruise ships, the *Morro Castle* and the *Oriente*, the latter named after a Cuban province. Displacing nearly 16,000 tons and priced at $5 million each, the twin liners represented the latest in marine engineering and decor. As the magazine *Marine Engineering* described the *Morro Castle*, she was "the finest and most luxurious...the safest ship of her size that it has been possible to build."

One had but to study the plans to appreciate that this was not an idle statement. Her engines, driving twin propellers, were of the latest turbo-electric design, providing smooth power for a top speed of twenty-one knots. Unlike yesterday's greasy, steamy domains, her engine room more resembled the control areas of some very modern electric generating plant, dominated by shiny banks of panels, gauges, and levers. Wireless, internal communications, navigating, and lighting systems had not long been off the drawing boards.

An especial object of boast by the designers and builders (the Newport News Shipbuilding and Drydock Company) was a far-reaching "Rich" smoke-detection network coupled with a fire-extinguishing system. The cargo holds, for example, were piped so that they could be flooded for extended periods of time with chemicals and water. For the passenger areas there was a total of about half a mile of conventional rubberized canvas fire hose, plus some one hundred hand extinguishers of varying sizes.

She was an elegant ship. As with the superliners of the turn of the

A vivid "before and after" contrast of the *Morro Castle*. The top photo shows the *Morro Castle* as the beautiful cruise liner it once was. At bottom, the abandoned, burned-out hulk of the ship drifted some five miles ashore right next to the Convention Pier, Asbury Park! (Both photos from the Steamship Historical Society Collection, from the collection of Everett E. Viez)

century, the first-class lounge set the mood. Consciously reaching for the mystique of Versailles in the reign of Louis XVI, furniture, drapery, white mahogany paneling, and modified Corinthian columns in this great, balconied lounge all harmonized with the decor that stamped the reign of that hapless eighteenth-century monarch. For contrast, the first-class smoking room was Italian Renaissance. Throughout the first-class areas, lavish use was made of paneling—redwood, satinwood, walnut, ebony, blended plywood—to provide false ceilings and doors, all heavily lacquered.

Tourist quarters were plainer. There were accommodations for only ninety, compared to four hundred passengers in first class. Their smoking room was simple Old English, the writing room modified Classical French blending with Empire. Here panels and carpeting were traded for paint and linoleum.

Passengers were pampered further by a "centralized" radio and phonograph system that piped music into public rooms and the more expensive first-class suites. Fares for the seven-day New York-Havana cruise started at a low $65—but for plain bunk beds and no music in the cabins.

Launched in March 1930, *Morro Castle* made her maiden cruise to Havana in late August. She swept under the crumbling stone battlements of her namesake in fifty-nine hours, nearly ten hours less than the best time of other Ward liners. But the honors for this run were held by the famed *Mauretania*, which had stroked the distance in just about two days—forty-eight hours—flat.

Still, *Morro Castle*'s owners could boast that their beautiful new vessel was the fastest with the innovative turbo-electric drive. And as the months wore on and she was joined by her sister, *Oriente*, she established a railroad-like reputation for regularity, sailing "every Saturday at 4:00 P.M....no passports required, no taxes."

That a crew was found to man the liner, however, was directly related to the desperation emanating from the Great Depression. Wages commenced at a low of $35 a month for ordinary seamen, working often an eighteen-hour day and living much as their forebears from sailing ships, in cramped, odorous fo'c'sles. Even her captain, Robert F. Wilmott, who had served under the company's flag since the turn of the century, received a monthly check of no more than $300. The cash value of the chief officer, William F. Warms, was pegged at $180, and the chief engineer, Eban S. Abbott, at $220.

The murderous turnaround—in Saturday morning, out Saturday afternoon—was wearing on men and machines alike. Neither had proper time for rest or "maintenance." If a crew member wanted a week's leave, he had to sign off and take his chances on his old berth waiting for him. The strain told—in tempers, efficiency, and general morale.

Food deteriorated, not only for the crew and those in second class but even for those who had paid full fare. More and more cuts of steak were returned to the chefs as too tough to eat. Fish spoiled and had to be thrown overboard. Milk went rancid, along with butter. Cheese turned moldy. Tourist-class travelers complained of cargo odors and bunker oil fumes drifting through the ventilators.

Worse, the Ward Line apparently turned its corporate back on the shipping of guns and ammunition—in large case lots—to Cuban revolutionaries. This was a legal as well as an ethical "no-no" for passenger ships. In November 1933 the liner herself was caught in a crossfire between rebel gunboats and shore batteries, causing passengers to tumble below and leaving bullet marks on the bridge. The more cynical quoted from a current Ward Line travel display ad, "How you'll revel in Havana's gay laughter…her cordial, hearty welcome!"

The vacationer had not been able even to go ashore this cruise.

Return cargoes into the United States were said often to include narcotics (smuggled by the crew?) and rum to slake prohibition thirsts. The opportunity to imbibe, if not become falling-down drunk—as many passengers regularly did—was one attraction of the *Morro Castle* that did not tarnish along with the quality of food and other services.

A few weeks before this shooting incident, in September 1933, the *Morro Castle* had been navigated through a hurricane off Cape Hatteras. The thoroughly frightened passengers later framed a resolution of appreciation for Captain Wilmott. Long a popular master with his passengers, the English-born Wilmott was a naturalized United States citizen. Mustachioed, overweight, he had to contend with worsening health—failing heart, it was said, "very high blood pressure." For this reason, probably, by the summer of 1934, Wilmott became an increasingly infrequent figure at the captain's table. His absence could not go unnoticed.

From mere inaccessibility, as September neared, Wilmott mutated into a recluse, going so far as to lock himself in his cabin. True, it was, and had been, a very unhappy ship. A crew currently of 230, representing at least eight nationalities, some of them speaking virtually no English, or to each other, was at the best sullen or at the worst actively agitating for more pay, better food, less intensive working hours. This morale malaise started at the top with Warms, the first officer, and Abbott, the chief engineer, barely speaking to each other.

But the apogee of internal disaffection had been attained in the wireless shack. There, the corpulent chief radio officer, George W. Rogers, had been waging a short but unremitting campaign not only to remove his assistant, George Alagna, but seemingly to slander and besmirch him beyond any hope of refutation or, certainly, salvation. To be sure, Alagna had done nothing to further his credibility—much less his reliability—when in early August he had approached several of the crewmen and junior officers, suggesting they walk off the ship in protest against working conditions. There was also the matter of the radio compass and his unwillingness to tune it.

One thing led to another so that by the first week in September 1934, in Havana, Rogers quoted the captain as saying, "Now, Mr. Rogers, you are my chief radio operator and I can talk to you, man to man.... What is the matter with your second radio operator, Alagna? I think the man is crazy...we have always had trouble with this man.... Now, I want this man removed in New York...I don't trust Alagna...he is vengeful. It has been reported to me that he declared there were ways of getting even with the ship."

This was fine with Rogers.

The captain, at about the same time, also confided in his first officer that "something was going to happen," adding he was afraid "that fellow Alagna will do something." He "understood" (probably from Rogers) that Alagna had brought two bottles of sulfuric acid into his cabin.

Apparently this came as no surprise to Warms since gossip from other channels had reached him that Alagna would "fix the officers and bust the Ward Line right open!"

But neither the master nor his second in command had been sufficiently concerned to pass his manifest concern on to the Ward Line, or even press for a showdown with Alagna himself. It was especially odd since on the previous outbound passage from New York on August 27, a fire in cargo compartment #5, "E" deck, had been detected by a watchman investigating the source of smoke. Whether the smoke breather tubes had as well alerted the bridge was not logged. A "pretty lively" blaze, by Warms's measure, was feeding from "burned and charred funnels of cardboard and burned newspapers."

When the captain suggested a cigarette may have been tossed in, the first officer pointed out that the metal door to the compartment had been securely dogged down, and that the conflagration was being fueled by tinder. It had beyond any reasonable doubt been set.

Nonetheless, as the *Morro Castle* sailed from Havana on Wednesday,

September 5, completing her 174th cruise, Captain Wilmott had put this incident out of his mind—completely. He ordered the smoke-sampling tubes to the cargo compartments shut down. A consignment of moist hides had been hoisted aboard in Havana. Wilmott feared their unpleasant odor might be wafted through the pipes to the passengers' sensitive noses.

Also, he had previously removed hoses and wrenches from the fire stations in the passenger areas because of a suit brought by a woman who had slipped on a wet deck. He had not yet seen fit to restore the hoses to instant readiness.

And so, carrying a passenger complement of 318 souls and a crew of 230, including officers, the *Morro Castle* plowed northward. On Friday morning the weather turned wet and sullen. By evening, the big liner was butting bow-on into a twenty-five-knot nor'easter. It was a common enough scourge along the Virginia, Delaware, and Jersey shores.

The captain's farewell dinner, as of late, was celebrated without the captain. Few passengers had glimpsed him the entire cruise. They merely assumed someone was up there on the bridge guiding the ship and their personal destinies. Wilmott had a tray sent to his cabin, as was increasingly routine of late.

About 7:45, either Warms or Fourth Officer Howard Hansen (there would be conflicting testimony), bearing some query, entered the master's cabin. He was in the small bathroom, half dressed, slumped over the tub.

Dr. De Witt Van Zile, the chief surgeon, was hastily summoned, then the chief engineer, other officers. Pronouncing him dead, Van Zile expressed the belief that Wilmott had expired some time before, from "acute indigestion, heart attack." Resuscitation did not seem a reasonable option.

If shocked, none present appeared altogether surprised. The fifty-five-year-old captain's health had been "indifferent" with his blood pressure and heart trouble. The last cruise he had taken sick, from eating finnan haddie, he thought.

The Ward Line was advised by radio, as Warms, eight years Wilmott's junior, assumed command of the *Morro Castle*. Those waiting for the final ball in the dining room were advised, first by loudspeaker, of the cancellation of the remaining festivities, then by an officer who personally announced what had happened. It produced the same stunning effect of a death in the household, even though virtually no one had met Wilmott or even knew what he looked like.

Lights were dimmed. The musicians commenced to pack up their instruments. The tourists slowly filtered back to cabins. Partying surely would continue, but in private groups.

With her acting captain on the bridge, *Morro Castle* bucked ahead into the nor'easter, maintaining close to her twenty-knot "service speed." While she was a steady ship and rode storms handsomely, as she had recently the hurricane, her boat and other exposed decks had become freshets of foaming, salty water. The liner dipped her nose into the seas and threw the churning wave tops back against the bridge and halfway to her mastheads.

By midnight, lights of the Jersey shore resorts winked through the scud to port. The New York channel should be raised before dawn.

Shortly after 2:30 A.M., Saturday, September 8, the *Morro Castle* was about twenty-five miles south of Scotland Light Vessel, at the approaches to New York's Lower Bay. This very early morning, about three hours before the first streaking of dawn, something altogether disquieting was noticed in two different locations and by at least two different persons. Arthur J. Pender, a night watchman, making his rounds on the port side of the high hurricane deck, bracing against the wind and rain slapping his face, noticed "what I first thought was steam," then realized was smoke issuing from a ventilator.

Assuming it led to a cargo hold, he started below deck to investigate. It had been a weird enough watch anyhow. Before going on it, Warms had summoned him with the semihysterical orders, "For God's sake, watch that fellow [Alagna] tonight. The captain thinks he is going to do something tonight…he has bragged that he was going to tie the Ward Line up and they would not run any ships!"

Simultaneously, a passenger put down his brandy and left a small gathering in the lounge. In the next saloon, the smoking room, he found the assistant beverage steward, Daniel Campbell, swabbing down the deck in readiness for the next sailing, this very afternoon. He asked Campbell if he smelled smoke and when the former said "no" the other man said he could "smell smoke very strongly."

The two started through the lounge, quiet and empty except for "a little party…drinking straight brandy," probably the one the passenger had just left. Not until Campbell entered the adjacent writing room did he see smoke, curling from around the door of a small "concealed" storage locker, on one wall, then hanging idly just off the ceiling.

"I opened the door and what I knew once as a locker was just one mass of flames, flames from top to bottom and from one side to the other side."

At this point, Pender, the watchman, had arrived. Campbell told him to "give the alarm!" which seemed obvious enough. He then phoned the chief steward, Henry Speierman, and raced out for an extinguisher. Apparently there was none in the writing room.

Word reached Warms on the bridge a few minutes before 3:00 A.M. either via the watchman, Pender, or by another crewman who also smelled the smoke coming from the port ventilator. The acting master, as he would recall, took three successive steps: He sounded the fire alarm, both to break out the crew and to alert the passengers; he aroused Ivan Freeman, the acting first officer; and he dispatched Clarence Hackney, the second, down to the writing room to see what the trouble was all about.

Warms, however, was not at the moment overly concerned, as he would observe. "I thought the boys could handle the fire." This belief was bolstered when the engine room reported all fine below, "no smoke." And he kept the ship slamming ahead, at a full eighteen knots, into the storm.

From then on, no one would ever know clearly just what happened, in what sequence, or when. For example, there were a number of passengers who would swear they never heard an alarm. But plenty would affirm that a heroic stewardess, Lena Schwarz, ran coughing down passageways that were rapidly filling with smoke, to bang on cabin doors.

When Hackney arrived in the writing room, just two decks below the navigating bridge and a bit aft, he found the fire, which had erupted into the entire saloon, already out of control. It smelled to him like "a paper or wood fire." Pender and Campbell were futilely attempting to fight the blaze with one or, at the very most, two medium-sized extinguishers. And there were no fire hoses handy on this deck. They previously had been removed.

A passenger, Doris Wacker, of Roselle Park, New Jersey, was certain, however, that the steward and the watchman were throwing buckets of water on the mounting inferno. In fact, already there was "too much fire," Campbell would testify, to enable him to close the fire-screen doors.

Since no smoke tubes or heat sensor wires led from the public rooms to the bridge, Warms had no appreciation of the seriousness until Hackney returned. The former then ordered a change in course to bring the flaming liner inshore, although the forward speed for the moment remained unchanged. The gale still screamed through the superstructure and into the many opened hatches and passageways, like combustion drafts in a furnace.

Morro Castle burning furiously at sea. About half of the liner's dozen lifeboats were aflame or dangled from their davits. To the author it seems strange that no one is visible in the foredeck, free of fire, since his was a similar experience in World War II when his tanker was also an inferno. For a long hour the bow was his sole place of refuge. (National Archives)

Only now, some twelve minutes after Hackney had been ordered to investigate, did the Derby fire alarm system begin to act: Red light after red light flashed on the bridge, and the bell rang. This delayed reaction had occurred *only* because the flames had leapt into the passageway and onto the deck, heating the thermostats inside the adjacent staterooms.

Chief Engineer Abbott was awakened by "the" or at least "an" alarm. Whatever, something roused him. He had to know there was an emergency and he *had* to smell smoke, since by now it was wafting up all around this forward portion of the superstructure. Then the chief engineer did a curious thing. He deliberately put on his dress whites and walked to the adjacent first engineer's cabin, that of Anthony R. Bujia. By telephone, or speaking tube, or perhaps both, he asked his assistant how things were below.

"Good," Bujia replied. "But we can't stay much longer."

There was no fire in the engine room, but smoke—being drawn through the ventilating system.

"Stay there," Abbott ordered, "and keep the men until you are driven out, then shut down everything but the fire pump!"

It was a curious order since Abbott's own emergency station was in the bowels of the ship—in the control areas of the engine room. It seemed a logical enough place. Although there was a small elevator he could have taken directly down to his post, he started a sort of walking tour along the passenger decks, slowly moving downward, toward "D" deck.

And while Arthur Stamper, third assistant engineer, supervised pressure buildup on the pumps, Acting First Officer Freeman himself went below to see if any progress was being made in fighting the fire. What he saw shocked him.

"There was a mass of flames along the aft rail and the ceiling was afire. Smoke was rolling back so we couldn't reach the fire in the corner. We couldn't even breathe. Two watchmen had a line of hose and were fighting the fire."

He referred to the area as the "lounge," but in the smoke and confusion he could have been looking at the writing room.

The chief radio operator, George Rogers, had been awakened about 3:00 A.M. as he would recall, by being shaken by the third operator, Charles Maki.

"Get up, chief!" he was shouting. "The ship's on fire."

Rogers, aware at once that the room was full of smoke, turned to Alagna, the second operator, instructing, "George, go up to the bridge and see what orders the mate has to give you." He still thought of Warms as "mate."

Alagna found the acting master "in a daze," running from the center of the bridge to the port side to stare at the flames. He kept muttering, "Am I dreaming, or is it true?" according to Alagna, as he continued to pace.

Unable to "break through the captain's bewilderment," the second radio operator for the moment despaired of eliciting any orders to transmit an SOS. So, on another tack, he suggested that Wilmott's body, dressed (by Warms) and laid out in his cabin, be placed in a boat. Hackney, who had returned to the bridge, shook his head, saying, "The living are more important than the dead."

Alagna quit the bridge as he heard Warms alternately ordering the boats to be lowered "to the rail" and calling for the chief engineer.

He stumbled back the fifty feet of cables, davits, and other obstructions, through the thickening smoke to the radio shack, then coughed:

"Come on, chief, get out of here. The whole damned place is on fire outside! We are going to get caught like a rat in a trap.... They're a bunch of madmen down there!"

Now, however—it was some time between 3:13 and 3:18—Rogers, on his own initiative, flashed a "CQ," or standby, with the call letters of the *Morro Castle,* "KGOV." He did this not only because of the smoke and the deteriorating condition of the ship, but also because he had heard the freighter *Andrea Luckenbach* calling Tuckerton, New Jersey, commercial radio, inquiring if there were "a large liner burning?" The *Luckenbach* was about ten miles distant.

The fire was also visible at shore points such as Sea Girt, New Jersey. A twenty-six-foot surfboat, not knowing what or who was in trouble, had just put out from the Coast Guard Station at that Jersey resort and headed through tossing seas and headwinds toward the ominous glow on the horizon.

The situation below in the passenger decks was at least as bad as on the bridge and in the radio shack. Since the fire had continued perhaps twenty minutes before any alarm was sounded, the flames had gained ferocious headway, leaping across the carpeting and polished veneer walls of the public rooms, licking along and devouring the flimsy false ceilings and spewing burning particles and hot ashes in their wake. The forward passageways on "B" (the promenade deck), also "C" and "D" decks, became choked with black smoke, and the two main stairways were impassable as the fire, demonlike, began tumbling down, stair to stair, deck to deck, consuming anything that was painted, carpeted, or padded. What was not combustible soon glowed white-hot.

With little or no direction from officers or crew to lead the passengers to the boat deck, the latter groped their way aft, milling like leaderless sheep, jammed ever closer together, some crying and screaming and all mortally frightened for their lives. Since no one had announced anything about boats, or what deck or decks from which they could be boarded, there was already mounting despair about quitting this inferno afloat.

Like many other passengers, Dr. Gouverneur Morris Phelps, well-known New York physician whose ancestry traced back to the Revolution, had been asleep only a little while. The noises attendant to many late cabin parties had kept him awake. His twenty-five-year-old son, Morris Jr., banging on his door, had roused him and his wife, Katherine. As Dr. Phelps recalled:

"I tried to go up to the companion way but was unable to do so because of the smoke, and I could hear the crackling of the fire. We then proceeded down toward the stern. This we soon reached. There we met a lot of other people huddled about, crying, screaming, and praying. The Heavens we could see were bright red with the fire.

"We stayed there for a little while and there was quite a mob of people...between the screaming and the terrific noise of the fire no one could hear anything practically except their own voices."

Phelps felt unmistakably that he had been here before. As an intern, he had ministered to the burn victims from the *General Slocum.* More than one thousand, mostly school children, had perished aboard her when she caught fire in the East River of Manhattan, 1904.

Some woman asked the cruise director, Robert Smith, tall and immaculate in his white uniform, "When are they going to lower the boats?"

"Lady, God knows..."

One lifeboat—#1—did get off in rather short order. It was occupied by twenty-eight crewmen, three passengers—and Chief Engineer Abbott, in his dress whites.

The senior engineer had been wandering the ship in a daze ever since he was awakened. On "D" deck he had encountered Bujia, who informed him that the smoke-filled engine room was being abandoned, everything shut down, "finished with engines." The chief seemed in accord, observing, "It is every man for himself! Let's get out of here." But some, even so, remained below about half an hour longer.

Abbott, on the bridge, told Warms he did not believe "we could run much longer," that the smoke below was "considerable." With that he climbed into the boat, which was in the process of being unlimbered. This was the only motorized lifeboat aboard.

"Lower the boat! Lower the boat!" Abbott was heard to cry out several times, alternating with invitations to Warms to join him. But the acting master in likelihood did not hear him since he was quoted by differing witnesses as shouting his own orders, which had to be contradictory. "Steer her into the wind, beach her!" was one, the other involved commands preparatory to dropping the anchor, which would check the headway and allow boats to be launched with more safety.

Since Abbott had "seen no more passengers around the ship," #1 boat was cast off. Because of a strong smell of gasoline in the bilge, the motor was not started.

Returning to the bridge, Alagna told the acting captain that the chief wireless operator was "dying in the radio room, almost unconscious." Now, at 3:24 A.M., approximately forty-five minutes after the fire had been discovered, Warms authorized an SOS. The position of the liner, moving only on its momentum, was twenty miles south of Scotland Lightship, or so Warms believed.

Rogers transmitted this message three times, adding, "Hurry, can't hold out much longer!"

There was so much smoke now in the radio shack that the operators could not read the big wall clock. One of them took a large flashlight out of a drawer and then started the auxiliary transmitter. There was a puff of smoke and a spurt of flame as one of the batteries exploded, apparently from the heat, spewing sulfuric acid onto the floor. A porthole curtain caught fire and fell onto a settee, which then began to burn.

Rogers tried wrapping a wet towel around his face, but since the little room was "permeated with smoke," this did little good.

Now, at about 3:30 this wet, stormy Saturday morning, the ship was in chaos. A crewman, Leroy C. Kelsey, would later sum up the scene: "Black smoke poured down stairways and there was a rush of running feet. Flames crackled and roared and the black windows were shot with red and yellow gleams...flames swept down upon us from forward and closed in from aft. She was no longer a ship. She was a flaming hell!"

He observed "one or two" passengers jump overboard, "then like a barrel of apples they began to go over the side until one hundred jumped."

Kelsey helped lower a boat, which had stuck at its falls, by grabbing a fire ax and severing the line. As the boat descended, plate glass from the ballroom windows buckled from the heat, then burst, showering the occupants with molten glass.

In no hurry to leave, Father Raymond Egan, of St. Mary's Church, in the Bronx, was praying and offering absolution for all who asked. It did not seem to matter their faith. Somewhat earlier, he had been struggling, with varying success, to calm the panic in the passageways.

Others had been equally deliberate. Dr. Theodore L. Vosseler, of Brooklyn, who had been aroused by the smoke rather than the alarm, spent some time searching for "a coil of rope." With it he planned to lower his wife, Kathryn, over the side. When a crewman helped him locate a length of hemp as well as a knife for cutting it he made his way with Kathryn to the bow.

At the opposite extremity, on the stern, "as soon as it got so damned hot," Dr. Phelps made up his mind to jump. "It was terrific. The smoke was stifling. I said, 'Love, I would rather drown than roast!' So she [his wife] shimmied over the rail, grabbed the flagstaff, went down. As soon as I saw her clear, so that I would not jump on her, I followed."

Their son, Gouverneur Phelps, Jr., chose, however, to cling to a stern line, expecting to be picked off sooner or later.

Right behind his parents were two sisters in their twenties, Gladys and Ethel Knight, from Shrewsbury, Massachusetts. Stroking out for the shore lights—those of Sea Girt—when they winked into view, Ethel, twenty, collided with a screaming, struggling young boy. She later learned that he was Benito Rueda, seven, of Brooklyn. She held onto him with one arm and kept dogpaddling.

Seemingly, the vast majority of the passengers had chosen the storm-tossed waters rather than the lifeboats. By 4:00 A.M., the last of six to float free (the liner carried a dozen boats) was gone. Others were aflame at their davits or dangled from a single falls, the products of clumsy or wholly ignorant launching. Less than one hundred persons were aboard the six, one-quarter of capacity. The majority of those in the boats were crew.

In the radio shack, meanwhile, conditions had degenerated from bad to worse. "Sort of in a coma," Rogers was "just staggering around." Conscious of his feet "burning," he felt the deck and it was "red hot." Aware that he "certainly could not hold out much longer," the chief radio operator "lay there across the table...I said to myself if I am supposed to be dying, it doesn't hurt very much...I'm just getting sleepy."

However, in this "coma," Rogers managed to repair a broken connection between the auxiliary transmitter and the batteries and apparently to keep transmitting his messages of distress. He was heard not only by the *Luckenbach*, but as well by the nearby *Monarch of Bermuda*; the *President Cleveland*; the *City of Savannah*; the Coast Guard cutter *Tampa*; a fishing vessel, *Paramount*; and a number of ships farther away, which nonetheless altered course in an effort to save a few lives.

Alagna returned and shook Rogers, calling out, "Chief, the mate says we are going to abandon ship, so get out of here right away! " With that he started to pull his 250-pound chief toward the door.

"I fell over the door coaming and skinned my leg," Rogers would remember. "I got up and got hold of the starboard bridge deck rail and I pulled myself forward. I looked aft and there was nothing but a sea of fire as far as you could see. It looked like just one big whole ocean of fire there."

Reaching the pilot house, he found it deserted, "completely afire." Spotting Warms below, moving through the smoke and debris toward the forepeak, the highest part of the bow, Alagna said to Rogers. "Look at the yellow rat. They are deserting us."

"It was a terrible sight to see the bridge in flames," Alagna thought. "They were just terrible at this time, huge yellow flames, and the whole forward deck was hot by the flames. We could see each other's faces plainly."

Inevitably, the two radio operators had to work their way to the forepeak, which appeared to represent the greatest distance from the fire. Since the *Morro Castle* was designed with virtually no forward well deck, it was no great journey from the bridge to the bow, once a person had descended the overhangs—like climbing down cliffs—of the sun or "A" deck; to "B," the promenade deck; and finally to "C" deck.

Once there, Alagna heard "a great deal of yelling and calling and Mr. Warms and the other officers motioning to someone at sea, and on looking I noticed that there were two or three of the ship's lifeboats out there…it must have been about a thousand to fifteen hundred feet…and looking a little closer noticed that there were several survivors bobbing up and down in the water approximately midway between the forepeak and the lifeboats, and all the men that were on the ship were motioning to the lifeboats to approach these people who were just floating around there…so this kept up for a few minutes and finally I went to Mr. Warms and suggested that he send a couple of swimmers over."

The acting master shook his head as he told Alagna, "No, we cannot do anything." The radio operator remained appalled, noting it was "a damnable state of affairs when people were permitted to drown within a few hundred feet of rescue."

Including Warms, Rogers, and Alagna, there were now about fifteen in the forepeak or nearby, all crew except for the Vosselers. Fortunately for her, the doctor had not yet resolved to tie the rope around his wife and lower her over. It was a long way down, even though the *Morro Castle* was not large or high compared with the new transatlantic giants, or even the older ones such as the *Aquitania* or *Leviathan.* However, the flaming liner had at least been halted in her careening course toward shore. Warms had already let go the starboard anchor. It touched bottom in about forty-five fathoms (270 feet), less than three miles off Sea Girt.

There were living passengers who remained trapped in their cabins. Rogers saw a woman halfway out of a porthole, crying, "Help, save me!" She was "practically naked and had pulled herself as far as her hips…finally after a lot of struggle she fell into the water, maybe twenty-five feet. She fell flat on her stomach, just lay there floating with her arms out and face down in the water."

Rogers started down a Jacob's (rope) ladder, kicked his shoes off, then paused. Someone else had already dived in, but the woman vanished aft into the darkness. Her would-be rescuer quickly found he was not up to the challenge, clutched out and caught a line, then hung on.

Seemingly determined to rescue *something*, the corpulent chief radio operator next stumbled into the smoky fo'c'sle. He emerged a few minutes later clutching the bos'n's canary, a towel wrapped around the cage.

"It was the only thing living down there," Rogers gasped out.

Dawn was nearing—about 5:30 A.M.—when the hulking silhouette of the *Andrea Luckenbach* materialized out of the murk. Using a flashlight, Rogers blinked in code a message of distress. It was hardly necessary. At the same time, tossing in the sea, the surfboat from Sea Girt neared the flaming cruise liner, followed by several steamships. These included the *President Cleveland, City of Savannah, Monarch of Bermuda,* the cutter *Tampa,* and a New York pilot boat, although witnesses did not agree on the order of their arrival.

Soon, the rescue vessels had put over their own boats and were plucking survivors out of the water, from stern lines—to which some such as Gouverneur Phelps Jr., had been clinging for several hours— and from the *Morro Castle*'s lifeboats. That a number of the latter were nearby was testament to the fact that virtually none of their occupants, including crewmen, knew how to row. Also, Warms had called to them to remain in the vicinity, even though it was unlikely that many aboard had heard him.

For the next several hours the Coast Guardsmen on the *Tampa* struggled to put a towline onto the liner, while those on the latter's bow labored to saw through the two-and-a-half-inch anchor chain links, using "five-and-ten-cent-store saws." They kept breaking, according to Alagna. It was, altogether, "a damnable thing to do."

One by one, the remaining crewmen were taken aboard the *Tampa* until Warms, in the best traditions of the sea, was by himself. Then, satisfied that he was the last living soul on the *Morro Castle,* he slid down a rope onto the Coast Guard ship, shortly before his late command was taken under tow. His right knuckles were cracked; he was burned about the face, shoulders, and other parts of his body.

Rogers, in the cutter's sick bay, was delirious, "kind of tipsy," Alagna thought, as he rambled on about "those damn murderers!" One could only speculate whom he had in mind.

Meanwhile, the survivors, through various means, commenced coming ashore. Chief Engineer Abbott, whose boat touched the beach at Spring Lake, five miles south of Asbury Park, was probably the first to land. Still resplendent in his whites, the ranking officer of the doomed liner appeared to be quite embarrassed. Too many of the local citizenry, newsmen, and police were on hand as a now unwelcome party. He was quoted as vainly urging crewmen to attempt to move the boat farther down to some sparser spot.

Dr. Charles Cochrane, prominent Brooklyn surgeon, was among the three passengers in this boat, as well as some twenty-eight crewmen. His sister, Catherine, had perished in an adjacent cabin despite efforts at rescue.

A Hartford couple, the Abraham Cohens, swam all the way in, collapsing on the beach at Sea Girt. To those who assisted her into an ambulance, Mrs. Cohen confided the obvious, "My vacation is over."

Dr. Phelps and his wife, clinging to oars, were sighted in the dawning light by a circling Army plane. In it was New Jersey's governor, A. Harry Moore. Smoke flares directed a Coast Guard launch to the pair. It was now about 11:30 A.M., and they had been in the water some six hours.

The two sisters from Shrewsbury, Massachusetts, Gladys and Ethel Knight, also were picked up nearing shore. They had taken turns holding up the seven-year-old Brooklyn boy, Benito Rueda. He had lost his father, although his mother was rescued by the converging fleet. (For twenty-year-old Ethel Knight the strain had been too much. She was dead within weeks of a heart attack.)

The fourth officer and now acting third, Howard Hansen, had the unenviable distinction of enduring possibly the longest in the storm-tossed Atlantic—seven and a half or even eight hours before being hauled out by the fishing boat, *Panama.* Hansen, who could not remember ever hearing an order to lower boats, had finally jumped from "B" deck. He had managed to hold a woman's head above water for more than an hour until his arms weakened and she slipped away.

About 1:30, *Tampa* had the flaming carcass of the cruise liner under tow. The New York pilot boat steadied her by a stern line.

Thus hooked up, the *Morro Castle* careened northward into the continuing gale for nearly four hours. Then the stern rope burned through. Next, the twelve-inch (in circumference) towing hawser snapped, leaving the ship, again, a derelict. There was nothing more either the *Tampa* or the pilot boat could do except keep out of the way.

Morro Castle's ill-fated voyage was almost over. Shortly after 6:30 P.M. on Saturday she drifted ashore right off—of all places!—Convention

Pier, Asbury Park. The still-flaming, smoking hulk was so close that a gangplank could have been stretched to her from the new $3 million structure.

The shutters that had blacked out the boardwalk stores and snack places after Labor Day came down. Soft drinks, popcorn, hot dogs, and ice cream were being hawked again before midnight, as tens of thousands of people streamed down onto the beaches in this wholly unpredicted Roman holiday. Admission was charged for those sections of the sand closest to the blistering hot hull—they came all through the wet, windy night, clogging the roads from the big cities: Philadelphia, Newark, New York. Morbid curiosity soared, fevered, irrational….

The Sunday morning papers devoted columns and columns to the disaster, complete with photographs and survivors' accounts. It was too late to edit the feature sections or kill stories. The travel pages of the *New York Times* carried a big display ad of the Ward Line, starting: "Step into the whirl of gay shipboard activities…sail on one of the newest, finest liners in exclusive Havana Service…."

It read like an obituary, somehow gone amok.

The "finest" was not only a twisted, blackened hulk, but a charnel house as well. A total of 124 had perished either aboard the liner or in the surrounding waters. Of this number, 90 were passengers. In proportion to crewmen/passengers, 80 percent of the crew was saved, 70 percent of the vacationers. It was not altogether a subject of pride.

In the sinking of the *Lusitania*, the ratio had been relatively equal. But the *Titanic*'s crew had suffered disproportionately: only some 23 percent saved. Steerage passengers aboard that liner fared little better, about 25 percent. Yet 41 percent of second-class passengers survived and 62 percent of first class. Apparently, prestige and affluence spoke its own message.

An investigation of the Ward Line's disaster was launched immediately by the Bureau of Navigation and Steamboat Inspection of the Department of Commerce. In the charge of Dickerson N. Hoover, the service's inspector, the probe continued through fifteen separate sittings and heard more than one hundred witnesses, passengers, and crew. It would fill twenty-one hundred typewritten pages.

Some who testified would spit out their own messages of recrimination and vilification. Alagna, for one, who had been arrested as a material witness, sought to place Warms in the worst possible perspective. As might be expected, the acting master retaliated in kind.

Warms was certain that the fire had been set deliberately in the writing room locker. But what kept it blazing in defiance of all efforts to extinguish it?

Warms held the belief that it was fueled by "gasoline or kerosene." Freeman and Hackney, his assistant mates, were in agreement. Freeman, for example, was convinced that "someone" had "saturated oil all around to feed it."

William O'Sullivan, a storekeeper, charged that the *Morro Castle* carried "illegal" inflammable polish. But he was wholly uncertain whether it was stored in the writing room locker.

On the other hand, some marine architect must have been nodding over his drawing board when he placed the locker close beside the flue of the forward funnel, going up right behind the writing room. There was plenty of heat, at all times.

(William McFee, respected writer on the sea and onetime chief engineer on British ships, concluded that the fire indeed must have found its origin here, assuming that "parts of the steel structure around the funnel had been red-hot for hours and were charring the woodwork, disintegrating the insulation....")

Warms could not explain to the bureau's satisfaction why the distress message was delayed and why he allowed the liner to plough ahead into the gale, fanning the flames, or, indeed, why "the ship's officers failed to control the situation with the strong hand that was necessary in such an emergency."

But *what*, once more, had started that fatal blaze in the locker?

The Hoover commission attempted not even an educated guess, more concerned with what happened, or did *not* happen, once the fire was underway. Its closest approximation to a conclusion was "the human equation failed."

It seemed the least the commission could conclude.

Perhaps William Floyd Justine, the chief electrician, had not entirely overstated the case during his own testimony. The fire, he asserted, must have been started by "troublemakers for spite." Then he postscripted, by inference, "half the ship" was suspect, even as in an Agatha Christie whodunit. However, as in a whodunit, the most obvious criminal might prove the most guiltless.

Considering the size of the crew on the *Morro Castle*'s final voyage, this meant that no less than 115 men and women could be considered potential arsonists until proven innocent.

But what about the passengers? Why could not one of them be equally capable of setting the liner ablaze?

Even before the hearings adjourned, newspapers had pushed

them into abbreviated paragraphs on back pages. There was reason. Bruno Richard Hauptmann had just been arrested in the Bronx and charged with the kidnapping two years previously of the infant Charles Lindbergh Jr.

As a consequence of the Commerce probe, a federal court found Warms and Abbott guilty of "negligence and inattention to duties" and sentenced both to prison terms. An appeals court, however, reversed the judgment, holding that Warms had stayed with his ship and thus was to be commended. Abbott was held not responsible for his acts because of the smoke he had presumably inhaled.

The only "hero" to emerge from the disaster was the chief radio operator. Rogers was awarded medals and presented with flowery commendations for sticking to his post as the ship burned out from under him. He went on a speaking tour.

In 1935 he opened a radio repair shop in Bayonne, New Jersey, leaving it the next year to join that city's police force. This in itself was remarkable considering his obesity—which by now had assumed the dimensions of deformity.

Yet just three years later, in 1938, Rogers was convicted and jailed for what the judge labeled a "diabolical" crime—attempted murder. He had, the court believed, maimed and almost killed his superior in the police station, Lieutenant Vincent Doyle, through a booby-trapped fish-tank heater. Only then did Rogers's criminal past, dating back to 1914 and his boyhood in California, become a matter of record. This involved charges and/or convictions of thefts, homosexual assaults, and even arson. The latest fire of suspicious origin had been in his own radio shop in Bayonne in 1935.

It came as a shock to many who tried to reconcile the stark paradoxical fact that a "public hero" was no less than a dangerous psychopath, in fact, the same man who had risked his life to rescue a canary. Nonetheless, World War II intervened, with its acute need for radio operators. Rogers was granted a conditional parole in 1942. While none of the armed services cared to take a chance on him, Rogers, it was reported, served a few months aboard a freighter traveling as far as Port Darwin, Australia. There, rumor had it, he was arrested on unspecified charges.

At or before war's end, the radio operator was back at his old premises in Bayonne. Until 1953, none outside of that New Jersey community had heard any more of him.

In that year a new charge against Rogers: murder. He was accused of the bludgeon deaths of two neighbors, William Hummel, an eighty-three-year-old retired printer, and his spinster daughter, Edith. The motive appeared to involve $7,500 he owed them. The jury believed Rogers had committed the terrible crime. The judge sentenced him to two concurrent life sentences in the New Jersey State Penitentiary.

In 1956 he was interviewed inside the prison in Trenton by Thomas Gallagher and possibly others. The former came to the conclusion, without Rogers confessing anything, that the radio operator had set the fire on the *Morro Castle* after, in likelihood, poisoning Captain Wilmott. Since his body was never positively identified and Dr. Van Zile presumably died in the disaster, this had to remain speculation. Gallagher published his well-researched account, *Fire at Sea*, in 1959.

Only the year before, on January 10, 1958, Rogers had died of a stroke. Thus, he carried to the grave whatever secrets he may have harbored in the addled and maddened recesses of his brain.

Other authors and journalists as well seemed to agree with Gallagher's reconstruction of the famous sea disaster. In 1972, for example, there appeared *Shipwreck*, by Gordon Thomas and Max Morgan Witts, a meticulous and serious study, which includes interviews not only with survivors and next of kin but also with noted psychiatrists.

But both the inquiry and the investigative authors neglected to probe an intriguing, pertinent question: *How* did Dr. Van Zile die? And, for that matter, had he actually perished? No testimony documents his last moments. No remains were identified. Too, what had been his relationship with Captain Wilmott?

Psychopath, arsonist, child molester, murderer, as well as attempted murderer, George Rogers surely was. He had even gone to the length of obtaining his chief operator's berth on the *Morro Castle* by frightening his predecessor off through anonymous warning letters. But did *he* set fire to the liner or poison its master?

There is absolutely no hard evidence—only surmise and suspicion.

Hal Burton, in his *The Morro Castle* (Viking, New York, 1973), wrote, "The only verdict has to be the Scotch verdict, 'Not proven,'...theories, and only theories. An incendiary device is far more romantic than a malfunction in the ship's funnel or spontaneous combustion in a pile of stored blankets.

"'An act of God,' the insurance companies called it, and that indefinite description best fits the *Morro Castle* disaster."

An individual concededly capable of dark and terrible deeds does not necessarily do them or do *all* of them. There was ample evidence to convince a judge and jury in Rogers's homicidal crimes. None could place Rogers in the writing room before the fire, or in Wilmott's quarters prior to his death. No grand jury could reasonably have been found to indict Rogers in either the start of the fire or the demise of the ship's captain.

Chief Electrician Justine had tossed out, perhaps bitterly facetious, that "half the ship" could be considered as suspects. And Acting Chief Officer Freeman would add his own frustrated amen, "God knows what the motive was!"

The Department of Commerce hinted at "spontaneous combustion," and let it go at that, although it flayed the lack of organization in fighting the fire or getting off the boats. The inquiry expressed profound wonder that Warms "continued on his course at 18.8 knots for 3.1 miles before sounding the fire alarm" and persisting "for some distance thereafter before undertaking to turn the ship."

The investigation found bungling and ineptitude, but not arson, at least not provable arson. Thus, more than sixty years after the tragedy, the loss of the *Morro Castle* remains a mystery no less profound than that, say, of the *Hampshire*.

* * *

Morro Castle was not the last liner to be destroyed by fire or from other causes. But none would leave the same legacy of enigma and suspicion.

Not quite four years later, on May 4, 1938, the 25,000-ton French liner *Lafayette* burned to a black hulk at her pier in Le Havre. The next year, on April 19, the larger *Paris* was also razed by flames at the same port. With World War II but a few months away and the receipt by the French Line of threatening letters, presumably of Nazi origin, sabotage was suspected in both disasters.

The French Merchant Marine would receive yet another and far mightier blow. The *Normandie*, at eighty-three thousand tons, was one of the largest and indisputably the most beautiful creation to sweep the seas. At war's outbreak she had raced to the sanctuary of her pier at New York's Hudson River. Under command of the Navy, she was being converted to a troopship on February 9, 1942, when a blaze was started in the grand saloon by a workman's torch. It spread rapidly, rushing out of control through the magnificent saloons and passageways.

The great liner's destruction was caused not by the fire alone, however, but also by the tons of water poured by firemen onto the flames. She rolled over onto her port beam, like a weary monster whale, into the rotten debris of the river. With Herculean effort, she was raised, minus her exquisitely sculptured superstructure. Her destiny had become the ship breakers.

After war's unprecedented carnage, travelers somehow regained their sea legs. Yet again disaster would intervene in their voyaging. Almost 350 perished in the fiery demise of two vessels between 1961 and 1963: the 5,000-ton *Dara* on April 8, 1961, in the Persian Gulf; and the 20,314-ton *Lakonia* in December 1963, near Madeira in the Atlantic.

The end of the famous old Boston-Yarmouth night "boats" came on a November evening in 1965, when the *Yarmouth Castle*, bearing some 550 passengers and crew, sank in flames. She had been on a Caribbean cruise when fire erupted supposedly in a cabin. Among the 87 casualties were 22 out of the 61 members of the North Broward (Florida) Senior Citizens Club.

Two decades later the *Achille Lauro* was to suffer the first act in a tragedy of the seas. The 23,000-ton Italian cruise liner was boarded October 9, 1985, by Arab terrorists in the Mediterranean. Before they were accorded sanctuary in Egypt, they had shot and dumped overboard an American, Leon Klinghoffer, confined to a wheelchair. (Years later, in captivity, the assassins would admit the murder was "a mistake.")

Almost a half-century old, the hard-luck *Achille Lauro* was cruising in the Indian Ocean one hundred miles off Somalia when it was this time swept by flames. It was the first day of December 1994. Only two persons were lost out of the more than one thousand aboard thanks to spectacular rescue efforts of U.S. Navy vessels and other nearby ships. A photograph taken from a low-flying airplane showed the vessel glowing with flames from stem to stern, eloquently reminiscent of the *Morro Castle*.

South African Air Force helicopters joined surface vessels to save more than five hundred persons from the foundering *Oceanus* on August 4, 1991. The Greek cruise ship had wallowed helplessly off the coast of East London and Durban in high seas following an engine-room blaze. No loss of life was reported in the sinking of the 7,554-ton *Oceanus*.

Liners grew bigger and bigger, but fewer and fewer were employed in transporting passengers from here to there. That had become the airlines' job. A burgeoning fleet of cruise liners weighed in with tonnages of seventy- to eighty-thousand-plus. They were tall, bulky creations, like resort hotels sitting atop flat hulls large enough for support. To one from the golden era of transatlantic voyaging, the cruise ship seemed ugly, like a rhinoceros compared to a gazelle. Although they were perhaps more fire resistant than their predecessors, they were not able to boast that they were "ignition-free."

The Carnival Cruise liner *Ecstasy* was lucky. She had just put the Port of Miami astern on July 20, 1998, when fire broke out in her high stern. It gained headway quickly and was a spectacular sight for those on shore, when Coast Guard patrollers joined city fireboats to douse her with tons of water. Despite heroic efforts, it required four hours to bring the blaze under control.

Unlike all other fires at sea, little or no anxiety was manifested on the *Ecstasy* by the some two thousand passengers in the distant bow area, in their cabins, or in a choice of cafes, pools, stores, or what-have-yous.

Television cameramen aboard helicopters brought the drama into the nation's living rooms and wherever there was a wide screen.

Similar to the *Normandie* before her, a workman's welding spark had ignited lint in the virtual forest of overhead ducts on the *Ecstasy*. Such was the finding of the National Transportation Safety Board.

The author, incidentally, is no stranger to fire at sea. Near the end of World War II, he abandoned his fiercely burning tanker in the North Sea with a long jump from her high bow to the tiny Dutch mail boat, which, finally and fortuitously, arrived.

7

SSN *Scorpion*

Death at "Point Oscar"

S*CORPION* WAS THE SIXTH naval vessel of that name but not the first to meet doom. Her predecessor, also a submarine, was lost in the Pacific during World War II.

Five years after the *Morro Castle* disaster, farther up the Atlantic seaboard, one of the navy's newest submarines, *Squalus*, No. 192, was continuing training runs and dives.

Under the steady, experienced hand of Lieutenant Oliver F. Naquin, Annapolis '25, *Squalus*, with fifty-nine aboard, was readying for her nineteenth practice dive. (For Admiral Naquin's comments on the *Scorpion*, see Acknowledgments and Bibliography.) She was off the Isles of Shoals, not far from the New Hampshire coast and the Portsmouth Navy Yard. The date was May 23, 1939, shortly after 8:00 A.M. The sea was choppy, the skies leaden.

She dove—and kept diving—in spite of the timely blowing of the ballast tanks, advancing her twin propulsion motors to full power, and the setting of the diving planes in the "full rise" mode. None of these actions was effective in preventing *Squalus* from sinking stern first at a dizzying angle of forty-five degrees. The four compartments abaft the control room had completely flooded.

As the submarine settled to the bottom, 240 feet down, at an increasing angle, the split-second judgment of a burly electrician's mate,

Lloyd Maness, held off closing the three-hundred-pound watertight door just long enough to permit several men from aft to gain the control room. With the door hinged toward the stern it meant that Maness had to lift the full weight of this door in order to latch it closed. Once dogged shut, the big hatch doomed the twenty-six men on the backward side. But the thirty-three officers and crewmen in the three forward compartments were saved by Maness's superhuman strength under stress.

Yet, unlike the dreary chronicle of most sunken submarines that would not surface, "lost with all hands" would not be the epitaph for *Squalus.* Thanks to red flares floating to the surface; even a telephone; a McCann rescue chamber (or "diving bell"); and the fast, heroic work of the salvage fleet, all thirty-three in the forward compartment were saved—within forty-eight hours of the sinking. The last to leave, Naquin, was brought to safety on the fourth trip of the McCann chamber. But it would never again be used for a submarine trapped "on the bottom."

A naval court would conclude, after the vessel was raised, that it flooded because of a false green light on the indicator panel, or "Christmas tree." It showed a big sea intake or induction valve closed when actually it was wide open.

Submarines were venturing into deeper, lonelier, and vastly more imperiled waters as America entered World War II. And afterward, a new generation, nuclear powered, would probe far beyond the reach of the rescue bell. No more noisy, foul-smelling diesels, no more sulfuric acid batteries and electric motors. Now a compact reactor provided heat to generate steam, which in turn powered a turbine to spin the propeller or propellers. A smaller turbine operated a generator for the boat's electrical needs.

On June 14, 1952, in New London, Connecticut, President Harry S. Truman dedicated the keel of the world's first nuclear submarine, *Nautilus.* The spirit of Jules Verne and Captain Nemo, possibly even the latter's giant pipe organ, seemed to hover in the wings. Two and a half years later *Nautilus* was operational, and in August 1958 she proved as capable of dramatic journeys as her namesake by passing under (or over?) the North Pole.

Congress and the public applauded. The submarine program was "flying" robustly into the future on atomic muscle. One class, alone, the *Thresher,* would consist of fourteen boats. But progress could exact its price. In this case, nuclear "wings" risked being clipped.

Commissioned in 1961, *Thresher,* SSN 593, standard-bearer for the class, was a 279-foot-long attack submarine. She displaced about 3,750 tons on the surface or 4,300 submerged. Her underwater, or fastest, speed was announced as some thirty-five knots, which was probably ten knots below her actual. Her "test" or maximum depth, while classified, was considered close to 1,500 feet, perhaps 500 feet more than her cruising depth.

When the $57 million vessel put out from Portsmouth on April 9, 1963, under Lieutenant Commander John Wesley Harvey, Annapolis '50, she was crowded with 129 persons, 35 in excess of her normal complement. No fewer than 17 civilian technicians were aboard hinting of major studies in progress or of certain functionings that were disturbing the navy and were being checked out.

As a matter of fact, the count would have been 133 had not four been left ashore. Lieutenant Raymond A. McCoole, reactor officer, had been granted emergency leave. His wife had accidentally spilled rubbing alcohol into her eyes. Two crewmen had been excused for personal reasons, while a sonar technician who received his orders late simply missed the boat. He professed to considerable dismay since his naval career had been marked by punctuality.

Some 220 miles east of Boston, the next morning, the rescue vessel *Skylark*, accompanying *Thresher*, logged a message by underwater telephone, "Experiencing minor difficulties." The time was 9:13 A.M. This was followed by, "Have positive angle. Attempting to blow. Will keep you informed."

Three minutes later there came a garble, from which only the words *test depth* were decipherable. Was another word *exceeding*? There was next the sound of compressed air rushing into the submarine's ballast tanks, and then one of those at the phones aboard *Skylark* heard "the sound of a ship breaking up...like a compartment collapsing."

Thresher, the United States's first casualty in its nuclear underwater fleet, was down in eighty-five hundred feet of water.

In the ensuing weeks, vigorous salvage operations, including dives to the crushed hull by the bathyscaphe *Trieste*, deep-water photographs, and other sophisticated probing provided enough information, including even tattletale wreckage, for a court of inquiry to conclude: "that a flooding casualty in the engine room is the most probable cause...and that it is most likely that a piping system failure had occurred in one of the *Thresher* saltwater systems, probably in the engine room.... In all probability water affected electrical circuits and caused a loss of power."

Admiral Hyman Rickover, waspish "father" of the nuclear submarine, had many sharp remarks to make. This surprised none. Delivered both before Congress and the naval court of inquiry, this is part of his criticism:

"There must be a change in the philosophy that the navy exists for its people and that the career of its people takes precedence...significant upgrading must be effected in our bureaus and shipyards in design, fabrication, and inspection...the *Thresher* is a warning made at great sacrifice of life that we must change our way of doing business to meet the requirements of modern technology...we must correct the conditions that permitted inadequate design, poor fabrication methods, and incomplete inspection to exist, if we are not to have another *Thresher*."

Not quite five years later, on Saturday, January 27, 1968, the Israel Defense Forces had an announcement to make about their 1,280-ton diesel-powered, 202-foot submarine *Dakar:*

"The communication with the Israeli submarine *Dakar* is broken since mid-day Monday (January 22) while the submarine was approximately 250 miles away from Israel and there is no information on its location. Searches are carried on. In those searches, in addition to the Israeli air force and navy, are participating ships and aircrafts of the U.S., Great Britain, and Greece, after those governments agreed to participate in response to our request. On the *Dakar* were sixty-nine crew members. The estimated time for her arrival was next Monday noon."

The position was some one hundred miles west of Cyprus, where the Mediterranean sinks to seventy-five hundred feet in places. Handed over to the Israelis only the previous year by the British, *Dakar* (*shark* in Hebrew) was the former HMS *Totem*, built in 1945. Eight days after the initial announcement, Israel declared the submarine to be lost. This left her navy virtually denuded of such craft.

On Sunday evening, January 28, about eight o'clock, twenty-five miles southeast of its naval base, Toulon, France, the 850-ton submarine *Minerve,* traveling just under the surface, using snorkel (for venting diesel exhaust) and antenna, advised an accompanying airplane that she would be at her berth in about an hour. Fifty-two, including six officers, were aboard.

She was never heard from again. The relatively small (190 feet long) "experimental ballistic missile" submarine was one of nine of the *Daphne* class. Diesel-powered, she could make no more than sixteen knots on the surface. Commander Philippe Bouillot, in turning over his four-year-old vessel to its last captain, Lieutenant Andre Faure, asserted he had logged a total of "seven thousand hours submerged" and "never had any trouble."

Minerve was approximately one thousand miles west of the *Dakar*'s last reported position, and some six days in time. Any conceivable connection in the tragedies of the two submarines was left for their respective navies to ponder. To this day the circumstances surrounding the disappearances and inquiries into them remain "top secret" in both naval departments.

Why should this be?

The world, if it had ever accorded much attention to the strange, almost simultaneous loss of two underwater vessels in the same area, quickly dismissed both. Public concern, centered in the seemingly endless war in Vietnam, focused the end of that January on the violent eruption of fighting within Saigon itself—the Tet offensive. For six hours Viet Cong fanatics seized parts of the U.S. Embassy, with resultant loss of life of the defenders before the area was cleared. Like a western movie, clerks and even ranking bureaucrats snatched rifles and revolvers to shoot it out in hallways and on the stairs.

February 1968 moved on as embattled Saigon struggled to rid itself of pockets of Viet Cong resistance. Attention slowly swung to an outpost, Khesanh, where Marines battled against a numerically superior foe that had surrounded them.

Forgotten in the greater, dramatic canvas were the more routine comings and goings, the background whisperings within the far-flung U.S. defense forces, the "silent service," for example. Thus, when *Scorpion* (SSN 589) put out from Norfolk on February 15 and plunged beneath the crests of a wintry Atlantic with 101 aboard, only those left behind and her immediate chain of command—Submarine Division 62, Squadron 6, U.S. Atlantic Fleet—were in any manner interested.

There would, necessarily, be especial loneliness in some of the homes of Virginia Beach and other "bedding places" for the huge naval base since aboard were several young newlyweds. It had to be expected in a predominantly youthful crew, chosen for endurance among other special factors peculiar to submarining.

The vessel would be gone for three months, "training with ships of the 6th Fleet" in the Mediterranean.

At 3,075 tons, the $50 million *Scorpion* was 700 tons smaller than the *Thresher* and some 27 feet shorter. But her speed of 35-plus knots was about the same, as was her cruising range of 60,000 miles. One of six of the *Skipjack* class, as an attack submarine she carried 24 torpedoes, some with atomic warheads. The navy did not care to say *how many*, or *when* the warheads were actually aboard.

This newest nuclear-powered submarine was launched in December 1959 in Groton, Connecticut. The sponsor was Mrs. Elizabeth S. Morrison, of Arlington, Virginia. Her father, Commander Maximilian C.

SSN *Scorpion* from the bow. (U.S. Navy)

Schmidt, was lost in the Pacific during World War II on a predecessor submarine, an earlier *Scorpion.*

Commissioned the following July, *Scorpion* was hurried out on patrol, next turning up at the big U.S. base at Holy Loch, on the Clyde, Scotland. In September there was brief panic as the Royal Navy lost contact with her. An "All ships alert!" was sounded by the Admiralty, then as suddenly canceled the next day. The new underwater craft was west of Ireland on NATO maneuvers, operating under radio silence. The Royal Navy apparently had not been informed.

In June 1961 *Scorpion* was host to a number of British newsmen. They would marvel, in their articles, at the silence and "motionless" illusion as she sped far beneath the surface. Impressive to the reporters also were the submarine's three decks and the "cinema" in the main mess hall. As to safety, her C.O., Commander Norman Bessac, boasted, "You receive less radiation in this vessel than walking about in the City of London."

The next year, 1962, *Scorpion* set a record for "sealed atmosphere endurance"—seventy days without surfacing. Late in 1963, along with all nuclear-powered submarines, she was carefully checked by ship-wrights and a virtual battalion of technicians after the loss of the

Thresher. Apparently, *Scorpion* was pronounced sound in all respects. For that matter, every unit of this ultramodern deep-sea fleet was the object of continuing scrutiny and monitoring by its officers and leading non-coms. Those who manned them were a wholly new breed of seafarers, bookish, studious: physicists, chemists, electronic wizards, and, of course, reactor scientists. How many of the submariners had distinguished themselves on the gridiron, or in the purely "muscle" brand of athletics?

Scorpion received a new skipper in October 1967 who handily fit this pattern. Commander Francis Atwood Slattery, Annapolis '54, was a student's student. He even looked like one—lean, quiet, with thoughtful, rather sunken eyes. To bone up for his Annapolis entrance examinations, "Frankie," as his friends knew him, went so far as to enroll in a correspondence trigonometry course. He was valedictorian, class of 1950, West Paris (Maine) High. But Frankie was not there to read his carefully prepared valedictory. He was hurrying down to Annapolis, unwilling to be so much as an hour late in commencing his plebe year.

When Slattery was piped aboard the submarine he was assuming his first command. (And like Benjamin Briggs aboard *Mary Celeste* almost a century before, he was preparing to take to sea a ship previously strange to him.) Familiarization with these special "boats," however, had commenced soon after graduation and included five years on the *Nautilus* and as executive officer for almost a year. As with fellow submariners, aviation had not appealed to Slattery. "Too dangerous," was a familiar submariner's commentary on the aeronautical branch.

Slattery had been in command but briefly when he conned *Scorpion* to sea for an all-day dependents' cruise. This was a navy custom when conditions permitted, with the object of making next of kin more familiar with an otherwise little-understood working place. In addition to the brides who made their appearance, there were several expectant mothers from growing young families.

After that it was all business for the *Scorpion*, which was ordered to New London, Connecticut, for refresher training. The navy would note of Slattery: "[He] had been absent from submarine duty for fifteen months between his tour as executive officer on *Nautilus* (all except three months of which was spent in a naval shipyard) and taking command of *Scorpion*, a faster and more maneuverable ship than those submarines on which he had previously served."

After New London, *Scorpion* underwent various drills, exercises, and inspections, extending in area as far south as the Caribbean. She received mixed grades, all the way from "outstanding" to "unsatisfactory," in these maneuvers and other operational conditions that could be measured. Nonetheless, when it was all over, the submarine was stamped with a "C-1" or "fully combat ready" status.

Slattery's first cruise as commanding officer was to accompany Task Group 83.4, part of Carrier Division 20, to engage in "controlled and free play exercises" in the Mediterranean. It wasn't exactly another Atlantic "milk run," but these underwater sorties at least did not separate crews from their families as long as, say, their shipmates on aircraft carriers were separated from theirs. The big, porpoise-shaped submarines had the potential for crossing the ocean in three or four days, and they also touched at United States or NATO bases whence mail could be sent home.

One letter on this voyage was mailed May 10, 1968, from the western Mediterranean by Robert Violetti, a torpedoman 3C, to his mother, Mrs. Salvatore A. Violetti, in Broomall, Pennsylvania.

"Ever since we left Naples," he wrote, "we have been circling the Isle of Crete. I can't tell you why. All I can say is that for thirteen days we have been going around it again and again."

What really impressed him, however, was a Russian destroyer that rode "alongside" the surfaced *Scorpion* "one hundred feet away with every gun trained." Noting that a "U.S. aircraft" arrived and "chased off the Soviet vessel," Robert postscripted, "Boy, was that an exciting experience!"

He believed the submarine had surfaced primarily to exchange mail via helicopter from a 6th Fleet carrier.

Whatever had been happening off Crete, it did not seem to mesh with the official purpose of her mission—"controlled and free play exercises." She had called at Taranto and Naples, in Italy, and Augusta Bay, Sicily. On May 16, *Scorpion* hove to off the breakwater of Rota, Spain, location of a U.S. Naval Base especially for submarines. Two men were transferred, reducing the complement to ninety-nine, representing three officers and two enlisted men over her "allowance."

Four of the officers apparently would just as soon not have been aboard. They had submitted their resignations from the navy. Three were in the engineering department, one in weaponry. It would take a little time for the Navy Department to act upon this request, considered "greater than average" for one submarine.

Before she departed Rota the next morning, May 17, *Scorpion* was again certified as "fully combat ready" by U.S. Navy operations officers at that base.

On Tuesday, May 21, *Scorpion*, reporting her position as some fifty miles south of the Azores, advised her arrival time in Norfolk as 1:00 P.M., Monday, May 27. She was about twenty-one hundred miles east of her base and making eighteen knots, which would indicate she was traveling on the surface. At that speed, she could easily raise Norfolk Monday morning—or even by Saturday, if Slattery decided to submerge part of the voyage.

Scorpion's estimated arrival was conveyed, as customary, by the submarine division to the commanding officer's wife, Dottie Slattery, also from West Paris, Maine. It thus became her responsibility to commence a word-of-mouth chain of communications. For example, when she told the wife of the "exec," she could assume the latter would pass the word along to the wife of the third officer, and so on until the families of all twelve commissioned officers on board were aware when husband or father or brother was coming home. News would trickle in much the same manner via the noncommissioned officers down to the most junior ratings—assuming their families were in the area. Otherwise, they could await a familiar voice on the telephone or themselves call the squadron duty officer.

Sunday night, in many homes of Virginia Beach, Ocean View, and other Norfolk suburbs, traditional welcome-home dinners were prepared. Refrigerators were stocked with beer and liquor cabinets replenished. For some men, at least, three and a half months without a drink was a long thirst. Mothers made arrangements to excuse their children from afternoon classes—to meet Daddy on the pier.

Monday dawned cool, rainy. A light fog hung just above Hampton Roads. It was a morning of muted nervous tension, even though many of the wives—perhaps the majority—had waited before and had been rewarded by the sight of the bulbous black hull sweeping in from the Atlantic to the great, gray base, redolent with the sea and the generations of warships it had served—and mothered.

Protocol in the navy was as timeless as it was unreal. If the wife of the third officer had wanted to confirm the latest arrival information, she should have called the wife of the second officer, or "exec." But Judy Stephens, whose husband, Lieutenant Daniel Peter Stephens, was third officer/navigator, knew Dottie Slattery quite personally. She shortcut protocol and called the C.O.'s wife directly.

"*If* anyone asks, the *Scorpion* is due back at noon," Dottie told her.

"*If* anyone asks...." Somehow those words impinged on Judy's mind and left a question mark imprinted. "Pete" Stephens, Annapolis '59, a big, heavy man, was on his last cruise aboard *Scorpion* after three and a half years with her. His lieutenant commander stripes were awaiting him and at least the "exec's" spot on another big boat, maybe even command of an older, smaller one.

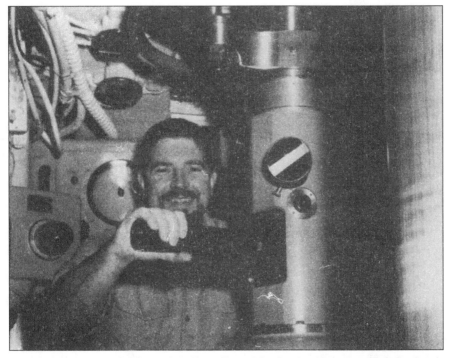

Lieutenant Daniel Peter Stephens, navigating officer of the *Scorpion*. (Courtesy of Judy Stephens)

The families, including some children, gathered before noon at a destroyer pier—No. 22—just in case the submarine pushed in early. After all, the captain could be expected to try to beat his own ETA on his homeward voyage. The drizzle continued, keeping most in their cars. Every time a yard tug or even a work boat coughed by the slip, a little thrill would go through those waiting, hoping the little craft was about to assist the *Scorpion* to her berth.

Noon came and passed, as did 1:00 P.M. Nobody knew anything. But then there were only a few guards around, and the lower ratings whose sole excuse for existence seemed to be hauling hawsers over bollards or casting them loose. By 1:30, the wives and others began to drift away, to the Ship's Service snack bar, to the Officers' or other clubs, even to their homes. Judy Stephens, for example, drove all the way back to Virginia Beach with her two little boys.

The rain continued.

But none in this complex warren of naval high commands that was Norfolk had seen fit to advise that *Scorpion*'s arrival message of nearly a week ago was the last one received. Further, since that time, nine messages were transmitted "on the submarine broadcast" to *Scorpion*. Although she was operating under "electronic silence" except as necessary "for safety and certain other specified situations," replies were specifically requested for three of the messages. None was received.

If not actually secretive within its own chambers of command, the navy was, at best, tardy. For example, shortly before one o'clock, Captain James C. Bellah, skipper of the submarine tender *Orion* and acting Commander Submarine Squadron 6, advised the commander of submarines of the Atlantic Fleet that he "had not established communications to obtain her [*Scorpion's*] berthing assignment and arrange tug services." This was how Bellah presumably became suspicious that something was wrong.

Now the Atlantic Fleet submarine chief "initiated an intensive communications check...." This might have been considered singular in light of the fact that nothing had been heard from *Scorpion* in upwards of 136 hours, and in spite of requested replies.

Why, anyone might have asked, had not "intensive" checking or concern been triggered several days before?

Bellah, a gray-haired Georgian, observed the families, back in their cars or on the dock, holding umbrellas against the miserable, incessant drizzle. He invited them on board. The crew lounge on the tender was comfortable enough, with upholstered chairs and settees and vending machines. But there wasn't much Bellah could, or was allowed to tell his guests.

"As the afternoon wore on," he would recall, "it became obvious we had a problem"—indeed one that continued to keep the radio operators at Atlantic Fleet, the squadron, and on the *Orion* doggedly calling *Scorpion* over and over.

"There was only worry," one of those present would observe, "no outward distress, no hysteria. It would have been almost an act of disloyalty to suspect the worst too soon."

About 3:15 P.M., "SUBMISS," a missing submarine alert, was declared. It so happened that "COMSUBLANT," Vice Admiral A. F. Schade, commanding submarines of the Atlantic Fleet, had just left New London on the SSN *Fargo*, a new, larger nuclear-powered submarine of the *Sturgeon* class. He set course to follow the "Great Circle Track" assigned *Scorpion* after Rota. Ordering a search to start immediately, Schade assumed duties as "Officer in Charge of Search and Rescue." His administrative offices remained in Norfolk.

This would soon involve some eleven destroyers, eight submarines, eight other fleet ships, and many aircraft, indirectly supported by carriers. About two-thirds of the emergency fleet would put out from Norfolk.

While on the *Orion*, rationalizing or theorizing provided a measure of solace. The *Scorpion* was encountering trouble with her transmitters, with her engines…the storm raging offshore, with waves reportedly twenty feet, was keeping her at sea…or even, the arrival time had been taken down erroneously. It should have been Tuesday the 28th, not Monday the 27th …?

But even so, by late afternoon the families began to go ashore, even as they had quit the pier earlier in the day. Barbara Foli, for one, wife of Electrician 3C Vernon Foli, had to return to her apartment in Ocean View to relieve her baby-sitter. Judy Stephens, "exhausted," took her two boys in hand and started home—for the third time. But a few, like Ann Morrison, wife of Quartermaster Raymond Morrison, would not move, as though being physically within the palpable womb of the submarine tender somehow lent proximity to the *Scorpion*—and to her husband.

On the pier, a sailor took their names and telephone numbers as they left and promised to call if he heard anything.

All in all, the scene at Pier 22 and aboard the *Orion* had been reminiscent of a similar drama at a municipal airport when a plane is overdue, off the airways radars, and "presumed down." In the latter case, however, there tends to be scant reason for any hope whatsoever. None was yet certain as to the fate of the *Scorpion*.

About 6:15 P.M. Judy Stephens received a phone call from a friend, asking, "What's this I hear about the *Scorpion* being overdue?"

She had been listening to the six o'clock news on WTAR-TV when the brief, if laconic, bulletin had been aired. Credence was lent through quoting the Chief of Naval Operations, Admiral Thomas L. Moorer.

At the same time, in Ocean View, a neighbor of Barbara Foli knocked on her door, bearing the same word, while a friend of Ann Morrison's jumped in her car and drove to base with the news. She found Ann still on the *Orion*, now accompanied by her sister, Florence Clark.

Judy, as did other wives, experienced difficulty in getting through to the squadron or to the Atlantic Fleet. Those who did learned little or nothing. For want of a better course of action, she finally drove to Dottie Slattery's, where several of her friends had already gathered. They opened the champagne that had been intended for a welcome-home party. But now there was nothing to celebrate. It was like a wake.

By 11:00 P.M. only Ann Morrison was left aboard the *Orion*, along with her sister. She had been in tears all evening. Now, she was persuaded to go home and get some sleep, if possible.

At 6:30 A.M. Tuesday, she and Florence were back on the tender. Telephones were already being installed, and volunteers among the crew preparing to call the families of the *Scorpion*—even though at this time no one had told them what to say.

Reporters, frustrated at the almost total absence of information from the fleet or squadron, wandered about the *Orion*, seeking incidental interest, or "sidebars," from anyone who would volunteer. As the day brightened under clearing skies, one writer looked at the red fender, which had been put in position for the *Scorpion*, and mused that it "bobbed angrily."

Judy Stephens had gotten her older son off to school when she looked out of the window and saw a gray navy sedan stop in front of her house. Out of it stepped a young officer, a chaplain's gold cross plainly evident on his collar. She knew then—it was all over.

Nonetheless, the navy mounted a search of historic proportions involving thirty-seven ships of the fleet, supported by "twenty-seven flights per day of long-range patrol aircraft!" It was far greater than the navy's fruitless quest in the Pacific in 1937 for Amelia Earhart. This search was conducted primarily by aircraft from the carrier *Lexington*, which was accompanied by a few destroyers.

A "close-in area" from about 120 miles to sea to offshore depths of about 180 feet was "intensively searched" for the missing submarine under the assumption it might have crossed the Atlantic. Some excitement was momentarily sparked when *Pargo*, presumably with sound-tracing devices, discovered the wreck of what was at first identified as a sunken World War II U-boat. Subsequently, it proved to be a small merchant ship.

On June 5, while efforts at locating continued, the *Scorpion* was "presumed lost." Arbitrarily, all aboard were declared dead.

Summer turned into fall. Some of the widows returned to their hometowns. Many of them would rejoin parents until they figured out how to piece back together their fragmented lives. Yet others would remain in Norfolk, in Portsmouth, in Ocean View, or Virginia Beach, whichever was home. They had friends. Their children in school had friends.

All of them had wedded their fortunes and their futures to an extremely hazardous service, yet none was really ready or even fully comprehending when the worst happened.

From the navy's perspective, the loss of two nuclear submarines in five years was far too many. How could this latest disaster have happened? Department hopes of finding an answer were centered primarily

Wreckage of the *Scorpion,* more than two miles deep. The navy has described this portion as the *Scorpion's* bow section. (Naval Photographic Center, Naval Station, Washington, D.C.)

around the two-thousand-ton civilian oceanographic research vessel *Mizar.* It possessed the tools—underwater camera and floodlights for sniffing, looking at, and especially hearing the great ocean depths. It had helped in locating *Thresher.* It was present in 1966, along with small deep-diving craft ("midget subs") such as the *Alvin* at the retrieval of a hydrogen bomb from the Mediterranean off Palomares, Spain. The missile had plunged twenty-five hundred feet into the sea following the collision of an Air Force B-52 bomber and a tanker plane.

   Mizar probed the Atlantic south and west of the Azores all summer. In fact, probably unknowingly, she retraced the route of the derelict *Mary Celeste.* In this operation, *Mizar* located on the ocean floor (at an undisclosed position) "a piece of twisted metal about two feet long…shiny, uncorroded, and not covered with silt." In August and September, fifty individual "artifacts" in a "random pattern" were spotted off the Azores.

   But none of these, nor the shiny metal found in June, could "with certainty…be associated with a submarine." *Mizar* kept on through

October. Then, on the thirtieth of that month, experts on board scrutinizing underwater films identified "portions of a submarine hull."

The position was some four hundred miles southwest of the Azores, the depth about eleven thousand feet, or more than two miles. If this were indeed *Scorpion*, she had traveled in radio silence for twenty hours, at least, after her final message.

The major wreckage—and it was soon identified as that of the *Scorpion*—was found in an area "of about six hundred feet diameter." However, the full "debris field" extended for "about three thousand feet," with a width of "about twelve hundred feet." This lent credence to an earlier report that the ill-starred submarine had "imploded" (burst inward) twice during her final plunge. It was also rumored, but not confirmed, that NATO warships, with underwater listening devices, had recorded the implosions at the time.

Shown quite plainly, considering the great depth, was a forward section of the lost submarine and her "sail," or conning tower. She seemed to be largely on even keel. There was an opened or partially opened hatch on her deck and a coiled rope, possibly belonging to a messenger buoy. Unlike the *Thresher*, nothing was retrieved.

At least enough had been found to quench a number of rumors, some of them bordering on fantasy. Among the more imaginative was the story that the *Scorpion* had been captured intact by the Soviets, and that the crew was imprisoned in Russia, their submarine added to the Red fleet.

The navy's court of inquiry opened hearings. Ninety witnesses would be called during its some three months of hearings.

Years passed without a public report from the court. Those whose lives were intertwined with that of the *Scorpion* struggled along the hard road back. Some widows remarried; others were wedded only to be divorced. Yet others remained where they were or returned to their childhood homes. A few attended an anniversary memorial service annually in the naval base chapel. But nothing really helped to lessen, much less eradicate, the hurt in their hearts. The loss was forever.

Finally, after continual importuning, the navy's judge advocate general released a long, thoroughly "sanitized" (in his own words) script. It was characterized by extensive deletions, even entire blank pages. It dealt with the hull itself and its equipment, the nuclear reactor, crew, and "the enemy." It was all to nothing, as the judge advocate concluded: "The certain cause of the loss of the *Scorpion* cannot be ascertained from the evidence now available."

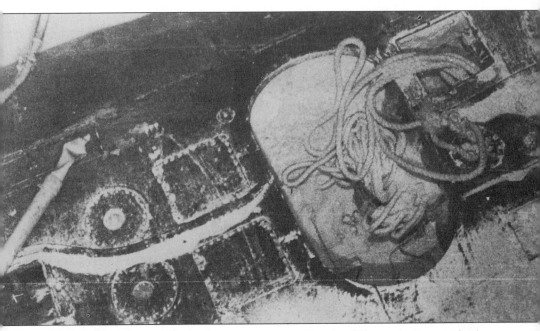

Another photo of the *Scorpion* wreckage. The navy notes a "large hatchlike opening" more or less in the center of this remarkably definitive photograph. Also shown, according to the navy, is a mooring line partially coiled, circular ballast tank vents, and damaged snorkel exhaust piping. The U-boats in World War II used the snorkel for venting diesel exhaust while submerged just beneath the surface. It could, as well, be an air vent. (Naval Photographic Center, Naval Station, Washington, D.C.)

But as the navy would tacitly admit, this was a lie. It was a lie because of a failure to acknowledge a basic truth: The *Scorpion* and all of its command belong to the people. The sea service is but the caretaker.

The truth or its closest approximation would come after the *Norfolk Virginian-Pilot and Ledger-Star* employed the Freedom of Information Act to learn—the navy considered a torpedo malfunction as the most likely cause of the *Scorpion*'s loss. According to the newspaper, "The crew of the Norfolk-based sub was attempting to disarm the Mark 27 (nonatomic) torpedo, which had been inadvertently activated by a mechanical malfunction in a piece of testing equipment when it was detonated."

Before the explosion, Commander Slattery had ordered a 180-degree turn—a procedure that was designed to "shut down the torpedo." The system either did not function or the submarine failed to complete the turn. This conclusion was based on the position of the submarine on the bottom. *Scorpion* was heading east, instead of west for the home port.

The bathyscaphe *Trieste* made dives to the wreck for photographic purposes. However, an attached device, a "swimmer," for penetrating the interior of the *Scorpion*, failed. Thus, any conclusions had to be based on rather imperfect exterior photographs.

The lack of interior photographs was in itself the subject of considerable debate within the court of inquiry. Only two possible causes were ruled out: malfunction of the nuclear reactor or underwater collision. Although the navy obtained "thousands" of photographs from the *Trieste* and the other submersible, *Mizar*, none released to the public (such as reproduced in this book) was of such quality as to reveal a cause of destruction.

That the eastward heading of the submarine could have inspired the torpedo scenario was discussed. Wholly out of control, could not the *Scorpion* have whirled around many times in its death throes?

More certain and "telltale" were the underwater explosions picked up by the navy and private acoustic devices, such as hydrophones. The information thus gained consisted of an initial explosion followed within about a minute by a series of "implosions" as the submarine sank below "crush depth." Triangulation of the "hearing angles" from the acoustic recordings produced "Point Oscar," or the approximate position of the source of the sounds.

That the two-thousand-ton privately owned *Mizar* was sent on a search for the *Scorpion* was a fact told to the author. That it was actually navigating toward "Point Oscar" was not revealed. The existence of the navy's super-secret sound system was common knowledge in the service's investigative crypts during the author's many efforts to ascertain this very sort of intelligence. The elaborate and sensitive underwater sound system had been hastily created and set in operation in answer to the Cold War's Russian "threat."

Only in likely condescension to the Freedom of Information Act did the navy reveal these conclusions "reached…soon after the sinking." And "soon after the sinking" did the author commence his requests for pertinent information…requests that were ignored insofar as the cornucopia bestowed upon the Norfolk paper.

Even so, until the interior of the lost submarine can somehow be penetrated, the mystery of its demise will persist. And so SSN *Scorpion* rests in Point Oscar, the grave of love and hopes, and of what might have been.

8

SS *Poet*

"Sudden and catastrophic"

IT WAS MISTY THAT Thursday evening when Barbara Schmidt drove her son, Alfred Jr., to the Tidewater Grain Pier at Girard Point, on the Schuylkill River, just north of the Philadelphia International Airport. There existed, as well, a presentiment in the chill atmosphere of worse weather to come.

Al, who was twenty-five years old, considered himself lucky. Jobs were less than plentiful. Laid off at a steel mill two years previously, he had attended merchant marine school and was now signed on his second ship—as ordinary seaman. This was the freighter *Poet*, chartered to carry a cargo of corn to Egypt under the State Department's Food for Peace Program. This program meant work for many merchant marine personnel like Al, since Public Law 480, which created it, specified that at least 50 percent of the cargoes be carried in U.S. flag vessels.

The date was October 23, 1980, and young Schmidt could still talk exuberantly on but one principal topic: The Philadelphia Phillies won the World Series, over the Kansas City Royals, just two days previously.

The vessel, seaworn and increasingly nondescript, was a "retread" of the ocean's pathways, one of a fleet that had sailed on long after its designed purpose in World War II—anachronisms even as certain human counterparts, such as the Civil War veterans who could be found marching in Memorial Day parades in the 1920s and even the

'30s. Yet, some estimated that in 1980 these deepwater "retreads" still accounted for nearly 40 percent of the U.S. merchant fleet.

Between the World Wars, mass-produced freight and troop carriers, including the U.S. Hog Islanders and the British Empire class remained familiar sights on the seven seas, along with newer, sleeker ships, both liners and cargo vessels. After World War II, the guns and gun tubs were removed from Liberty ships, C-2s, C-4s, and T-2 tankers. The primary workhorses of the sea supply routes, east and west, were repainted and sent off on peacetime pursuits. They flew the flags of many nations, large and small, especially of those whose merchant marines were decimated in the conflict.

None was fancy. All were designed for rapid construction, and in quantity—by the hundreds. The stub-nosed Libertys, for example, were powered by reciprocating steam engines with a basic design going back to steamships of, at least, the Civil War era. The *Poet*, a C-4, was driven by steam turbines turning a single propeller shaft. Although her top speed was listed at fifteen knots, like all wartime "emergency" mass-production ships she was a hard ship to control. Because the *Poet* had only one screw (propeller), it had reduced maneuverability in docking, in navigating narrow channels, and in meeting heavy seas on port or starboard bow.

The C-4 transports were late bloomers in the war. The bulk of our forces had already been ferried overseas in converted liners, notably the greyhounds, *Queen Mary* and *Queen Elizabeth,* either one of which was capable of carrying virtually an entire division. (While the Liberty ship *Joseph Le Conte* was loading for India at the Army Base, Brooklyn, this author, who was her armed guard officer, watched the *Queen Elizabeth* sail twice, bulging to her boat deck with troops.)

Many luckless GIs were packed on Libertys as a kind of afterthought. Some five hundred had been billeted aboard the Liberty ship *Hamilton,* otherwise fully burdened with ammunition. All died when a German bomb went down her funnel in the Mediterranean.

Obviously, one objective in creating a class of ships designed exclusively as transports—the C-4s—was to avoid a repetition of similar tragedies; randomly mixing men with freight, especially lethal freight.

The *Poet* (to-be) was not built until 1944, one of thirty of her class launched by the Kaiser Shipyard, of Richmond, California. Commissioned the *General Omar Bundy,* the new C-4 did not enter service for the army until the following June, after hostilities in Europe had ended. Four years later, the *Bundy* was returned to the Maritime Commission, languishing in the James River as part of the National Defense Reserve Fleet until 1964.

The *Poet,* in her wartime role as the USS *General Omar Bundy.* The author served as a gunnery officer on the tanker version of this ship, a T-2. (U.S. Navy)

Converted for the carrying of steel products, knocked-down houses, grains, and other bulk commodities, she became the *Portmar*—in effect just another tramp of the sea-lanes. Since she was not quite 12,000 tons displacement, and 522 feet overall, her cargo capacity had to be less than impressive. And her best speed of fifteen knots was exceeded by as much as ten knots by the fast new freighters and tankers being built around the world, especially in Japan.

But she was cheap. Her insurance indicated a market value of $1.25 million, and a crew of only about thirty could take her to sea.

In 1979 she was purchased by Henry J. Bonnabel, principal stockholder and president of the Hawaiian Eugenia Corporation and of other steamship companies. He was, on a far wider scale, sort of a modern-day counterpart of shipper James Winchester, part owner of the *Mary Celeste.* A graduate of the Merchant Marine Academy, Bonnabel described himself as having "worked" with the "maritime trade" for more than thirty-five years.

At the change of ownership—*Portmar* had already become simply *Port*—the erstwhile C-4 had sustained what might be termed only normal wear and tear for an aging ship in her kind of trade. She had plate and frame damage from colliding with another vessel. There had been a fire in No. 2 cargo hold, resulting in a crack in the main deck. Temporary repairs, largely through welding, were effected, but permanent correction was deferred. A "considerable amount of erosion" on the sternpost was noted by a coast guard inspector. But he postscripted it was not "excessive."

In June 1980, the old C-4 ran aground in Santo Domingo harbor. The bilges were checked. She had not sprung a leak. Now, she had become *Poet* instead of *Port*. Her seamen theorized it was an economical way of name changing, substituting only one letter. As *Poet*, she also won a namesake, which was a floating Soviet fish factory.

On October 16, of the same year, she arrived in Delaware Bay in ballast after a two-month voyage to Port Said carrying 5,606 tons of bagged flour. Her new orders were to load a 13,500-ton cargo of No. 2 yellow corn for Port Said under State Department Food for Peace contract. This was a last-minute bonanza for the operators of the *Poet*, which was normally homeported in Galveston. The value of the grain was $3 million, or nearly three times the worth of the aging freighter.

There were repairs to be made, but none said to be crucial to the safety of the ship—stop an oil leak on a crane, provide some spare parts for the same piece of machinery, replace a couple of boiler gaskets, "fabricate" a new winch gear cover, make a few repairs to the main deck, minor adjustments on a midship's fire main—a local firm, Phillyship, was contractor.

Some fairly routine radio maintenance was effected, together with the installation of a LORAN C for long-range radar navigation. The RCA service representative who checked over the radio and radar equipment would observe that it was in "rather good condition." This included an "EPIRB," or Emergency Position Indicating Radiobeacon, designed to float free from a sinking ship and transmit signals allowing other ships or aircraft to home on it.

EPIRB is a cylinder sixteen inches high, with an antenna that rises automatically into position. Its greatest deficiency: the range is no more than twenty-five nautical miles, and its frequency is largely for aircraft. Few ships are capable of picking up EPIRB signals.

However, this weakness seemed to be more than compensated for by backup radiotelephone and radiotelegraph transmitters and receivers. The *Poet*'s main transmitter, for example, tested up to one hundred nautical miles and the high-frequency set to three thousand—all the way across the Atlantic. Even the little lifeboat radio checked in at nearly fifty miles. Uninterrupted electricity was apparently assured by a 240-volt emergency diesel generator. It was sufficiently powerful to supplement the ship's lighting and even to operate the steering gear.

But Joseph Vyhnak, the fifty-two-year-old radio operator who had come aboard only in Port Said, was not easily satisfied. Observing that he was accustomed to more "sophisticated" equipment, Vyhnak, master chief petty officer and a thirty-year veteran of the navy, asserted obliquely that he was "not too happy" with the work. Something of a perfectionist, he carried his own digital short-wave receiver.

Meanwhile, still berthed at Pier 2, Girard Point, the *Poet* was undergoing a scraping and scouring of her holds "because of water, rust scale, and residue of the previous cargo." This was a precaution, as well, against rodent and weevil "infestation," ordered, sometimes routinely, by Department of Agriculture inspectors.

On October 21 the freighter was moved to adjacent Pier 3, and loading commenced. The coast guard would comment:

"Grain is among the most basic of commodities and must have been a cargo very early in marine trade (grain vessels are mentioned in the commentaries of Julius Caesar). Grain can be shipped in bags but, today, grain is shipped in bulk...[grain has] long been recognized as a problem cargo requiring special precautions to avoid shifting...."

Ships were lost or endangered because holds believed to be full actually had empty—"void"—spaces, causing shifting of hundreds of tons of the grain. This could give the vessel a dangerous list. Amendments to the 1960 Safety of Life at Sea Convention involving "Bulk Grain Cargoes" detailed how trimming should be done during the loading and "stability calculations" made carefully at the same time.

Actually, three inspectors from the National Cargo Bureau were present at various times before and during the loading of *Poet* to work on these calculations with the chief mate, Norman Currier. This bureau, formed privately in 1952 as "a public service organization," works primarily with the coast guard to check on the proper loading of grains "and other dangerous cargoes," other than tanker cargoes.

On Thursday, October 23, loading was completed—an estimated 13,538 long tons of corn. The *Poet* was down by the bow—drawing thirty-four feet, eight inches—by about two feet, eight inches. The chief mate, Norman Currier, was certain, however, that the trim could be better equalized by transferring fuel oil. There was also a question whether the freeboard was some one and a half inches "light"—the loadline or

Plimsoll too low—for winter regulations. However, this would pose no apparent problem since the ship would be back in the summer loading zone in a week, and normal fuel consumption should result in an inch less draft per day.

As the crew tightened the hatch cover gaskets and started sealing them with a heavy adhesive tape, a Cargo Bureau representative, Captain Geyser, signed a certificate of loading, indicating his organization's approval. Before he went ashore about 5:00 P.M., he routinely shook hands with the master, Leroy A. Warren, who observed in passing that he planned a rhumb line—straight—course to Gibraltar, 145 degrees, rather than a circle route.

Warren, almost sixty, a former American Export Lines skipper and thirty-year veteran of the oceans, had been with the *Poet* since August 1979, although he had alternated with a relief master. While Warren, a resident of Belair, Maryland, had remarked to his wife, Kathryn, that the *Poet* was a "rustpot," his confidence in her was implied by his continued presence. But in the jargon and paradoxes of seafaring, "rustpot," could easily have been construed as a term of endearment. (The author, for example, more or less affectionately alluded to his two Liberty ships and one T-2 tanker as "bolt buckets" and the like, even though the two former were not long off the ways and he took the tanker out from Chester, Pennsylvania, on her maiden voyage.)

Warren was comfortably situated. Money was no desperate need. From the company's point of view, Warren was a good captain in many respects. Meticulous, he was accustomed to communicating by radio with the owners every forty-eight hours: position, amount of fuel in her bunkers, estimated arrival time….

Shortly before 6:00 P.M., *Poet* was "buttoned up" and awaiting only the next high tide. On board were thirty-four officers and crew.

Later in the evening, the owner's representative appeared to receive any last-minute comments and to wish the captain bon voyage. He was advised by Warren and by the radio operator that both were satisfied with repairs and were ready to sail. Vyhnak did not repeat comments previously made to the RCA representative that he was "not too happy" with the repair work.

At least one other in "officer's country" was apparently not so happy himself. Anthony Bourbonnais, thirty-two-year-old third engineer from Newark, Delaware, had signed on only that week. When he returned home to say good-bye to his wife, Alice, and two small daughters, he commented on what he described as the indifferent condition of the ship, observing, "I think I may have made a mistake."

Before Bonnabel's agent left, Noel McLaughlin, an Alabaman and the ship's baker, asked if he would be home by Christmas. He was assured he would.

At 1:00 A.M., Friday, October 24, the *Poet* backed out into the murky darkness of the Schuylkill and then into the broader Delaware. There was a light fog. The docking pilot observed the freighter was "sluggish," or slow in turning, but he attributed this to shallow water and the fact that the *Poet* was down by the bow. Captain Gary Harper, the river pilot, noticed the same thing at first, but then, in the deeper water of midchannel, the vessel became more responsive. The master assured the pilot that the engineers had already commenced trimming.

After a late night and early morning passage down the refinery-studded river, and then into the bay described as "uneventful," Pilot Harper left the ship at 8:20 A.M. She was abeam of Cape Henlopen, one mile east of the Harbor of Refuge. The mate on watch had just logged an east wind of twenty knots and a three-foot sea. The clouds were heavy.

As a matter of fact, the National Weather Service Offshore Forecast had already broadcast a storm and gale warning from northern Florida right up to Nova Scotia. Any ship crossing the Atlantic and that had left East Coast ports from Jacksonville to Boston could expect the disturbance within the next twenty-four hours.

At 9:00 A.M. Captain Warren ordered a message transmitted simultaneously to the U.S. Coast Guard's Voluntary Automated Mutual Assistance Vessel Rescue System (AMVER) and then to the required U.S. Maritime Administration Merchant Vessel Locator Filing System (USMER). It stated that the *Poet* had departed Philadelphia at 1:00 A.M. and was sailing a rhumb line to Gibraltar at fifteen knots, then coastal to Port Said.

The message was received by the coast guard radio station in Puerto Rico, perhaps elsewhere, too.

Under USMER, messages were to be transmitted at noon of the second day following departure and every forty-eight hours thereafter. However, both AMVER and USMER fed more or less identical information into different computers. There existed no procedures by the coast guard, navy, or other services to ascertain if the reports were actually being submitted as programmed. There was a U.S. Maritime Administration general check or survey, but only every three months.

Also about 9:00 A.M., Warren advised the ship's owner via Chatham (commercial) Radio Station, in Massachusetts, of his departure from Cape Henlopen, bunkered with 6,218 barrels of fuel oil. He gave his ETA, or estimated time of arrival, in Port Said as 6:00 A.M., November 9.

Late that Friday night, when the *Poet* should have been more than two hundred miles at sea and heading into a mounting storm, the third mate, Robert Gove, made a radiotelephone call to his wife, Donna, in Red Bank, New Jersey. They were newlyweds. As Donna would recall, Robert did not mention the ship, where it was, or—significantly—the weather. The substance was "personal."

But early the next morning, Saturday, the twenty-fifth, the Weather Service was warning that the coastal storm had accelerated. It was roaring northward with winds of up to fifty knots and seas as high as twenty-two feet.

How, one might speculate, could Bob Gove have failed to comment on this?

Upwards of twelve vessels along the *Poet*'s stated track were caught in the fury of this storm. Some had to reduce speed and even alter course. Two, the ketch *Wandering Angus* and the yacht *Polar Bear*, were so buffeted that both foundered the next day, Sunday, the twenty-sixth.

The crews were saved. Bart Dunbar, captain of the ketch, spoke of a "rogue" or off-rhythm wave, upwards of fifty feet high, which had capsized his ship.

The 14,400-ton freighter *Columbia*, war-built herself, en route from Norfolk to Alexandria, Egypt, had observed the seas building since the twenty-fourth, when the *Poet* sailed. On the twenty-fifth, the mate of the *Columbia* logged winds of fifty-five knots howling through the rigging and "shipping seas starboard side main deck and over bow, occasionally, on bridge deck."

The force by Sunday had in no manner diminished. Shortly after midnight, Earl Johnson, operator at WMH, a commercial marine radio station in Baltimore, heard an auto alarm signal such as the EPIRB, the floating-free emergency transmitter, would emit. These were four- to six-second dashes at one-second intervals. Johnson thought the transmission "clear but weak," and it did not fade until it ended "abruptly."

Without equipment to "home" on the signal for either distance or direction, Johnson called the Coast Guard Communications Station at Portsmouth, Virginia. No, the alarm had not been picked up there. He assumed other stations or ships listening in, or had been—and he left the matter there.

About 4:30 the next afternoon, Monday, the twenty-seventh, Edward R. Mashburn, radio operator aboard the *Columbia*, was eating an early supper when notified of a similar alarm crackling in. He listened to determine if other vessels and shore stations had turned off their own transmitters in order to hear. Since "normal communications" were continuing, Mashburn concluded that these were false signals, somehow attributable to the static and lightning during foul weather.

The same Monday, Henry Bonnabel, the *Poet*'s owner, called up Chatham radio and asked it to contact the *Poet*. This was unusual since the freighter was but three days out of harbor. Even so, Bonnabel would insist, and insist again, that he was "not concerned."

Obediently, Chatham repeated its call every two hours, even as the great storm subsided along the Southeast and East Coast, and now lashed at the fishing fleets of Maine, Nova Scotia, and Newfoundland.

The week moved ahead. On Thursday, October 30, Bonnabel was again in touch with Chatham radio, which advised him that *Poet* had not responded to its call flashed out every two hours since Monday. The owner of the silent vessel would admit that "the first slight concern" now "came to my mind." Not receiving his forty-eight-hour reports—the ship having been gone one week—he thought to be "rather strange," though even so there was not "a serious question in my mind."

For one consideration, Bonnabel maintained faith in the seaworthiness of his big ship and in the competence of her crew.

He asked Chatham to relay a "routine message" regarding the discharge of cargo in Port Said, and requesting that Captain Warren advise him when *Poet* passed through the Strait of Gibraltar. After he hung up from talking with Chatham, Henry Bonnabel started making calls to the seamen's union offices. He knew that crewmen frequently would cable or radio their unions with requests such as "Please see that my wife gets $50" or the like. He continued his calls on Friday, October 31, with negative answers.

The ship's owner, the same day, sent off an "urgent" message via Chatham asking the master to supply him at once with the *Poet*'s position. Even so, as Bonnabel would testify, "there was no need to think that the ship was in trouble." He would rationalize that there existed "all sorts of emergency ways of handling messages on the ship had she been in trouble." He speculated, for example, that the antenna "could have been carried away," or atmospheric conditions could have "interfered." Indeed, the radio operator may have become ill.

And so November arrived, and the hours ticked on, inexorably, beyond recall.

Not until November 3, ten days after *Poet* had put Cape Henlopen astern, was the Coast Guard Rescue Coordination Center (RCC), in

New York, advised by the Hawaiian Eugenia Corporation that the *Poet* remained unreported, that it should be passing Gibraltar this very day. The coast guard instituted a number of preliminaries including checking Chatham, the AMVER reporting center (also in New York), the navy, the Delaware Pilots Association, the Defense Mapping Agency, and a unique organization known as Lloyd's of London Intelligence Service. This latter network had long maintained an international check on merchant ship operations.

But the idea of search manifestly was not considered at all by the coast guard, patiently waiting the next four days "for some positive response" from its routine signals. Actually, the coast guard recognized little cause for concern. Its chief of operations would observe that "only very few ships of the size of the *Poet* are ever reported overdue or even unreported each year and they eventually do turn up."

...the *Cyclops* all over again.

Responses to the coast guard's signals all were negative. One of its aircraft, searching on October 25 and 26 for a missing sailboat along the *Poet*'s route, spotted neither the object of its quest nor any vessel resembling the grain-carrying freighter. It had received no automatic radio alarms.

Lloyd's reported that none on "the Rock" had sighted the *Poet*. This gloomy intelligence was confirmed during the next forty-eight hours by other sources on that same austere and strategic listening post.

On November 6, Bonnabel decided to check his agent in Piraeus, Greece. This was across the Mediterranean from the *Poet*'s destination and relatively close.

On Friday, November 7, the agent replied that the *Poet* was unreported in his area. This inspired Bonnabel to request that the coast guard initiate "an intensive air and sea search along the entire route from Cape Henlopen to Gibraltar."

Word, however, had already spread through union halls that something was wrong with the Hawaiian Eugenia freighter. In fact, a number of these seamen's representatives themselves expressed concern this Friday to the coast guard, pointing out the *Poet*'s past punctuality in reporting every forty-eight hours.

One union representative telephoned Barbara Schmidt that the *Poet* was some five days overdue, but probably "would turn up." Her reaction was one of numbed disbelief. Al's last words to her were that he would be home for Christmas—and she just assumed he would be. Her faith had been firm.

The coast guard informed an ailing Katharine Warren, in Belair.

And so, through various sources, the families of all of the thirty-four aboard the *Poet* had been notified by that Friday evening.

Saturday afternoon, more than two weeks after the freighter had sailed, the coast guard commenced its search. But it had required some twenty-four hours to crank up the ponderous search machinery, a veritable grab bag of facts that were fed into computers. As the National Transportation Safety Board would reconstruct:

"The coast guard…began to look back to October 24, 25, and 26 when the *Poet* began its voyage. A severe storm had passed along the Atlantic coast during that period and the coast guard had been very busy searching for vessels in distress…the coast guard may have experienced some problem during that period…the RCC contacted the navy's oceanographic center in Norfolk and was advised that the *Poet* would have encountered the heaviest weather conditions [between October 25 and October 26, when the freighter would have passed through the cold "North Wall" of the Gulf Stream where storm winds are frequently fifteen knots greater and seas five feet higher than outside this "Wall"]…it was assumed that the *Poet* experienced trouble in the first forty-eight hours of its voyage during the severe storm and that it traveled its stated rhumb line course from Cape Henlopen to Gibraltar. However, the coast guard planned to search the entire trackline…in the event the *Poet* was proceeding at some reduced speed due to machinery problems…it may not have reached Gibraltar by November 7. Lloyd's of London told the RCC that it had missed some ships at Gibraltar on occasion."

When this and other information—some detailed, some general—was "digested" by the computers, the initial answer was for a block search of the Atlantic to cover almost two hundred thousand square miles over a period of six days. However, to obtain a realistic readout, the tapes would have to be updated daily.

The aircraft sent on this mission—coast guard, navy, air force, and even a few Canadian—varied in number from as many as nine to as few as two. The first day, November 8, more than 34,000 square miles were combed, 85,000 the next, only 16,000 on the tenth, as manifest discouragement set in because of the negative results. Not a hint or a whisper of the *Poet* was encountered.

A meeting, which included Lyle Clemens, alternate master of the *Poet*, was held on the tenth by the coast guard for evaluation. It was decided to continue for three more days, though the effort was already reaching huge proportions by the measure of the coast guard's chief of operations, Rear Admiral John D. Costello.

"In my memory, and the memory of everybody that was involved here," he added, "we had not conducted such a massive search for a long time."

On the thirteenth, when the search was due to end, relatives, union representatives, U.S. senators, and congressmen began begging the coast guard to continue. By the time the operation was terminated, on November 17, nearly three hundred thousand square miles had been studied, and under great difficulties. For example, the coast guard said they needed ten times the aircraft. And even to arrive at the area, navy aircraft required three to four hours' flying time from bases in the Azores or Bermuda. Nor was there any position report or distress signal to offer a reference point.

"The search," reported the Transportation Safety Board, "covered the entire estimated tracking of the *Poet* from Cape Henlopen to the Strait of Gibraltar. If the *Poet* had still been afloat during that period it probably would have been detected. The total area searched was 297,400 square miles—an area approximately the total area of the eastern United States from Maine to South Carolina, including New York and Pennsylvania...any lifeboat, life raft, or significant concentration of debris should have been detected in the detailed search area [the first seventy-two-hour period] but because of the search pattern needed to cover so vast an area, anything smaller would have been difficult to detect.

"Although crew members may have survived for two weeks in a lifeboat or life raft if the conditions were favorable, a person would survive for less than a day in the water in October in the North Atlantic. Therefore, the possibility of finding any survivors or debris smaller than a life raft by November 17 was very small."

The board postscripted that the "probability" of locating either survivors or debris would have been "greater" had the air search commenced sooner.

The Transportation Safety Board's hearings began rather quickly, on November 19. They were jointly conducted with the coast guard in Philadelphia. Not adjourning until December 12, the inquiry heard a procession of individuals who had any connection whatsoever with the *Poet*, from radio repairmen and grain loaders to next of kin and former crewmen.

The maritime board admitted the "disappearance of a 523-foot-long ship such as the *Poet*" was "unusual," but "not unique." Other losses were recalled, especially the big West German barge carrier *Munchen*, 335 feet longer than the *Poet* and far newer. It went down in the North Atlantic off the Azores in December 1978 with all twenty-eight aboard.

The Marine *Sulphur Queen*, a converted wartime T-2 tanker, sank in the Gulf of Mexico in February 1963, taking her crew of thirty-nine to the bottom. Coincidentally, her last wireless message had been a personal phone call from a crew member.

But neither was lost fully "without a trace." A distress message from the *Munchen* had been picked up, a raft was found. Two life rings, part of a man's shirt, assorted debris, and some "yellow material" were observed by search vessels floating in the last estimated position of the *Sulphur Queen*. Her cargo had been molten sulfur.

The *Poet* left behind not so much as a hint. Her accident was "sudden and catastrophic," theorized the investigators. At the same time, however, they did not attribute the disaster to structural failure, improper loading, cargo shifting, or even "a sudden explosion." In sum, the governmental probers were "unable to determine the probable cause of this accident since no distress signal was ever heard and no trace of the ship or its crew has ever been found. Based on assumed sea conditions, ship speed, and ship heading, calculations indicate that "the *Poet* may have capsized suddenly due to synchronous rolling."

Computers, inevitably, had played their role in the hypothetical reconstruction.

"The computer simulation showed that in less than three minutes the *Poet* would have capsized in three out of four quartering seas conditions investigated. As the wind and waves shifted through the south to the southwest on October 26, the master would have resumed an easterly heading exposing the ship to quartering seas. The Safety Board believes that the capsizing in beam or quartering seas on October 26 is the most likely explanation...in both cases, the ship could have capsized and sunk within a matter of minutes."

Bonnabel's role was mentioned more or less as an aside, while the coast guard, as might have been anticipated, received the equivalent of but a wrist slap.

"The delay until November 3 by the *Poet*'s owner in notifying the coast guard that the *Poet* was unreported since October 24 may have contributed to the loss of life. The coast guard's failure to make adequate preparations once notified of the *Poet*'s disappearance on November 3 and its failure to begin an active search until November 8 decreased the probability of finding survivors."

In profound frustration, a number of next of kin wrote that winter to the president, to other high executives in government, and to members of Congress, voicing the broadest latitude of suspicion and asking the FBI as well as the CIA to investigate. For one, Mrs. Liselotte Zukier

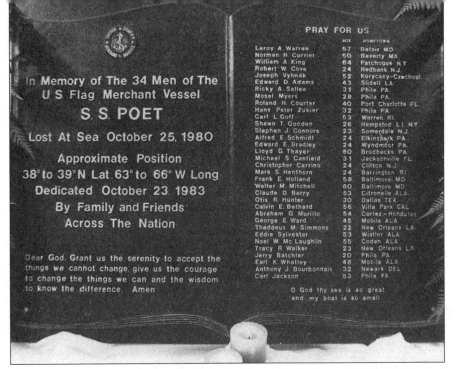

PRAY FOR US

	AGE	HOMETOWN
Leroy A. Warren	57	Belair MD.
Norman H. Currier	50	Beverly MA.
William A. King	64	Patchogue N.Y.
Robert W. Cove	24	Redbank N.J.
Joseph Vyhnak	52	Korycany-Czechost
Edward D. Adams	43	Slidell LA.
Ricky A. Sallee	31	Phila PA.
Mosel Myers	28	Phila. PA.
Roland H. Courter	40	Port Charlotte FL.
Hans Peter Zukier	32	Phila. PA
Carl L. Goff	53	Warren RI.
Shawn T. Gooden	26	Hempsted L.I. N.Y.
Stephen J. Connors	23	Somerdale N.J.
Alfred E. Schmidt	24	Elkinsbark PA.
Edward E. Bradley	24	Wyndmoor PA.
Lloyd G. Thayer	60	Brodbecks PA.
Michael S. Canfield	31	Jacksonville FL.
Christopher Carrino	24	Clifton N.J.
Mark S. Henthorn	24	Barrington RI.
Frank E. Holland	58	Baltimore MD.
Walter M. Mitchell	60	Baltimore MD.
Claude D. Berry	53	Citronelle ALA.
Otis R. Hunter	30	Dallas TEX.
Calvin E. Bethard	56	Villa Park CAL.
Abraham G. Murillo	54	Cortez - Honduras
George E. Ward	45	Mobile ALA.
Thaddeus M. Simmons	22	New Orleans LA.
Eddie Sylvester	53	Wistler ALA.
Noel W. Mc Laughlin	55	Coden ALA.
Tracy R. Walker	23	New Orleans LA.
Jerry Batchler	20	Phila. PA.
Earl K. Whatley	48	Mobile ALA.
Anthony J. Bourbonnais	32	Newark DEL.
Carl Jackson	53	Phila. PA.

In Memory of The 34 Men of The
U S Flag Merchant Vessel

S. S. POET

Lost At Sea October 25, 1980

Approximate Position
38° to 39° N Lat. 63° to 66° W Long

Dedicated October 23, 1983

By Family and Friends
Across The Nation

Dear God, Grant us the serenity to accept the
things we cannot change, give us the courage
to change the things we can and the wisdom
to know the difference. Amen

O God thy sea is so great
and my boat is so small

Plaque in the Church of Gloria Dei, Philadelphia. (Courtesy of Mrs. Liselotte Zukier Fredette)

Fredette, of Philadelphia, told President Ronald Reagan that she was a "desperate mother."

"My son, Hans," she noted, describing him as a thirty-two-year-old able seaman of fifteen years' experience, "was a respectable citizen—he was an altar boy, an Eagle Scout, and chose the merchant marine as his career. During the American conflict in Vietnam and Cambodia, he made many trips up the Delta River, in convoys; his vessel loaded to capacity with ammunition for our armed forces—like sitting ducks in a shooting gallery for the Viet Cong."

[For Lotte Fredette, however, personal tragedy had only begun. On Thanksgiving Day, 1983, just one month after she had participated in the dedication of a plaque to the lost men of the *Poet*, another son, Holger Christopher Zukier, died in a hunting accident. He was twenty-six. Like his brother, Hans, Holger had been a Boy Scout and an altar boy.]

The U.S. Congress did not enter the probings until April 1981. At that time the House of Representatives Committee on Merchant Marine and Fisheries opened its own inquiry as Chairman Walter B. Jones, a North Carolina Democrat, averred, "The loss of a U.S. flag vessel of this size without a trace is unheard of...."

Bonnabel, as a primary witness, was examined at some length. Reporters present described him as often emotional. The vessel, he was convinced, was "probably the victim of a killer storm...suddenly capsized without warning and there was no opportunity for anyone to do anything at that particular point."

He defended the freighter as "a good ship manned by officers who homesteaded the vessel. Some of the officers have sailed on this vessel for long periods of up to fourteen years. It is inconceivable that they would knowingly take a vessel to sea if they had the least feeling that it was not seaworthy in every respect."

At the same time, the ship's owner cited "outrageous stories and innuendo that appeared in the media alluding to allegations of marine fraud, hijackings, or trading heroin in collusion with Iran, or carrying secret explosives for the U.S. military to Egypt."

Captain Arthur W. Gove, a retired coast guard captain and merchant master who was the father of Robert Gove, the third mate of the *Poet*, was certain that "whatever happened was momentous and rapid to preclude a radio message and possible launching of lifesaving equipment." At the same time he echoed the Transportation Safety Board in asserting that "the owner's failure to report that one of his vessels was unaccounted for nine days or so cannot be excused," while the coast guard's "compounding of the delay...for another five days is inconceivable."

Much was introduced at the hearing, without conclusion or resolution. For example, the Seafarers International Union of North America castigated the quality of coast guard inspections and the expertise of the inspectors. Frank Drozak, its president, charged that the inspector in Philadelphia who sent the *Poet* on her way was "a reservist who did weekend duty. He had no special qualifications. His regular work was that of a detective...most coast guard inspections are usually superficial and not done with any depth."

But any merchant skipper could quickly counter, "The master has the last word on the seaworthiness of his ship. He is not supposed or expected to sail unless he is completely satisfied." None possessed other than the highest accolades for the ability, experience, and judgment of Captain Leroy Warren.

Some discussion was accorded the condition of other ships owned in whole or in part by Bonnabel. He bristled when it was suggested that he picked up an old freighter, the SS *Pilgrim*, "on its way to a ship graveyard" in order to accept a Food for Peace grain charter for Zambia.

"It was not true," Bonnabel told the committee, "that the ship was en route to a graveyard." He as well denied that the *Pilgrim* had developed a forty-five-degree list as suggested by Congressman Thomas Foglietta of Pennsylvania.

However, the entire line of questioning on the seaworthiness of other ships in which the lost cargo carrier's owner might have had an interest was abandoned after the awareness by the committee that the fate of only one vessel—the *Poet*—was the subject of the hearings. Then the investigation was concluded on a somewhat anticlimactic note: "Our responsibility is not to accuse, but to correct and help...and with that the committee stands adjourned."

But however earnest and constructive might have been the legislators' purposes, the hearings accomplished little other than to reaffirm the Transportation Safety Board's musings and, indeed, they even reprinted verbatim much of what that executive agency had already published.

The coast guard's Marine Board of Investigation did not release its own report for another year, in April 1982.

"The precise time and location of the vessel's loss are unknown and cannot be determined," although the board estimated the *Poet* may have encountered the highest seas and winds of sixty knots on October 26; "a credible flooding of No. 1 hold."

There was, as well, "a credible possibility...that a major structural failure occurred. A detailed critical analysis of design and actual hull strength serves to discount this possibility, but other considerations are of concern to the board, including the possibility of an undiscovered hull structural defect of a size and nature adequate to lead to a major hull structural failure."

Thus, the coast guard differed with the Transportation Safety Board: "The *Poet* probably did not experience a massive structure failure because calculated stress levels were well below design standards."

Shifting of the grain cargo was virtually eliminated as "a significant factor in the loss of the vessel." So was an explosion of grain dust.

Positive recommendations centered around communications with and from merchant ships, both in routine reporting and emergency. The board believed, "There is a need to look at safety radio communications with ocean-going ships, and the current applicable laws and regulations...."

The commandant of the coast guard, Admiral J. B. Hayes, while endorsing some and discounting or questioning others of the board's findings, personally held that "some loss of hull integrity occurred. The age of the ship, the fact that it deferred repairs to both underwater hull and topsides, and the severity of the storm are factors to be considered."

He believed in the likelihood of the *Poet*'s capsizing, or even "plunging" bow first.

The investigations were concluded. No one, no individual, corporate, or governmental group was charged with anything. No blame was fixed. Insurance monies had been paid. The demands of the next of kin were settled out of court.

The books, for all practical purposes, were closed. There was not even a "*Poet* desk," like the navy maintained on the *Scorpion*, established within any of the three investigative bodies. A chorused sigh of relief was all but audible.

A very few of the bereaved, such as Barbara Schmidt and Lotte Fredette, continued to haunt maritime hearings, anywhere, related in some manner to safety at sea. Occasionally, Barbara admits, she walks down to some handy pier where an old cargo ship is loading, to ask the crew:

"Do you *really* think this vessel is safe?"

Obviously, her concerns have a certain foundation. Ships continue to sink in storms—or from other causes, such as fire and collision. On February 12, 1983, the wartime T-2 tanker *Marine Electric*, running as a collier, went down in a raging blizzard (that also paralyzed eastern cities) some thirty-five miles southeast of Ocean City, Maryland. She carried all but three of her crew of thirty-four with her.

Unlike the *Poet*, apparently, the *Marine Electric* remained afloat almost an hour and a half after the first message of distress. Divers reaching the wreck in 120 feet of water found the old vessel in two pieces. Later, the Transportation Safety Board blamed "flooding...as the result of undetermined structural failure."

Could this tragedy somehow be related to the *Poet*? And if so, in what respects other than the obvious that she never made port? And who could provide any yardsticks of comparison?

Like the *Waratah* and *Cyclops* long before her, the *Poet*'s voyage into oblivion has become unique in the annals of the sea, rare and unenviable. When two major investigative bodies could not agree even on a primary question—*Poet*'s structural stability—it was obvious that gropings for an answer remained in the realm of surmise and only deepened the mystery.

Synchronous roll? And if so, since in retrospect it seemed so absurdly simple to the probers, how come any ship, large or small, old or new, can voyage very far in any kind of sea without commencing this killer rhythm and falling victim to it?

Flooding of No. 1 hold? Plunging? Capsizing? Foundering? Cargo shifting? All conjecture.

And the computer simulation that *Poet*, given the same conditions of wind and sea, would have capsized "in three minutes"—was it not computer "intelligence" that forecast, just prior to election, a race between Carter and Reagan "too close to call"? And, from what information has been made public, did not an erring computer lead a Korean airliner to its doom over Soviet restricted territory? Also, according to the air force, an erring computer sent a $100 million satellite, launched by the space shuttle in April 1983, on literally a cockeyed course. Has not computer failure darkened big cities and disrupted rail and air traffic?

The investigators were asked (by the author) why no weight at all was accorded sabotage. There was "no evidence," was the reply. Then, there *was* "evidence" that the *Poet* was lost from "natural causes" in a storm? No.

The war atmosphere, or climate in the Middle East, to which the old C-4 steamed was as real as that when the *Lusitania, Hampshire,* and *Cyclops* put to sea. Hatred, murder, and mass destruction, especially through "infernal machines," had become a shocking way of life in that part of the world. Both materials and technique had shown deadly progress since World War I, even since World War II. A plastic bomb that a man could transport by suitcase could level a building—and frequently has, both in the Middle East and in Northern Ireland.

Such a device, anywhere near a ship's boiler room, for example, could tear the vessel in half, so that it would sink in minutes.

"I don't recall anyone stopping us that evening," asserts Barbara Schmidt, concerning taking her son Al to the *Poet*. "I don't remember if there was any security at all on that pier. No one asked me for a pass or identification."

But even if there had been some security, it would not have mattered. Determined saboteurs have placed bombs—and large ones at will—in areas thronged with onlookers such as airports and shopping streets, even inside U.S. embassies and marine command posts which are supposedly well guarded. Consider Oklahoma City, the New York Trade Center bombings, and the August 1998 car bombings at the U.S. embassies in Kenya and Tanzania that resulted in heavy loss of life.

Sabotaged? Synchronous roll? Neither can readily be proven or disproven. Obvious only is the fact that twenty-six thousand tons of ship and cargo—with all living souls aboard—were swallowed by the great oceans in some fashion and for some presumably logical reasons.

Poet is the latest profound mystery of the sea. But surely she will not be the last, not so long as there are those who "must go down to the seas again."

Acknowledgments, Bibliography, and Author's Notes

Chapter 1   *Mary Celeste*

Captain Briggs's ill-fated half-brig sails on sturdily in the National Archives. More than a century after the fact, enough interest persists so that the legislative and diplomatic branch there has prepared an eight-page "finder." The author of this ambitious project is Kathryn M. Murphy, archivist, whose compilations fill fourteen volumes and several microfilm rolls. They embrace the voluminous correspondence of Consul Sprague, the rather fabulous Solly Flood, and other principals in the disappearance; special reports such as those concerning the bloodstains; crew lists; clippings; etc.—179 items *in toto*. Encompassed as well as the Department of State and Consular Post records are those of the Division of Customs (Treasury) and Bureau of Marine Inspection and Navigation.

In 1938, under the Secretaryship of the celebrated Cordell Hull, bureaucrats in "State" decided that the files of its far-flung consular posts must be much too cluttered. Genoa, for example, had sent nothing home since 1822, when the post came into existence. Even to the unimaginative, that seemed far too long a time. Thus, in February 1939 Consul General Warden McK. Wilson packed up the ghosts of 117 years into seven sturdy crates and shipped them to Washington. The freight charge aboard the SS *Excalibur* came to exactly $33.47.

Historians of those pre-World War II months who might have expected some light to be shed on the *Mary Celeste* mystery encountered only chill disappointment. Not only was the missing log not in Consul Spencer's files of the pertinent period, but one might conclude that this long-ago diplomat had never heard of the *Mary Celeste*.

Nonetheless, researchers and perhaps, as well, those who simply savor a real-life mystery continue to find their way into the cramped little cubicles over which Kathryn Murphy continues her patient and helpful reign. Assisting her, among others, is Ronald Swerzek.

"We do not own the logbook of the *Mary Celeste*," writes Ardie L. Kelly, (former) librarian of the Mariners' Museum, Newport News, Virginia. "I have also checked a couple of lists we have of logbooks owned by other collections and do not see it listed."

This splendid and beautiful museum has long assisted the author in his various research projects. Its library contains material on *Mary Celeste* perhaps second only to that in the National Archives. This includes copies of the Admiralty's futile, if not farcical, investigation in Gibraltar. Still, an authentic set is not easy to come by.

Some cross-checking was accomplished, also, at the Mariners' Museum on the *Lusitania, Hampshire,* and *Cyclops* chapters.

"I do not know what happened to the *Mary Celeste* log book," writes Mrs. Chester T. Cobb, of Hyannis, Massachusetts, a daughter-in-law of Dr. Oliver Cobb. "The melodeon went to James Briggs, brother of Capt. Briggs. I saw it many years ago in Frank Briggs's home in New Bedford. I believe he was a son of James. I presume it has been passed down through the family.

"I am eighty-three years old and my memory is not what it used to be."

Thomas Wolfe wrote a short story, "Only the Dead Know Brooklyn." By the same token, it would appear that only the dead know what happened to the half-brig's missing log.

The author also acknowledges the assistance of the late Alexander C. Brown, of Newport News, marine author and book reviewer; Mary Cabral, New Bedford, Massachusetts, Free Public Library; Katherine E. Dibble, Boston Public Library; Peter Fetchko and Kathy Flynn, Peabody Museum (Salem, Massachusetts); Mrs. Myrtle Finison, Public Library Association, Easthampton, Massachusetts, who helped to solve lineage problems of the Cobb family, and as well supplied excerpts from *Rose Cottage,* by Oliver Cobb, and a copy of an article he wrote for *Yachting Magazine,* February 1940, "The 'Mystery' of the *Mary Celeste*" (a similar piece in the *Outlook* for September 1926); Caroline Preston, manuscript librarian, Essex Institute, Salem; and Madge Trundy, of Stockton Springs, Maine, already alluded to in the chapter.

A definitive book, *Mary Celeste, the Odyssey of an Abandoned Ship,* by Charles Edey Fay, was published in 1942 by the Peabody Museum. It contains much of the *Dei Gratia*'s log, something of the Briggs family and the crew, excerpts from the Admiralty Court, and a bibliography on what's been written on the subject, starting at the time. But the book needed a very sharp, if not merciless, editorial pencil. It is so badly organized (going back and forth in time) and poorly written that it almost defies reading.

Certainly more readable is George Bryan's *Mystery Ship, the* Mary Celeste *in Fancy and in Fact,* published in 1942 by J. B. Lippincott (New York). Other books or books with chapters on the mystery include:

Baldwin, Hanson. *Sea Fights and Shipwrecks.* New York: Hanover House, 1938.
Bradford, Gershom. *The Secret of Mary Celeste and Other Sea Fare.* Barre, Massachusetts: Barre Pub. Co., 1966.

Cobb, Oliver W. *Rose Cottage.* Easthampton, Mass: privately printed, 1940.

Furneaux, Rupert. *What Happened on the Mary Celeste.* London: Max Parrish, 1964.

Keating, Laurence J. *The Great Mary Celeste Hoax.* London: Heath Cranston Ltd., 1929.

Lockhart, John G. *Mysteries of the Sea.* London: Philip Allan & Co., 1925.

————. *A Great Sea Mystery: The True Story of the Mary Celeste.* London: Philip Allan & Co., 1930.

Newspaper and periodical treatments of the half-brig have been no less than voluminous over the decades. *Mary Celeste* is discovered anew by writers of every generation. In addition to those mentioned in the chapter, these two should be noted: P. T. McGrath, "The Terror of the Sea," May 1905, *McClure's;* and a paper presented before the Old Dartmouth Historical Society, New Bedford, by James Franklin Briggs in 1944, "In the Wake of the *Mary Celeste.*"

Libraries: It should be noted that reference material for most of the chapters was consulted in these principal libraries: Boston Public Library, District of Columbia Public Libraries, Library of Congress, Maine State Library and Archives (Augusta), Montgomery County Public Libraries (Maryland), New York Public Library, University of Rochester Library, also the Rochester Public Library (New York).

Chapter 2   *Waratah*

The Board of Trade's inquiry on the *Waratah* somehow became lost, strayed, or even stolen, even as the subject of its probings. It cannot be found other than in the columns of the London *Times.* Fortunately, that journal covered the sessions in much detail, as assiduously as it would the sinking of the *Titanic,* just fifteen months after the *Waratah* inquiry adjourned. These columns in the *Times* provide the basic information on the Lund's liner.

A distinguished South African journalist, Eric Rosenthal, of Fish Hoek, already alluded to, has done as much contemporary research on the *Waratah* as anyone, but with the solution obviously eluding him as it has others, including this author, who wishes to thank Mr. Rosenthal for his assistance.

He is also grateful to Lloyd's and to Guildhall Library, Aldermanbury, London, which made available Lloyd's early ship casualty records; and to the Naval Archives, Provincial Administration, Pietermaritzburg, which located photos of the Durban port area at the turn of the century.

Considering the many unusual aspects of the disappearance of the *Waratah,* its modernity in her day, and the implication of such a loss along Britain's stretching lifelines of empire, little has been written about the ship. Perhaps her chronicle is not to be found in magazines or newspapers, for example, because the disappearance was so quickly overshadowed first by the *Titanic,* next the *Empress of Ireland* two years later (in the St. Lawrence, with more than one thousand dead), then the *Lusitania,* and by the Great War itself.

However, there is mention of the *Waratah* in a number of books on the sea, including Lockhart's (previously listed), and dealing with the history of South Africa. Chapters or allusions are to be found in these books in particular:

Bennett, William E. *Last Voyage.* New York: John Day, 1956.
Breed, Bryan. *Famous Mysteries of the Sea.* London: Arthur Barker, 1965.
Hoehling, A. A. *Great Ship Disasters.* New York: Cowles, 1971.
Malherbe, Janie. *Port Natal.* Cape Town: Howard Timmins, 1965.
Rosenthal, Eric. *Schooners and Skyscrapers.* Cape Town: Howard Timmins, 1963.
Villiers, Alan. *Posted Missing.* New York: Charles Scribner's Sons, 1956.

Chapter 3 *Lusitania*

The road, which was really a lane, wound through a cluster of little houses and up an easy hill toward the Old Head of Kinsale. We stopped a man who was on in years, walking his dog and steadying himself, inevitably, upon a gnarled stick; we posed a question he had surely been asked before:

"Do you remember the *Lusitania,* or know of anyone who saw her sink?"

He said his name was O'Connell, and that he had been a boy of five that fateful spring morning in 1915. Although he lived here, he could recall nothing, nor think of anyone in the area now who might.

This was a bright May afternoon, too, in 1983, with the shadows, however, lengthening. We continued along the road, and at its end the spectacular promontory—the Old Head, ruins, candy-striped lighthouse, and all. Not only could we have seen the Cunarder without binoculars, but we realized at once what a wonderful backdrop was the Old Head for lining up a target.

Not the Old Head but the fishing village of Kinsale offered refuge for some of the first victims to come ashore. Outwardly, Kinsale appears unchanged since that emotional evening of May 7 long ago.

The fishing fleet still puts in, and sets sail, at dawn or well before. The pace of life remains something short of rapid, except perhaps Saturday night when couples arrive from many kilometers around to dine at the spread of gourmet restaurants—and this in spite of gasoline selling at the equivalent of some $3.50 per gallon.

It is rumored, but without ready verification, that widely varied memorabilia from the *Lusitania* are tucked away in more homes than not. Salvage or would-be salvage expeditions have berthed here. So far as is known, nothing of real worth has ever been exhumed from the wreck, surely not one dollar or pound of the purported millions in gold.

In the yard of St. Multose Protestant Church of Ireland—a dominating ancient stone edifice—rest three victims of the "*Lusitania* outrage," an unidentified woman and two men. Just down the hill is the old Town Hall, now the Kinsale Museum. Its relics on display date back several centuries before this century's "outrage."

As far as the curator, Eugene Gillen, is concerned, the English are at least as guilty of the crime as the Germans. While not necessarily seconding the "plot" theory, the retired lighthouse keeper poses a number of questions about the movements of the Royal Navy as *Lusitania* steamed down the coast toward her date with destiny. He alludes to sightings from lighthouses of the U-20 and possibly other submarines as well. He indicates that the keepers also had been marking the progress of the big liner. On the other hand, although other promontories, such as Brow Head and Cape Clear, are themselves commanding, the fog during early and mid morning leaves elements of doubt. Was the ship visible from land?

Gillen, the personable Irishman, cannot be convinced, should one try so to do, that Schwieger's encounter with the Cunarder was chance. Why, he repeatedly asks, did the Admiralty keep its patrol in port?

It was farther along the coast, Queenstown, for which the "ghastly procession...of rescue ships" set course. Only the name of the city has been changed, to Cobh, pronounced "Cove." (Whose queen, anyhow?) A somber file of horse carts bearing wooden coffins moving along the waterfront could encore the dismal scene today in front of buildings facing the harbor that appear almost exactly as they did in 1915. Only the names of the shopkeepers have been altered with time.

The road, still indifferently paved, curves sharply up the steep hill past dominating St. Colman's Cathedral. It pushes straight through the city and on out to the Old Church Cemetery. But the 120 graves are forgotten, literally caving in, weed-strewn, unmarked but for a crude plank of wood, on which someone has scrawled *Lusitania* 7th May, 1915.

The author has been unable to interest the Department of State, Ireland's emissaries, or Irish or English newspapers in somehow correcting this deplorable neglect.

Perhaps, after all, these dead indeed died in vain?

In 1956, A. A. and Mary Hoehling published *The Last Voyage of the Lusitania* (originally with Holt, New York; now with Madison Books, Lanham, Maryland). The authors were so extremely fortunate as to talk or correspond with some sixty-five survivors of the lost Cunarder. Most of these charming people became pen pals, as it were. We exchanged greetings at least at Christmas, dropped by for a cup of tea in London, or elsewhere. Then the cards thinned out. Letters were returned "addressee unknown." There was a new resident of the familiar house outside of, say, Liverpool.

"My son was born four months to the day, on the 7th of September, 1915," wrote a survivor, Mrs. Florence Padley, of British Columbia, in 1978, to the author. It was her last letter. But all, at least almost all, are gone now, as the First World War recedes ever further into the misty recesses of history.

This book, which remained in print over a quarter of a century in various editions and in several languages, was an attempt to reconstruct the disaster through the eyes of those who were involved. The direction of the present study is quite different. Through focusing on the master, it is hoped that some light, thereby, will be shed on the mysterious aspects of the torpedoing.

Not a great deal of documentation exists on William Thomas Turner. In life, he was "a private person." Yet, looking to German sources, in the original World War I archives, less can be found on Walther Schwieger even than on Captain Turner. He did not survive the war to explain what made him a dread U-boat ace. He went to whatever his reward on September 7, 1917, commanding U-88 when it ran into a minefield off Denmark. Thus, the author noted with raised eyebrows the arrival in 1983 of a "historical novel," titled simply *Lusitania*, from which, after hundreds of pages, none other than Kapitanleutnant Schwieger emerges as quite a sympathetic figure.

One might speculate that the same British journalist who gave us this offering may next treat with warmth and understanding Count Dracula or Jack the Ripper.

The *in camera* hearings before the Wreck Commissioner, Lord Mersey, declassified after the war, in 1919, published by His Majesty's Stationery Office, London, provided primary research for this chapter and the only probings that can be found into the workings of Captain Turner's mind as he navigated *Lusitania* along the Irish coast. The U.S. Department of State's own files in the National Archives were studied again, proving especially valuable for a copy of the cargo manifest and personal accounts of many survivors.

There was an extensive bibliography in the authors' original book on the *Lusitania*, in addition to the names of the survivors. Since that time a scholarly study accenting the diplomatic aspects of the torpedoing was published by Thomas A. Bailey and Paul B. Ryan: *The Lusitania Disaster* (The Free Press, New York).

The two historians were in contact with this author both before and after the publication. Their extensive files, including many illustrations and drawings, are now archived at the Hoover Institution on War, Revolution and Peace, Stanford University (even as the research material of this author, and his wife, Mary, is to be found at the Mariners Museum).

In addition to those already mentioned, others aided in the preparation of this chapter, among them:

Kieran Burke, head, archives section, Cork Corporation Central Library, Cork, County Cork, Ireland.

Mrs. Robert J. Clarke, of Naples, Florida, the widow of a young survivor of the *Lusitania* who entered the ministry. He was pastor of an Episcopal church in Fort Lee, New Jersey, prior to his retirement.

Ronald D. Clifton, U.S. Embassy, Dublin.

Rose Coombs, longtime special collections officer of the Imperial War Museum, London, and a recognized research authority on World War I. Recently retired, the affable and able Rose has unstintingly aided this author from his first book—that on the *Lusitania*—right on through others in some way involving the British Empire and its affinity for conflict.

James S. Lucas, of the Imperial War Museum's photographic department, is to be thanked for locating that dramatic last photograph of Lord Kitchener on the rainswept deck of the *Iron Duke*.

Millicent Fenwick, former member of the U.S. House of Representatives from the 5th Congressional District, New Jersey. A child of five at the time, Millicent lost her mother, Mary Hammond, with the sinking of the Cunarder.

A. J. Francis, Naval Historical Library, Ministry of Defense, London, who kept the author well "clued in" on what was on file on both the *Lusitania* and *Hampshire*, volunteering several times to advise of declassification of new bits and pieces. Unfortunately, the mysterious aspects of both sinkings remain sturdily protected both by the sea and their Royal guardians.

Also Mac Lochlain, librarian of the University College, Galway, who has long kept sort of a mental card file on who knows what about the *Lusitania* or who may be planning a new probe into the wreck.

Richard O'Brien, press attaché at the Irish Embassy, Washington.

Two books quoted in this chapter should be referenced: *German Submarine Warfare*, by Wesley Frost (New York: D. Appleton & Co., 1918); and *Parnell to Pearse*, by John J. Horgan (London: Browne and Nolan Ltd., 1948). The author had the pleasure of meeting Mr. Frost when he was living in retirement in Florida. Horgan remains a well-known name among the adult population of Kinsale.

Chapter 4   *Hampshire*

The evil spirit which obviously had jinxed the Orkneys in 1916 returned in the early weeks of World War II. A U-boat, commanded by the daring Guenther Prien, penetrated the east channel in October 1939 to torpedo and sink the battleship *Royal Oak*, at anchor in Scapa Flow. More than eight hundred crewmen were lost in this, Great Britain's first major naval disaster of the second conflict with Germany. Some said a Swiss watchmaker at Kirkwall had supplied Hitler's Kriegsmarine with maps of the steel nets and minefields "protecting" the great anchorage. He had vanished with the declaration of war. Old salts tended to credit pure luck that Prien had transited the thick maze of heavy mines without being blown to scrap.

Shortly afterward, the aging *Iron Duke*, Jellicoe's beloved flagship relegated to a depot ship's role, was so damaged in a Luftwaffe bombing that she had to be beached. Nonetheless, the defenses of the anchorage were beefed up and not abandoned by the Royal Navy until 1956.

Appropriately, the *Hampshire* has been designated a gravesite by the Imperial War Graves Commission—much as the USS *Arizona*, in Pearl Harbor. When a German television crew recently attempted to film the wreck or—worse—obtain artifacts, the cameramen were ordered away by the Royal Navy.

The Orkneys are no longer as inaccessible as they were when Lord Kitchener met his doom in attempting to get to Russia. Kirkwall boasts an airport and scheduled service. There is also a car ferry from Scotland and smaller mail and passenger boats. But the islands can scarcely compete for tourists with other portions of the British Isles or Ireland. They remain bleak, windswept, sparsely populated, with more than vestiges of yesterday's lifestyles. The incessant rains beat at the Kitchener Memorial Tower atop Brough Head, with none to come to lay wreaths at the base, much less to weep. It remains a monument to loneliness, austerity, and, surely, to a major, unfulfilled mission.

The Admiralty's white paper, "The Loss of the H.M.S. *Hampshire*" (His Majesty's Stationery Office, London, 1926) is the only official documentation on how that mission failed. Largely bare bones, it is still waiting to be fleshed out…though the trail has grown very cold.

Donald McCormick's *The Mystery of Lord Kitchener's Death* (Putnam's, London, 1959) became the first serious book-length probe into the loss. From his home in Beckenham, Kent, this prolific man of letters has written that the whole matter remains obscure to this day, nor is he convinced that all surviving files have been made public.

Another British author, Oswald S. Nock, of Batheaston, Bath, was not so much concerned about what happened after Scapa Flow, but how Lord Kitchener got there in the first place. Mr. Nock furnished not only the timetable of the Kitchener special but photographs of the types of locomotives that hauled his train through the Highlands to Thurso. Among his books on British railroads are *The Great Northern* and *London and Northwestern*, both published by Ian Allen Ltd., London, the former in 1958, the latter two years later. The author is most grateful for Mr. Nock's assistance.

Once again, Ardie Kelly, of the Mariners Museum, came to the rescue with copies of pages from William Charles Phillips's graphic account as a survivor. His hard-to-find *The Loss of the Hampshire* was privately printed in London in 1917.

A vast amount of historical literature, as well as memoirs, exists on the World War I shelves, which would be eclipsed only by that on the second global conflict. The following is a highly selective list pertaining in various degrees to the *Hampshire.*

Arthur, Sir George. *Life of Lord Kitchener.* Vol. 3. New York: MacMillan, 1920.

Cassar, George H. *Kitchener: Architect of Victory.* London: William Kimber, 1977.

Chatterton, E. Keble. *Danger Zone.* Boston: Little Brown and Co., 1934.

Corbett, Sir Julian. *History of the Great War* (cont. by Henry Newbolt after the author's death). London: Longmans, Green & Co., 1920-31.

Courtney, Charles. *Unlocking Adventure.* London: Robert Hale, 1951.

Esher, Reginald N. N. *The Tragedy of Lord Kitchener.* London: John Murray, 1921.

Gibson, R. H., and Maurice Prendergast. *The German Submarine War.* London: Constable & Co., 1931.

Hendrick, Burton. *Life and Letters of Walter Hines Page.* New York: Doubleday Page & Co., 1924.

Hoehling, A. A. *The Great War at Sea.* New York: Thomas Y. Crowell Co., 1965. (Currently in print, Barnes and Noble)

Jellicoe, Sir John. *The Crisis of the Naval War.* London: Cassell & Co., 1920.

———. *The Grand Fleet.* Cassell, 1919.

Magnus, Sir Philip. *Kitchener, Portrait of an Imperialist.* London: John Murray, 1958.

Scheer, Admiral Reinhard. *Germany's High Seas Fleet in the World War.* London: Cassell & Co., 1920.

Statistics of the Military Effort of the British Empire During the Great War. London: His Majesty's Stationery Office, 1922.

Wood, Clement. *The Man Who Killed Kitchener.* New York: William Faro, 1932.

Many books on espionage and intelligence-gathering during the same period were consulted. Some appear to be weighted on the side of fancy, rather than fact. These are a sampling:

Aston, Sir George. *Secret Service.* New York: Cosmopolitan Book Corp., 1930.

Barton, George. *Celebrated Spies and Mysteries of the Great War.* Boston: The Page Co., 1929.

Beesley, Patrick. *Room 40, British Naval Intelligence 1914-18.* London: Hamish Hamilton, 1982. (This was the code-breaking, wireless intelligence unit that received warning of the High Seas Fleet sortie before Jutland. There is a chapter on *Lusitania,* critical both of the Admiralty's lack of protection and meager communications to the liner.)

Berndorff, H. R. *Espionage.* New York: D. Appleton & Co., 1930.

Boyce, Burke, as told to by George Zimmer. *K-7, Spies at War.* New York: D. Appleton Century Co., 1934.

Carl, Ernst. *One Against England.* New York: E.P. Dutton & Co., 1935.

Felstead, S. T., ed. *The Kaiser's Master Spy, as Told by Himself, John Land.* London: The Bodley Head, 1930.

Gross, Felix. *I Knew Those Spies.* London: Hurst & Blackett, 1940.

Holst, Bernhard P. *Spies in the Great European War.* Chicago: privately printed, 1916.

Landau, Capt. Henry, *Spreading the Spy Net.* London: Jarrolds, 1938.

Nicolai, Colonel W. *The German Secret Service.* London: Stanley Paul, 1924.

Rintelen, Franz von. *Dark Invader.* New York: MacMillan, 1933.

Singer, Kurt. *Gentlemen Spies.* London: W. H. Allen, 1952.

———. *Spies and Traitors.* W. H. Allen, 1953.

———. *Spy Omnibus.* W. H. Allen, 1959.

Snowden, Nicholas. *Memoirs of a Spy.* New York: Scribner's, 1933.

Voska, Emanuel. *Spy and Counter Spy.* London: George Harrap and Co., 1941.

Wood, Clement. *The Man Who Killed Kitchener.* New York: W. Faro, 1932.

Yardley, Herbert O. *The American Black Chamber.* Indianapolis: Bobbs-Merrill Co., 1931.

Chapter 5   The *Cyclops*

In the summer of 1983, Dean Hawes, a retired navy diver, set out in a sixty-five-foot fishing launch on a mission that had been foremost in his mind for some fourteen years. In 1969, the Norfolk resident was investigating a wreck seventy miles northeast of Cape Henry, in 180 feet of water, which the navy thought to be a U-boat sunk in World War II.

He located something. But it was not a submarine, rather a "strange vessel," with a "boxlike bridge and twin masts." Later, reading some World War I identification charts, he came upon the *Cyclops*. This so piqued his curiosity that he prevailed upon his commanding officer (with a little congressional prodding) to send out a salvage ship equipped with underwater TV. With relatively little effort, an image appeared on the screen. It was obviously a torpedoed merchantman from the last global conflict, its radar antenna lying beside it, around which schools of fish swarmed.

This, Hawes insisted, was *not* the wreck on which he had walked. The navy lost what little interest it ever had. An auxiliary collier that disappeared in 1918? Why should anyone care at this stage of history? Hawes ultimately discovered someone who did care—Clive Cussler, author of *Raise the Titanic* and other sea adventure novels. His foundation, the National Underwater and Marine Agency, agreed to let Hawes have another try, by funding the short '83 probe.

But the area is spotted with true frustrations for any diver: some six wrecks on the charts, at least half of them unidentified. Quite aside from this confusing factor, the story has a very sad ending. Just a few weeks after his fruitless search, Hawes died suddenly. The listed cause was pneumonia, contracted during treatment for a tumor. None could say if deep diving could have aggravated his condition.

"He was buried at sea, as he had always wished," said his widow, Patricia, adding pensively, "Now he knows where the *Cyclops* is—and, I believe, all secrets of the sea."

Wherever the collier may be resting, however, chances are she is not off the Virginia coast. If she had journeyed that far, she almost certainly would have been sighted by the navy's offshore patrol, increasingly numerous by this stage of the war, or by some other ship.

The author, like the late Mr. Hawes, has himself been probing the disappearance for some years. He has chapters on the subject in two books: *They Sailed into Oblivion*, first published in 1959 by Thomas Yoseloff, New York, and, later, in *The Great War at Sea*, already noted.

As with the *Lusitania* and *Hampshire*, the author commenced his research anew, hoping that some unnoticed tidbit may have found its way into the files. The declassified Naval Intelligence inquiry, at the National Archives, remains the basic source material on the *Cyclops*.

But even as with the *Lusitania*, living memory has almost vanished since the author initially commenced research on the *Cyclops*. Answers to queries today follow much the pattern of this letter from Edward H. Pollard, of Hanover, Virginia, a relative of Edward Spottswood Pollard, lost on the *Cyclops:*

"I know very little. I was fifteen years old at the time. My father spoke of it, he was lost at sea. No one knew what happened, just that the ship and all its crew were lost.

"His father used to visit my father and they conversed on the front porch..."

Mr. Pollard then went on into family genealogy and the names of the Pollard homesteads, including "Zoro" where apparently Ed, who was lost on the *Cyclops*, grew up.

Scant documentation on Brazil's very secondary role in World War I can readily be found. However, there is a Brazilian Green Book, published by the Ministry of Foreign Affairs in 1981 (London, Allen & Unwin Ltd.).

Brief allusions to German problems in Brazil appeared in the London *Times* and the *New York Times*.

Chapter 6 *Morro Castle*

With all the speculation and theorizing, earnest and serious as most of it has been, since that flaming September night off the New Jersey coast, the report of Dickerson N. Hoover of the Bureau of Navigation and Steamboat Inspection, Department of Commerce, remains the only solid and substantial documentation on the burning of the *Morro Castle*. Dog-eared, worn, and torn from use—and overuse—the massive document reposes in the tomb that is the National Archives to tease and taunt the researcher.

Is the answer somehow there, eluding only the reader's capacity to translate and interpret the innuendo from the staggering profusion of facts and testimony?

This author has battered his way through the inquiry no less than three times. He certainly feels an affinity with Dickerson Hoover, deceased some four decades now. This, by the same token, is true of all of the principals in the disaster. They are all gone now.

By chance, however, the author met one—William Warms—while the erstwhile acting master of the *Morro Castle* was commanding a navy section base at Corpus Christi, Texas, in World War II. Much as he might have liked, even then, this young naval officer was in no position to pose questions to the lean, gaunt, silent merchant mariner. It was obvious, should he have been so brash—a very junior to a very senior officer—he would have received no answer.

Lieutenant Commander Warms appeared the very stereotype of someone who is haunted.

While researching a chapter for *They Sailed into Oblivion*, noted already, the author contacted a number of survivors, including the lucky Dr. Cochrane, at that time still in medical practice.

"It's a dead issue," he wrote, brushing off the whole matter as though it were some minor traffic accident, like a dented fender. Apparently, the state of New Jersey feels the same way. For example, in answer to a request for the criminal record of George Rogers, the State Police wrote:

"It is a long-standing practice...to purge the entire record of any individual reported dead to the Bureau."

The same proved true at the Department of Corrections and elsewhere in New Jersey where law enforcement and judicial files are kept.

The *Morro Castle*, however, is not a "dead issue." Until someone comes forth with a reasonable explanation of the source of that fire in the writing room, as well as the death of Captain Wilmott, and perhaps the total disappearance of all physical evidence of Dr. Van Zile, the "issue" remains at least an open one.

Correspondence with the authors, Thomas Gallagher and Gordon Thomas and Max Morgan Witts, alluded to in this chapter, is acknowledged. Their books:

Gallagher, Thomas. *Fire at Sea.* New York: Rinehart and Co., 1959.

Thomas, Gordon, and Max Morgan Witts. *Shipwreck: The Strange Fate of the Morro Castle.* New York: Stein and Day, 1972.

The brief quotation from William McFee comes from *The Aspirin Age*, edited by Isabel Leighton (New York: Simon and Schuster, 1949).

Chapter 7   SSN *Scorpion*

Researching the *Scorpion* chapter proved to be an experience of mixed bitterness and reward, wholly unprecedented in the author's career as a writer, editor, and newspaper reporter. Certainly he was unprepared for the resentment, antagonism, and suspicion he met. It was almost as though No Trespassing had been posted before the precincts of many memories, still painfully alive after so many years.

While he does not wish to belabor the point, he must nonetheless underscore it:

"I'm not in favor of talking with you, as I feel you are trying to write some type of exposé," wrote the widow (since remarried) of one officer. "Whether or not Frank was a good skipper is immaterial at this point and that kind of speculation would serve only to hurt his beautiful children. You appear to be not interested in facts but rather in the type of 'sensational' journalism for which far too many writers are know [sic].

"I intend to contact all wives whose locations are known to me and advise them to use *great* caution in talking with you.

"I had hoped that my low opinion of most journalists/writers was [illegible] but, unfortunately, you have instead added strength to my feelings.

"There is no way that we will ever know what really happened that night in May. How much better to allow each of us to believe that possibility which has made reality acceptable for fifteen years."

Norman Bessac, the *Scorpion*'s first skipper, now retired as a commander, has written:

"At first I was reluctant to reply...and certainly do not want to be a part of any sensational journalism...I know the *Scorpion* was the result of a superb design, carefully and soundly built, and manned by the cream of navy personnel; however, she was a high-performance ship subject to all the hazards inherent in such a man-of-war. My personal opinion is that you would harm the reputations of fine submariners if you were to speculate on the possibility of human error causing the tragedy. To the best of my knowledge, there is no evidence leading to such a conclusion. Though I did not know Captain Slattery personally, one of the officers last served with me in another command and several of the enlisted men were shipmates of mine aboard the *Scorpion*. These were all fine men, who served their country well, and whose memory should not be clouded in doubt concerning their performance."

These and other misconceptions, unfortunately, stem from the fact that Commander Bessac had an opportunity to read a very few, rough pages, not the chapter as a whole. Thus, his impressions on physical prowess and personalities:

"I was relieved by Commander [Robert Y.] Kaufman, later vice admiral, who commanded *Scorpion* on the seventy-day cruise without surfacing...you appear to be characterizing nuclear submariners as bookish intellectuals with little concern for physical accomplishment. 'Yoggi' Kaufman, as an example, was a physical culture disciple without peer, who could, at the drop of a hat, execute more one-armed push-ups than most All-Americans could accomplish with two hands...I doubt whether Slattery was the 'Casper Milquetoast' you seem to imply...

"The incident concerning the 'all ships alert' deserves some amplification. *Scorpion* was engaged in an extensive NATO exercise around the British Isles. It was the first NATO exercise wherein a nuclear submarine was deployed and some shore-based communication personnel incorrectly interpreted *Scorpion*'s radio silence."

While pleading mystification at the "Milquetoast" analogy, the author might note that a next of kin was among those who mused on the intellectual model of today's submariner. This does not seem to imply that physically they need assists from a cane, or such.

From quite another tangent, and rationale, Admiral Naquin, of the *Squalus*, was kind enough to pass along his thoughts. Admitting that all perforce must be "conjectures, suppositions, probabilities," he continues:

"Let's say for the sake of argument, these two subs (*Thresher* and *Scorpion*) had attained a cruising depth of 1,500 ft. Frankly, I do not know at what depth they were assigned to cruise. Nor do I know their designed 'test depth.' What I do know is that for every foot of submergence the ship will experience 0.44 lbs./square inch of pressure. At 1,500 feet we are looking at 660 lbs./square inch.

"This would be the internal pressure in any pipe inside the hull and exposed to sea pressure. I would guess that whatever the *Thresher-Scorpion* difficulties were, they were not hull related but rather piping failure. True, all piping welds are X-rayed or [checked] by some such method to prove the soundness of the weld, but one cannot rule out human error in such tests."

Naquin went on to speculate that with piping failure, "main propulsion" would be lost and "without propulsion the only way to bring the sub to the surface is by blowing the ballast tanks...to expel the first bucket of water from a ballast tank such pressure must be attained by bleeding high pressure air from the ship's high pressure air tanks. This cannot be accomplished instantly. If we assume a piping failure of any considerable size, it would not be long before the ship would feel the effects of added negative buoyancy—sinking to a greater depth, thus requiring more air and pressure to expel water from the ballast tanks. Without propulsion the battle would most certainly be lost."

Another who sought to help is Judy (Mrs. Daniel Peter) Stephens, widow of the navigating officer. She graciously met with the author in her pleasant Annapolis home and assisted him to the best of her ability, and memory, as is indicated in the chapter itself.

Thanks to her and reporters from the *Norfolk Virginian Pilot*, the author was able to reconstruct that tragic day as families waited on the cold, rainy pier. Perhaps this mirror of life in its starker moments of despair is what has been alluded to as "sensational journalism."

Others have experienced the same rebuff and frustration in trying to lift the veil of secrecy from the *Scorpion* disaster. Close navy contacts, according to Clive Cussler, become "very evasive" when the subject is broached. Also, "some friends in the intelligence agencies, who have been most helpful in areas that are sensitive, are very reluctant to push for me on this one."

Cussler muses, "I suppose the truth will (come) out someday, but I frankly don't have a theory on the loss with the least substance."

Commander Bessac pointed out, quite correctly, that others of the *Scorpion*'s class are still operational, and thus a continuing reason for classification of performance and design data. Another submariner, who was highly honored for his World War II exploits, confirms that the breaking up of *Scorpion* indeed was heard by several other ships, and thus another aspect of secrecy. That is, the desire not to reveal the extent of the navy's ability to hear and communicate underwater; how far and how deep?

By the same token, if the moments of disaster were actually listened to and the object identified as *Scorpion*, why were the search and the announcement delayed for so many days?

For reasons that should now be amply clear, little or nothing has been written in hindsight of the *Scorpion*. The *Thresher*, yes, accenting Hearings before the Joint Committee on Atomic Energy, 88th Congress, June 26, 27, and July 23, 1963; and July 1, 1964, Washington. There exist, as well, two books:

Bentley, John. *The Thresher Disaster*. New York: Doubleday, 1964.

Polmar, Norman. *Death of the Thresher*. Philadelphia: Chilton Books, 1964.

Chapter 8   SS *Poet*

A cold, driving October rainstorm was howling up the Delaware that Sunday, October 23, 1983, and drenching the dock area of South Philadelphia, three years to the day after the *Poet* set course seaward from the same port. Just a few minutes' drive up along the river from the Tidewater Grain Terminal, more than two hundred persons were gathering in the historic Gloria Dei (Old Swedes') Church just across from the piers, deserted, glistening wet.

The occasion, one of mixed sorrow and sociability, was the dedication of a large bronze plaque to the memory of the thirty-four lives lost on the former C-4 transport. Family, friends, writers, reporters, perhaps even the merely curious composed the congregation that honored the crewmen in a service of the Episcopal Church (though the handsome brick structure, the oldest church building in Philadelphia, was Swedish Lutheran when founded shortly before 1700).

A fife and drum corps of a local American Legion post and sea chanty singers tended to leaven the mood of a gray afternoon and provide an upbeat of harmony. But sadness was inevitable, in children and grandchildren, as well as mothers, fathers, and grandparents. A father who had lost his only son, who was thirty-nine, wept in spite of all efforts of his family and others to comfort him.

"It's like opening the wounds all over again," observed another, Alfred Schmidt, father of Alfred Jr.

Among those not present were two widows: one in a psychiatric institution, another at home with terminal cancer.

Alice, the widow of the third assistant engineer, Anthony J. Bourbonnais, would note, "I wish I had more answers concerning my husband's disappearance. I may never know until I die." Philosophically, however, she adds, "I've had a chance to sit back and reflect on my life without Jim and have come to the conclusion that life must go on. I knew that intellectually all along but had to relay that to my heart."

While grief and tears even after three years might have been foreseen, the wonder and the disbelief persisted. Certainly, the total absence of anything whatsoever from the lost ship has contributed to this question mark in the minds of most next of kin.

It was something quite short of coincidence that among the many prayers of this service were those for the crew of a sister ship, the *Penny*, then preparing to sail from Tampa, Florida, with a cargo of phosphates for Kenya. The condition of the old C-4 had been the subject of a front-page article that Sunday morning in the *Inquirer* by reporter Robert Frump.

"The deck of the *Penny*," he wrote, "is not rusting. It is rust." According to the reporter, *Penny*, with a questionable record for dependability, was slated to go to some overseas scrapyard after this voyage.

Bob Frump has been of much assistance to the author in researching this chapter. Marine reporter for the *Inquirer*, Frump has never let go of the *Poet* story, which he has parlayed into a continuing investigation of the merchant marine. In one of his many articles since then in the *Inquirer*, Frump has written, for example:

"Many of the ships...are so unseaworthy they could not begin to pass U.S. Coast Guard safety regulations. They go to sea anyway. They do so with the complicity of industry, labor, Congress, and the Coast Guard itself.

"And sometimes they don't come back.

"Since 1963 more than 350 American seamen have died in major accidents on old ships operating close to or beyond the twenty-year recommended retirement age....

"Despite...billions in government assistance, the United States now has the oldest merchant marine fleet in the world. Twenty-two percent of U.S. merchant ships are more than thirty years old, a percentage far higher than of any other major merchant marine fleet in the world."

Those who had paid their final respects to the men of the *Poet* had but to drive along the facing waterfront to see what Frump was talking about: big, modern, glistening vessels, especially the container ships, all flying the flags of other nations.

Others who assisted are noted in the text.

It should be reemphasized that no blame or responsibility was even hinted at in the wake of the official hearings. The seaworthiness, or lack of it, of the *Poet* was in no way resolved. Legal claims were settled out of court.

In fact, if any one factor was emphasized, probably it was in looking toward better communications at sea for the future and improved float-free emergency transmitters.

Bearing in mind these considerations, the author wove the *Poet* chapter out of the fabric of the public record, using, as well, quite a number of verbatim quotes, much as he did with the *Scorpion*. Among the many obvious differences between these two vessels, however, is a signal one: The submarine was public property, the *Poet* was private property.

These are the three hearings on the disappearance:

Marine Board of Investigation, U.S. Coast Guard, to investigate the circumstances surrounding the disappearance of the SS *Poet* after departure from Cape Henlopen, Delaware, on 24 October 1980 with Loss of Life. Report released by the Commandant April 12, 1982.

National Transportation Safety Board, Department of Transportation, Disappearance of U.S. Freighter SS *Poet* in North Atlantic Ocean about October 25, 1980. Adopted June 23, 1981.

U.S. House of Representatives, Hearings before the Committee on Merchant Marine and Fisheries (97th Congress), on the Fate of the U.S.-Flag Freighter, the SS *Poet*, which disappeared with all Hands Aboard. Hearings held April 9, June 24, 1981.

DATE DUE	BORROWER'S NAME
	Weaver

THE LIBRARY STORE #43-0801